THE WEEK

HOW TO BE REALLY WELL INFORMED IN MINUTES

All you need to know about everything that matters from the popular 'Briefing' columns

EBURY PRESS

10 9 8 7 6 5 4 3 2 1

Published in 2012 by Ebury Press, an imprint of Ebury Publishing

A Random House Group Company

The Random House Group Limited Reg. No. 954009

Addresses for companies within the Random House Group can be found at www.randomhouse.co.uk

A CIP catalogue record for this book is available from the British Library

The Random House Group Limited supports The Forest Stewardship Council (FSC®), the leading international forest certification organisation. Our books carrying the FSC label are printed on FSC® certified paper. FSC is the only forest certification scheme endorsed by the leading environmental organisations, including Greenpeace. Our paper procurement policy can be found at www.randomhouse.co.uk/environment

To buy books by your favourite authors and register for offers visit www.randomhouse.co.uk

Project Editor: Steve Tribe
Commissioning Editor: Carey Smith
Editorial Assistant: Roxanne Mackey
Text design by ClarkevanMeurs Design Ltd

Printed and bound by CPI Group (UK) Ltd, Croydon, CR0 4YY

ISBN 978 0 09194 706 4

Contents

Foreword

The Briefing is one of my favourite pages in *The Week*. It nearly always tells me something I didn't know speedily and authoritatively. When I dreamt up the magazine in the mid 1990s, the idea behind it was a simple one. It seemed to me that our newspapers and magazines were full of extraordinarily interesting things which most people, with limited time on their hands, were simply unaware of. *The Week* would be a means to convey those things to an intelligent audience in a concise, accessible way.

But it also struck me that newspapers rarely give the background to a story or set it properly in context – understandable, of course, given that they are produced in a tearing hurry and face a formidable task each day gathering news from all over the world and then passing it on.

The Week, I knew, could stand back a bit more, and I thought it would be very useful to have one page in it which explained the background to a particular issue. No one could possibly be an expert on all aspects of world events, and *The Week* needed to assume that its readers did not know everything about the background to them. My hope was that the Briefing would become one of the hallmarks of the magazine – something distinctive which would mark us out from other journals – and, to judge from the reaction of readers, so it has proved.

The success of *The Week* depends largely on our choosing the best stories and the most interesting analysis from a huge range of newspapers and magazines and then rewriting it all in our own distinctive style. But what makes our Briefing pages different is that they are entirely original. Written and researched, for the most part, by Katharine Ramsay, and skilfully edited by Jeremy O'Grady, our editor-in-chief, they are an essential part of our mix, and one of the parts of which I am most proud. This book contains the best of our Briefings in a handy and attractive format. I am delighted we are producing it and hope you will enjoy it as much as I have.

Jolyon Connell
Founder and Director, *The Week*

Does
aspirin
prevent cancer?

It just might. *A landmark study published in the* Lancet *in 2010 showed that taking an aspirin every day for several years can reduce the risk of dying from cancer. Doctors have suggested this before, but the* Lancet *study confirmed it. Researchers at the University of Oxford studied the cancer death rates of 25,570 people who had taken part in eight randomised trials of aspirin up to 20 years ago, and found noticeably fewer deaths among those who had taken the drug. Overall, death rates among those who had taken a daily dose of aspirin for five years were 34 per cent lower than they were among those who had not taken the drug. Stomach and bowel cancers showed even greater declines, with death rates falling by more than 50 per cent.*

How does it work?

No one knows yet, but the active ingredient of aspirin is a naturally occurring chemical – salicylic acid – which is known to have a range of effects on the body, including thinning the blood and reducing inflammation. One theory suggests that inflammation is connected to the development of tumours; another says that the drug may induce the early death of cancer cells. A third theory is that natural salicylic acid has disappeared from our diets because of the increased use of pesticides and fertilisers, and that a small daily dose of aspirin restores the body's defences.

When was aspirin discovered?

In a way, it has been discovered many times over. Salicylic acid is found in the bark and leaves of the willow tree, and people used both to alleviate pain in ancient times. The Hammurabi Code, a Babylonian document from 1700 BC, mentions the medical uses of willow bark, as do Egyptian scrolls dating from the same period. In 400 BC, the Greek physician Hippocrates said that pregnant women should take an infusion of willow leaves during labour. But the chemical properties of salicylic acid were not properly investigated until the nineteenth century, when a series of European chemists tried to isolate and manufacture a form of the compound that could be taken safely as a drug. In 1897, Felix Hoffmann, a German scientist working for Bayer, the chemical company (see box), finally cracked it. Aspirin went on sale in 1899.

What was it sold for?

Bayer marketed aspirin as a painkiller alongside its other new wonder drug, a cough suppressant called heroin. It began to patent the drug aggressively around the world, but failed to do so in Britain before having to surrender its patents in allied states at the end of the First World War. Nevertheless, for the next 40 years, aspirin was one of the world's most popular and profitable medicines, recognisable in more than 80 countries for the Bayer cross stamped into each tablet. It was not until the late 1950s that a new generation of painkillers, including ibuprofen and paracetamol, appeared, and briefly threatened aspirin's future. The new drugs could reduce inflammation and pain just as quickly, but without some of the side effects.

What are those side effects?

Aspirin can upset the stomach, and cause ulcers. It also thins the blood, leading to excessive bleeding. These were the downsides that rival drugs sought to avoid – but they also laid the basis for discoveries about potential new uses for aspirin in the 1970s. In 1971, John Vane, a British pharmacologist, realised that most of the impacts of aspirin – positive and negative – were caused by the way it impeded prostaglandins, a powerful group of chemicals in the body. Prostaglandins produce pain, fevers and swelling – but they also regulate the acidity of the stomach, and cause blood to clot. Vane suggested that small doses of aspirin could be used to keep blood moving round the body, thus reducing the risk of clots that might cause strokes and heart attacks.

Was he right?

Yes, he was. Vane's insight made aspirin standard treatment for heart-attack sufferers and stroke victims. He won the Nobel prize for medicine in 1982 and saved countless lives. Millions of healthy people also started taking an aspirin a day to reduce their risk of heart disease. But in recent years, doctors have become increasingly sceptical that the benefits outweigh the risks from side effects in the wider

population: an estimated 5,000 people a year are hospitalised for internal bleeding caused by aspirin. In 2009, the *Drug and Therapeutics Bulletin* (DTB) said that only those actually suffering from cardiovascular disease should take a pill every day, prompting new guidelines from the British Heart Foundation and Diabetes UK. The cancer breakthrough, however, reopened that debate.

'Around 60 people would have to take the aspirin continuously for around five years to prevent one death from bowel cancer during a 20-year period.'

So should all now be taking it?

The authors of the *Lancet* study say that aspirin has positive effects even in small doses – at just a quarter of a typical headache pill – but this will not suit everyone. 'These results do not mean that all adults should immediately start taking aspirin,' said Professor Peter

Rothwell, who led the research and now takes a low daily dose himself. 'But they do demonstrate major new benefits.' Meanwhile Dr Ike Iheanacho, editor of the DTB, points out that all effects of aspirin in low doses, benign and otherwise, are so slight that they will probably only be noticed across the population as a whole.

'Around 60 people would have to take the aspirin continuously for around five years to prevent one death from bowel cancer during a 20-year period,' he says. 'While that remains a considerable benefit, it could clearly put a very different perspective on things for an individual deciding whether to take aspirin for this purpose.'

BAYER: 273 MILLION ASPIRINS A DAY

To celebrate a century of selling aspirin, in March 1999 German chemical giant Bayer wrapped its 32-storey Leverkusen headquarters in fabric to make it look like an aspirin box. Around 100 billion tablets of the drug are still produced each year, making it an extraordinary constant for the company – which was founded in 1863 by a salesman, Friedrich Bayer, and a master dyer, Johann Weskott, to develop new textile dyes during Germany's industrial revolution; and which spent the twentieth century buffeted by war and controversy before helping to lead the country's post-war economic revival.

In August 1897, the same month that he synthesised aspirin, Felix Hoffmann also created heroin – a drug that Bayer hoped might be a non-addictive alternative to morphine, but which proved even more devastating.

After the First World War, the company was hit by the loss of its aspirin patents and foreign subsidiaries, and the cloak-and-dagger poaching of four of its leading chemists by its US rival DuPont. During the unstable 1920s, Bayer was merged into I.G. Farben, the conglomerate of German chemical companies that became notorious during the Second World War for the production of Zyklon-B gas, and for cruel medical experiments. But in 1951, Bayer emerged again as a single company, with fertilisers, synthetic fabrics and aspirin, to revive the German economy. In 2009, it had revenues of €31bn.

Are **our** bosses **overpaid?**

At a time when most people's salaries were frozen, directors in Britain's blue-chip FTSE 100 index enjoyed an average pay rise of 50 per cent in 2011, taking average pay packets to £2.7m. As a result of these stratospheric rises, corporate bosses risked being viewed as 'aliens' by the general public, warned former CBI chief Sir Richard Lambert. 'For the first time in history,' he noted, 'it has become possible for a manager – as opposed to an owner – of a large public company to become seriously rich.'

Are British pay packets the biggest?

No. UK executive pay awards still pale in comparison to the USA, where Bob Iger of Walt Disney, 2011's top corporate earner, scooped $54.9m. But they are growing faster than anywhere else. Executive salaries in FTSE 100 firms have risen by some 4,000 per cent since 1980, compared with an average of 300 per cent for their employees. In 1979, BP's chief made 16.5 times the company's average pay packet; the multiple today is 63. The gap is even wider in banks such as Barclays and Lloyds, where top pay is now 75 times that of the median wage.

Why this widening gap?

Defenders of executive pay levels argue that, far from engaging in plutocratic pocket-lining, British boardrooms have been playing catch-up with rates commanded by the global 'talent pool'. They also note that globalisation and new technology have squeezed out skilled manual workers and middle-ranking white-collar staff, thereby increasing (at least in theory) the productive potential of their bosses. But equally inflationary have been the fads engineered within management – the 1990s cult of 'the Superstar CEO', for example, and above all the rise of an incentivised bonus culture. This took off in the City after Big Bang in the 1980s, and quickly spread to blue-chip boardrooms. Basic salary now often accounts for just 20 per cent of a FTSE boss's overall remuneration, with bonuses and 'discretionary payments' justified on grounds that talented executives deserve additional rewards for, in the jargon, 'going beyond the day job' to transform a company's performance.

What evidence is there of this?

Not much. On the broad measure of long-term shareholder value, boardroom pay and executive performance lost touch with each other years ago. Despite ever more complex incentive packages (see box), the FTSE 100 is some 20 per cent lower than it was at the turn of the century. Meanwhile, the 'contagion' of high pay has seeped into the public sector, amid the usual arguments that rewards must keep pace with the private sector to attract the best candidates.

Who decides on boardroom pay?

A company's remuneration committee – typically comprising non-executive directors, often moonlighting from executive roles in other companies. They in turn are advised by independent pay consultants on the going rate for a particular role in the wider market. Given Britain's smallish executive pool and the intricate criss-cross of relationships within it, the potential for conflicts of interest is clear: a non-executive sitting on one board may be setting the pay of someone in another company who may have a role in setting theirs. In practice, such direct boardroom swaps are rare, but critics argue that pay is still hatched in a sort of closed-shop, back-scratching environment and that it's high time this cosy club was bust open.

Who should police corporate pay?

Shareholders. As the company's owners, they have both a duty and

Executive salaries in FTSE 100 firms have risen by some 4,000 per cent since 1980. In banks such as Barclays and Lloyds, top pay is now 75 times that of the median wage.

an interest in ensuring executives don't feather their nests at their expense. Until now, large institutional shareholders have sat back – not least because the fund management industry also has a record of giving executives big rewards for mediocre performance. But now that even the Institute

of Directors is expressing alarm over the 'unsustainable' rate of executive pay, there's a new sense of urgency for root-and-branch reform – an urgency matched by increased shareholder activism. The number of revolts against executive pay proposals has doubled this year, with some 15 FTSE 100 firms targeted – including BP, HSBC and Diageo. However, since shareholder votes on pay are only advisory, boards have typically ignored these tilts.

How might pay-outs be curbed?

Some ideas under review (such as following the German example of putting employees on remuneration boards, or closer government monitoring of pay) have been slammed by critics, who claim that since workers and governments do not own companies, they shouldn't have a say in what CEOs are paid. Judgements based on economic worth will be sacrificed, they argue, to the politics of envy. But there is consensus that shareholders should be given more teeth – by making their votes on pay awards binding, and giving them more powers to claw back undeserved bonuses. The government set out its proposals in January 2012: more shareholder power, and transparency and greater diversity on company boards were the main measures.

Why the sense of urgency?

Because the widening pay gap isn't just an ethical problem. IMF research has found that countries with a narrower gap between rich and poor enjoy longer economic expansions than less equal ones, as the latter are more vulnerable to financial crises and political instability. Economist Andrew Smithers goes further: a corporate bonus culture, in which pay-outs are typically triggered by short-term profitability targets, risks driving a country into economic decline, he argues, because the focus is always on cost cutting. The last three years in the USA, he notes, is the only period ever recorded in which a fall in output has been matched by record profitability, a pattern now evident in Britain. For all their protestations to the contrary, it seems bosses are more inclined to slash jobs and investment than to sacrifice their pay.

HOW TO INCENTIVISE AN EXECUTIVE

Anyone doubting the ingenuity of British companies should check out their skill in finding ways to reward executives whatever the corporate weather – for example, by setting performance targets risibly low and with plenty of leeway built in for 'extraneous factors'. And the complexity of pay packages – which usually involve a host of different targets and share options – means that if one pay stream goes belly up, another is sure to hit the jackpot.

Then there are 'discretionary' payments: thus although BP's former chief Tony Hayward (basic salary £1m) was denied his 2010 cash bonus after the Gulf of Mexico oil spill, he still got a £1.045m payment as 'compensation for loss of office'.

Another recent fad is 'pity bonuses': paid to bosses who fail to qualify for pay-outs under existing schemes because of the diving economy.

Necessary incentives? Not according to former Shell boss Jeroen van der Veer who, in a candid moment, once admitted: 'If I'd been paid 50 per cent more, I wouldn't have done it better. If I'd been paid 50 per cent less, I wouldn't have done it worse.'

Yet given the tight grip maintained by remuneration committees and the pay consulting industry, even bosses willing to take a pay cut are dissuaded on the grounds that it might disrupt 'differentials' with other executives and companies.

 Is it
the end
for email ?

For several years, *students of the internet have noticed that young people are abandoning email in favour of other electronic ways of staying in touch. 'High school kids don't use email,' noted Mark Zuckerberg, founder of Facebook, in 2010. In 2012, the leading US internet research firm ComScore reported a 59 per cent decrease in the use of internet-based email services (such as Gmail and Hotmail) by 12- to 17-year-olds, an 18 per cent decline among 25- to 35-year-olds, and an 8 per cent fall among 35- to 44-yearolds. There are even signs that email is starting to lose favour in the workplace.*

In which workplaces?

Europe's largest IT company, French firm Atos Origin, intends to scrap internal emails by 2013. Its 49,000 staff will still use email to correspond with clients and other businesses, but to talk among themselves they'll adopt a variety of newer (e.g. instant messaging services) and older methods (talking face to face). Thierry Breton, a former French finance minister and the company's CEO, prompted headlines around the world when he mentioned he had not sent an email in more than three years.

Why is the company giving up email?

In part to reflect the preferences of its workers, many of whom are under 30, but also because – in Breton's words – the volume of email is becoming 'unsustainable'. Employees, who typically get 200 emails a day, spend between 5 and 20 hours a week just clearing their inboxes. 'Companies face a deluge of information. It's time to think differently,' said Breton. The perils, distraction and time-wasting of email have been a regular part of office life for more than a decade. More than 107 trillion are now sent each year, of which about half are spam (see box). The rest are a dubious mix of round-robins, personal messages and badly written memos that pile up in archives and do little to boost productivity. Research shows it takes 64 seconds to regain concentration after reading an email, and when you consider that US office workers have been measured checking their emails and swapping windows on their computer screens an average of 37 times an hour, that adds up to major distraction. To its detractors, email – 40 years old in 2011 – has had its day.

So what is the alternative?

'Employees will be expected to use collaboration and social media tools instead of email to communicate with co-workers,' said Atos. In English, that means newer types of electronic messaging services. One such – particularly popular with the young – is instant messaging. Devised in the mid-1990s by people playing games on the net, instant messaging, or 'IM', is much simpler, quicker and more responsive than email. Rather than having to wait until someone opens, reads and replies to an email, IM users can see when colleagues are online and then communicate in small, continuous trails of dialogue on their screens, much more like a phone call. These messages tend to be deleted as they go, thus avoiding clogged-up email inboxes and archives. Less formal than email, they're also a far more efficient way of, say, trying to arrange a meeting. IM or 'chat' facilities often form part of larger social networks – of which the best-known is Facebook.

Why are social networks so popular?

Because they enable people to stay in touch and broadcast information to each other – their location, activities, plans, schedule for the day – without the need for constant emailing. 'Status updates', in which users post a simple message that can be read by all their contacts, enable people to see and share information that might not be worth an email but can be useful nonetheless. (This is one of Twitter's uses.) All such 'easy chat' services were born of an engagement with the internet that just didn't exist when email overtook the world of communication in the 1990s: increasing numbers of us are connected – at work, at home, on our mobile phones – all the time.

Is any of this good for our attention spans?

Probably not. Until the mid 1990s, most neuroscientists thought the brain stopped developing after childhood. But the constant distraction and torrent of information that we subject ourselves to – via email, surfing the web, TV, multi-tasking – is now thought to alter the way we think. The new technology 'is rewiring our brains', says Nora Volkow, director of the US National Institute of Drug Abuse. Scientists have drawn parallels between the use of electronic communication and addictions to drugs, food and sex – all stimulants that release small amounts of dopamine in the brain. We feel a buzz of excitement when a message arrives, which

---

The volume of email is becoming 'unsustainable'. Employees, who typically get 200 emails a day, spend between 5 and 20 hours a week clearing their inboxes.

---

then fades, leaving us feeling flat and bored until the next one comes. But whether this makes us less productive is open to question. Research has found that people work better in bursts of concentration interrupted by breaks – even for pointless emails – than in long sustained spells.

So email still has it uses?

Undoubtedly. There are still an estimated three billion email accounts in the world, a figure that dwarfs any other form of electronic communication. Facebook has 20 per cent of that number, Twitter 5.5 per cent. Email also retains several vital distinguishing qualities. Unlike the galaxy of social networks and IM services on the internet – all requiring different accounts and often their own software – email is fundamentally compatible. It doesn't matter which programme you send it from. And even its annoyances contain advantages: email archives have proved to be hugely valuable, while the 'asynchronicity' of the medium (recipients choose when to open their messages) means that we can try and preserve some control over our time. This is not the end of email, it is just the end of its monopoly.

SPAM, SPAM, SPAM, SPAM

Spam gets its name from a Monty Python sketch set in a café where everything comes with servings of Spam. But the idea of using modern technology to send unwanted messages and dodgy business offers goes back to the nineteenth century. *Time* magazine notes that questionable propositions – the forerunners of today's Nigerian '419' scams, which ask for help in transferring money from one country to another – were being sent by telegraph to rich Americans in 1864.

The first modern spam was sent in 1978, on the US military network Arpanet (a forerunner of the internet), advertising a new kind of computer. In 1994, two US lawyers, Laurence A. Canter and Martha S. Siegel, successfully defended their use of unsolicited email adverts as an exercise of freedom of speech.

In the intervening years, spam has mushroomed. By 2009, 89 per cent of all email was spam, much of it containing viruses, malicious software or 'phishing' messages (attempts to trick recipients out of their personal details or money). Since then, filtering technology and internet security companies have held back the tide. In October 2009, a US court fined Sanford Wallace, America's self-styled 'King of Spam', $711m for illegally obtaining the details of Facebook users. A survey by Symantec in June 2011 found that 73 per cent of email was spam – a noticeable fall.

How did
Kinsey get
interested in sex ?

In 1938 Kinsey *was teaching zoology at Indiana University (specialising in the study of wasps) when he was drafted in to give a course on 'marriage' and was appalled to find how little his students knew about sex and how much they feared it. According to a study at the time, 96 per cent of young Americans didn't know the word 'masturbation'; when told what it meant, 40 per cent thought it caused insanity. The most popular marital guide of the day called oral sex within marriage 'the hell gate of the realm of sexual perversion'. Kinsey's students often asked him if their habits and desires were 'normal'; he had no answer, since no one knew what people did behind closed doors. Kinsey resolved to find out.*

What did he find?

Having devised a questionnaire of some 300 questions about Americans' sex lives, he travelled the country with four trusted colleagues, jotting down 18,000 'sexual histories'. His knack for gaining people's trust (see box) and keeping them honest was vital to his success, but his truly revolutionary breakthrough was philosophical. He approached the sexuality of what he called 'the human animal' as a biologist, without imposing any moral judgements. He discovered that Americans were far more sexually adventurous than anyone had previously been willing to admit. In 1948 Kinsey published *Sexual Behavior in the Human Male*, in which he reported that 85 per cent of white men had had premarital sex, 50 per cent had had extramarital sex and 69 per cent had visited prostitutes. The Kinsey Report, as it became known, sold 270,000 copies and Kinsey became a celebrity. He was compared to Darwin and Copernicus, and became a favourite punchbag for cartoonists and comedians. But it was one statistic in particular that brought the former zoologist instant notoriety: his contention that 10 per cent of men are gay.

Is that true?

No, and Kinsey never said it. In fact, Kinsey didn't even believe there was such a thing as 'a homosexual' or 'a heterosexual' – only homosexual or heterosexual acts. What he found was that 37 per cent of men had had at least one homosexual experience, that 10 per cent had been 'more or less exclusively homosexual' for at least three years, and that 4 per

cent were exclusively homosexual their whole lives (that last figure has been largely verified). Kinsey also developed a scale of 0 to 6, with 0 being purely heterosexual and 6 being purely homosexual. People who fell at the extremes of 0 or 6, he said, were rare. Moral traditionalists were outraged, accusing Kinsey of deliberately promoting homosexuality. That charge was buttressed years after Kinsey's death, when biographer James Jones revealed that Kinsey, though married, frequently had sex with men.

Did Kinsey have an agenda?

Yes, but it wasn't just about homosexuality. Kinsey was raised in a strict Methodist household, and grew up wracked with shame about his body and his adolescent urges. He wanted to persuade the world that sex was natural, and was determined 'that no one else should suffer as he had suffered,' said biographer Jonathan Gathorne-Hardy. Kinsey liked to point out that because America's morality laws prohibited oral sex and other 'deviant' acts, even within marriage, 95 per cent of the people

19

he met were sex criminals. Though he posed as a neutral observer, he believed that social mores should be more in line with actual behaviour, and promoted tolerance for everything from masturbation to, in some cases, paedophilia. 'There are only three kinds of sexual abnormalities,' he once said. 'Abstinence, celibacy, and delayed marriage.'

How did that go down?

Not so well. Critics said his data was skewed by the way he purposely sought out fringe groups, including prisoners and men who frequented gay bars. In fact, Kinsey's findings were fairly sound. He weighted his sample to minimise the influence of non-typical groups. But he did play fast and loose with the way his results were presented. He encouraged the media to sensationalise his findings, and always spoke as if more and varied sex was inherently preferable to the opposite. The grumbling about Kinsey's first book, however, was nothing compared with the storm that followed its sequel.

What was his second book?

Sexual Behavior in the Human Female. The typical pre-Kinsey attitude toward female sexuality was summed up by a marriage manual of the time: for men, it said, sex was as easy as falling off a log, for women, it was 'as simple as being the log'. In 1953 many men did not know that women could have orgasms, and those who did assumed that sexual

---

Kinsey liked to point out that because America's morality laws prohibited oral sex, even within marriage, 95 per cent of the people he met were sex criminals.

---

intercourse was the sole means to that end. Kinsey showed that most women needed some form of direct clitoral stimulation. He also reported that 63 per cent of women masturbated, and that 14 per cent were capable of multiple orgasms. He also revealed that half of married women had had premarital sex, and that of those, 77 per cent had no regrets. A nymphomaniac, said Kinsey, is 'someone who has more sex than you do'.

What was the reaction?

Horror. American men were not ready to hear that their mothers and daughters were sexual creatures. 'It's impossible to estimate the damage this book will do to the already deteriorating morals of America,' said evangelist preacher Billy Graham. The backlash included congressional hearings, obscenity charges, and an FBI investigation. Kinsey was branded a communist out to destroy the American family. Depressed and stressed, he

died of heart failure at 62.

Did he die a failure?

He thought so, but his work changed the world and paved the way for the sexual revolution. One by one, states undid laws against fornication, adultery, and sodomy, usually citing Kinsey as their authority. Schools began to teach sex education based on his principles. Today, people who see the sexual revolution as a giant step forward and those who see it as the beginning of America's descent into moral degeneracy agree on one thing: Alfred Kinsey was the man who got it all started.

THE SECRET LIFE OF A SEX RESEARCHER

Kinsey earned America's respect in part because he looked the very model of a conservative academic. With his grey suit and polka dot tie, said Gore Vidal, who was one of his early interviewees, he just 'looked terribly grey'.

But appearances, as James Jones revealed in his 1997 biography, were deceptive. Kinsey and his wife were both virgins when they married, but his work transformed them into sexual enthusiasts. Kinsey had sex with men in his inner circle and

encouraged others to have sex with his wife. In fact, Kinsey's staff and their wives had sex with one another in every conceivable combination.

He also used his attic to film hundreds of people engaged in a wide variety of sex acts. For example a 60-year-old woman called Alice was roped in for sex with his researchers, because she was able to have dozens of orgasms during intercourse. All of this, Kinsey insisted, was a necessary part of the research.

Did the West know
about Mao's
'secret famine'?

The famine is *usually called the Great Leap Forward. That was how the regime characterised the period between 1958 and 1962, when Mao Zedong pursued his plan to transform China from a backward agrarian economy into an industrial powerhouse. Directed ruthlessly from the centre, and fuelled by false reports of impossibly high production targets being met by motivated farmers and factory workers, the Great Leap Forward has long been known as a grand folly, but it is only in recent years that the true scale of the suffering it caused has come to light. Frank Dikötter, a Dutch historian based in Hong Kong who won the Samuel Johnson Prize for his book Mao's Great Famine, revealed that 45 million people died – making it a catastrophe of a similar order to the Second World War.*

What was the source of the catastrophe?

Mao ordered the Great Leap Forward after the Sino-Soviet split, when he became convinced that the USSR's model of socialism had failed. He resolved that China should follow its own path and 'walk on two legs' – meaning it had simultaneously to revolutionise both its agriculture and its industries. Overnight, private ownership and private farms were abolished, and peasants were forced onto vast state-run communes where they were paid 'work points' instead of wages. Millions stopped farming altogether after being made to set up furnaces in their backyards in order to meet Mao's steel quotas – he had decreed that steel production must double within a year. Everywhere people melted down pots and pans – but the brittle metal produced was unusable. Further millions of peasants were dragooned into working on large-scale dams and reservoirs, leaving traditional irrigation and drainage systems to disintegrate. Dikötter's book exposed in new and horrifying detail how the massive disruption in food production this caused led to catastrophe – the book begins: 'China descended into hell.'

How did Dikötter's book change our understanding?

By meticulously researching the records of China's Public Security Bureau, the author was able to lay bare the sheer scale of destruction. Mao's Great Leap precipitated the biggest waste of manpower and the greatest demolition of property in all history: some 40

per cent of housing was turned to rubble, at some times in the hope of using it for fertiliser, at others simply to punish the householders. It also produced the most extensive destruction of the environment: deforestation, floods, soil erosion, landslides and droughts. Insect infestation was chronic: although Mao declared war on flies, mosquitoes, rats and sparrows, there were no longer peasants available to control the locusts and grasshoppers that devoured millions of tons of food as people starved to death.

Why did so many starve?

Because all farms were stripped bare to feed the workers in the factories that were mushrooming in the cities. In the worst-affected provinces, people took to eating bark, leaves, poisonous berries, mud and human flesh. Dikötter tells of a father selling his child for a bowl of rice and two sacks of peanuts, and a mother giving up her son for a few pennies and four steamed buns. And those who didn't starve were often killed by the regime.

Why were they killed?

Often for tiny crimes. The father of a boy in Hunan who stole a handful of grain was forced to bury his son alive. Workers unable to complete tasks were forbidden to eat in their canteen – a death sentence. Exhausted party cadres fretted about their failure to meet targets for executions. 'It's impossible not to beat people to death,' one noted. Dikötter estimates that 2.5 million were killed by the state, and nine million jailed. As many as three million committed suicide.

How much did Mao know about this?

The received wisdom even now in China (see box), is that the Great Leader's advisers, desperate to assure him that the Great Leap Forward was producing miraculous results, never told him. But Dikötter shows that for years China's leaders regarded the country's peasants as mere 'digits', expendable in the name of development. 'When there is not enough to eat, people starve to death,' Mao said. 'It is better to let half of the people die so that the other half can eat their fill.' In the summer of 1959, one year into the four-year famine, Mao was confronted about the extent of the suffering by Peng Dehuai, his defence minister and the former commander of China's forces during the Korean War. Peng was dismissed and placed under house arrest.

So did the West know what was happening?

Reports from refugees did get

Millions stopped farming to meet Mao's steel quotas. Everywhere people melted down pots and pans – but the brittle metal produced was unusable.

---

out, although the Communist Party hid most of what was taking place. Communism had 'ended the traditional Chinese famine cycle', enthused Lord Boyd-Orr, former director of the UN Food and Agriculture Organisation, after vising the country in 1959. Others – such as the philosopher Bertrand Russell – were less credulous, but it was not until 1996, when British journalist Jasper Becker published *Hungry Ghosts*, that the silence was truly broken. Even now, some struggle to accept the scale of the disaster. Henry Kissinger's 600-page book *On China* devotes one line to the famine.

How did it end?

In 1962, Communist Party Vice-Chairman Liu Shaoqi visited his home village and was shocked by what he saw. A 'manmade disaster' had occurred, he admitted publicly, for which 'the central leadership'

was responsible. Mao retreated from public view as Liu, premier Zhou Enlai and future leader Deng Xiaoping rebuilt the economy, but in 1966 the Chairman emerged again with his next reformist programme – the Cultural Revolution – which over the following decade destabilised the country and killed millions more. During those years, Mao made sure to have his revenge: Peng, who had spoken out in 1959, was beaten to death; Liu was starved and later cremated under a false name.

THE GREAT HELMSMAN

The publication of Dikötter's book and its international impact coincided with the ongoing celebrations in China to mark the 90th anniversary of the founding of the Chinese Communist Party (CCP). Mao, a co-founder of the party in 1921, has been a central figure, and a portrait of the 'Great Helmsman' still overlooks Tiananmen Square, despite the party's official condemnation of the 'mistaken leadership of Mao Zedong' during the Cultural Revolution.

Connecting Mao in the Chinese imagination to the millions of deaths of the famine is another

matter entirely. The official CCP verdict is that his rule was '70 per cent good, 30 per cent bad', and the country's current leaders continue to invoke 'Mao Zedong Thought' to justify their policies.

But there just may be signs that his allure is weakening. *Beginning of a Great Revival*, a two-hour propaganda film released to mark the 90th anniversary of the CCP, featured Mao at its centre, but, to the surprise of the government, it had few fans. Audiences stayed away, and more than 90 per cent of users on pirate film website VeryCD described the film as 'trash'.

Where can we find 'shale gas'?

Tightly bound up *in the bedrock. The difference between a conventional and an 'unconventional' source of fossil fuels is how securely the oil and gas is trapped inside the earth. The less permeable, or accessible, are the rocks that contain it, the more unconventional is the reserve. For the past 100 years or so, it has been too expensive and technically complicated to extract unconventional gas reserves – many of which consist of methane trapped inside the sedimentary rock shale (hence 'shale gas'). But thanks to rising energy prices, and a clever combination of traditional drilling techniques, the last ten years have witnessed extraordinary advances and discoveries in the shale-gas industry. The International Energy Agency (IEA) says there are now sufficient unconventional gas reserves to keep the world in gas for the next 100 years.*

Is it everywhere, then?

Sweden, Germany, Ukraine, South Africa and Australia all have shale-gas reserves – but the real treasure lies in China, and even more so in the USA. An American engineer, George Mitchell, working on the Barnett Shale in Texas in the early 1990s, devised the drilling techniques that have revolutionised the industry. Since then, 2.3 trillion cubic metres of recoverable gas have been discovered in the

Marcellus Shale (a formation that stretches from upstate New York to Kentucky), which on its own could supply America with gas for the next four years. Shale-gas drilling, which already accounts for 22 per cent of US gas production, has driven down energy prices, created jobs and encouraged new technologies. Car-makers are now focusing on natural gas vehicles (NGVs). Academics speak of a 'Golden Age of Natural Gas'.

How many shale reserves does the UK have?

No one knows yet. The British Geological Survey thinks there are four significant 'plays' (as unconventional gas reserves are known) under UK soil. Official estimates put the amount of technically recoverable gas at between 150 and 560 billion cubic metres – enough to supply Britain with gas for anywhere between 1.5 and 5.6 years. A report by the Commons Committee on Energy and Climate Change described this as considerable but 'unlikely to be a 'game changer'' in the UK's energy mix. Shale-gas prospectors disagree. In 2010,

British firm Cuadrilla Resources began drilling in the Bowland Shale, five miles outside Blackpool in Lancashire, and says it has found up to 5.6 trillion cubic metres of 'gas in place' – ten times the official estimate.

So how do we get it out?

By a complicated process known as 'fracking'. As well as being locked more tightly inside rocks, 'plays' tend to be deeper underground and exist in broader, shallower plains than ordinary oil and gas deposits. To reach a reservoir, a drill is sent down vertically and then steered until it is boring horizontally through the shale. Hydraulic fracturing (fracking) is then used to extract the gas. A mixture of water and sand (and often diesel) is injected at high pressure into the rocks to create fissures through which the gas bubbles out. Although it sounds dramatically 'cutting-edge', hydraulic fracturing was in fact first performed in upstate New York in 1821 and is common practice in conventional oil and gas drilling. But that has not stopped it getting a terrible reputation.

What's wrong with fracking?

In the USA, where thousands of shale-gas wells have been drilled in the last decade, the concern is mainly about the impact on water supplies. Each well can consume up to 9 million litres of water a day, of which around 50 per cent can be reused – the rest becomes heavily polluted. The US Environmental Protection Agency (EPA) has warned that water withdrawn from aquifers on this scale can lead to 'destabilisation of the geology'. An even greater concern of fracking opponents – or 'fracktivists' – is what happens to the mixture of water, gas, metals and naturally occurring radioactive materials (Norms) that flows up to the surface once fracking has taken place. In heavily drilled parts of the USA, tap water has caught fire, while state officials have discovered methane and heavy metals in local streams.

What does the industry say about this?

That accidents have occurred in shale-gas plays, just as they have in conventional oil and gas drilling, but that fracking isn't the problem. The British Geological Society agrees: it's 'very unlikely', it says, that hydraulic fracturing could contaminate water supplies, because aquifers tend to be separated from shale by hundreds of metres of solid rock. As for 'fluid leak-off' – that is probably caused by poorly constructed wells or flawed storage pools at the surface. But such assurances have not stopped France and several US states from imposing

---

The US shale-gas industry seeks to allay fears about water pollution – the head of Halliburton Energy drank fracking fluids to show how safe they are.

---

a moratorium on fracking until more research has been carried out. A report by the EPA, ordered by Congress, will deliver its verdict next year. In the meantime, politicians will find it hard to resist the lure of an industry that promises jobs and clean fuel (see box). British MPs gave fracking the go-ahead this summer.

Is it full steam ahead?

Not quite, no. While the US shale-gas industry seeks to allay fears about water pollution – Dave Lesar, the head of Halliburton Energy, publicly drank a small quantity of fracking fluids to show how safe they are – in Britain the issue is earthquakes. In the spring of 2011, geologists detected two small 'seismic events' (magnitudes 2.3 and 1.4) at the Cuadrilla drilling site in Lancashire. And in an internal report, published in November 2011, the company admitted it was 'highly probable' that the tremors had been triggered by fracking at one of its exploration wells. Cuadrilla put the quakes down to unusual 'geological factors' that were unlikely to occur again, but the company subsequently had to wait for clearance to start drilling again. A report by government advisers gave the green light in April 2012.

THE LURE: MORE JOBS, FEWER EMISSIONS

In a different financial climate, the laboriousness of shale-gas extraction – the hundreds of wells that must be dug, the complex infrastructure involved in fracking – might be a disadvantage, but in depressed economies such as the USA and the UK, it means just one thing: jobs. Drilling the Marcellus Shale has led to 48,000 new jobs in Pennsylvania since 2010, plus billions of dollars in royalties for landowners in poor rural communities.

In the UK, oil and gas deposits belong to the government, but the promise of jobs is just as real. Cuadrilla Resources expects to create 5,600 highly skilled jobs, 1,700 of them in Lancashire.

Shale-gas proponents also point to their green credentials: natural gas is the cleanest-burning fossil fuel, producing 45 per cent less carbon dioxide than coal and 30 per cent less than oil.

Overall, however, a 'golden age of gas' would present the world with a dilemma rather than a solution to climate change. While a switch to new, plentiful supplies of cheap gas would offer a meaningful improvement on more polluting fuels, climate-change campaigners fear that it could significantly delay – or even prevent altogether – the transition to a truly carbon-free economy.

Who switched off the lights?

The European Union, *which in March 2007 agreed to phase out incandescent light bulbs by 2012. Proponents say that the old bulbs waste most of their energy (95 per cent) on heat, use up four times more electricity than the new breed of compact fluorescent lamps (CFLs) and are bad for the environment. Artificial light accounts for 19 per cent of the world's electricity consumption, producing 1.5 billion tonnes of CO_2 emissions a year, about 5 per cent of the global total. By switching its bulbs, Britain should save a million tonnes of CO_2 emissions a year, the equivalent of taking more than 150,000 cars off the roads. And if all the light bulbs in Europe are changed to energy-saving models, the continent will have reduced its CO_2 output by as much as 50 million tonnes a year: equivalent to planting ten million acres of forest.*

So how has it been done?

Each member state chose its own path. In Britain, the government asked retailers to help bring about a voluntary switch-over. The 150-watt bulb was scrapped in 2008; stocks of 100W and 75W bulbs were run down in 2009; 60W bulbs, commonly used for table and reading lamps, were phased out in 2010. From 2016, those who deal in old light bulbs will be committing a criminal offence. But the phase-out of the 100W and 75W bulbs initially led to a stampede as consumers tried to stockpile the old bulbs before the ban came into effect. In many parts of the country, it quickly became impossible to buy 100W or 75W incandescent bulbs.

Who came up with the bright idea of incandescent bulbs?

The glory usually goes to the American Thomas Edison, but it was the Briton Humphry Davy who, in 1802, created the first incandescent light by passing electrical current through a strip of platinum, a metal with a very high melting point. The light this gave was not bright or long-lasting enough to be practical, but it inspired dozens of inventors over the next 80 years. In February 1879, English chemist Joseph Swan revealed his invention: an enclosed bulb from which all air had been removed, with platinum lead wires and a light-emitting element made from carbon. Edison displayed his own bulb – with its famous 'filament' (the super-thin wire whose high electrical resistance generates a bright light) – six months later. It needed far less current than Swan's,

but Swan's patents were strong enough to win in British courts, and, in 1883, the Edison and Swan companies merged into the Edison and Swan United Electric Company.

What are the alternatives?

Most common is the CFL (compact fluorescent lamp), a coiled-up version of the strip lights found in offices. Rather than heating a metal filament, the electric current passes through a mixture of inert gases and mercury, producing a glow. Critics say the bulbs are ugly, expensive and simply not bright enough, that they take up to two minutes to warm up and that even then, the light given out has a blueish, harsh quality, unlike the warm glow of a traditional bulb. It's also said that CFLs flicker, causing headaches, eye strain, even seizures. And there's concern about the use of mercury, a substance the EU has otherwise banned as highly toxic, creating serious problems with disposal.

What did the government say?

That it's time to use less energy. The Department for the

Environment and Rural Affairs (Defra), which oversaw the change, said low-energy light bulbs would be a 'great way to help the environment and save money'. Because the new bulbs use less energy and last around 12 times longer than traditional ones, replacing a 100W one can save £60 over the new bulb's lifetime. Defra pointed out that the newest generation of CFL bulbs operate on a higher frequency than earlier models, which means a constant, flicker-free light. And as for concerns about mercury, Defra advised the public to take the new bulbs to council recycling plants, for disposal by specialist companies.

Are these cost and energy savings estimates reliable?

Not necessarily, argued Michael Hanlon in the *Daily Mail*. If a CFL is switched on and off frequently, it can shorten the working life of its electronic circuits. To reach full brightness at maximum efficiency, CFLs need to be left on for long periods, a bit like car engines. This negates any CO_2 savings if light is only needed for a short time. Others challenge their energy-saving credentials, pointing out

that the excess heat produced by incandescent bulbs is useful in a frequently cold country like Britain.

Has any non-EU country banned incandescent bulbs?

Cuba was the first to implement a ban, in 2005; Brazil and Venezuela followed suit – then Australia, Switzerland and Canada began their own phase-outs; in 2007, President George W. Bush signed legislation to consign incandescent

---

Artificial light accounts for 19 per cent of the world's electricity consumption, producing 1.5 billion tonnes of CO_2 emissions a year, about 5 per cent of the total.

---

bulbs to history by 2014. But many remain sceptical. The *LA Times* chose CFL bulbs ('a light source that does not render colour or texture') as one of the 'bad design trends we hope die'. By 2012, many Republicans were actively campaigning to repeal the law, with presidential hopeful Mitt Romney giving it as an example of President

Obama's over-mighty government. But a five-year phase-out has even been announced by China, which uses a quarter of the world's 3.85 billion incandescent bulbs.

Can we learn to love the new bulbs?

You can make CFLs warmer by using coloured shades; the latest versions can now be dimmed. Besides, CFLs are not the only option (see box); far better mercury-free LED lights are on their way. In any case, argued David Randall in the *Independent*, much of the initial resistance was based on our old friend, fear of change. 'The spirit of 1940' was being invoked by papers like the *Daily Mail* and *Daily Telegraph*, he said. 'The forces of eco-scepticism, anti-Europeanism, and those who oppose the Nanny State, have mustered. The cry has gone out that this is Lighting Correctness Gone Mad.' In the end, the reaction to the new bulbs is not that different to the reaction when incandescent bulbs became widespread a century ago. They were considered dangerous (a permanent risk of electrocution) and far too bright for any respectable household.

LOW-ENERGY OPTIONS: WHAT BULBS TO BUY

CFLs: The most common type of eco bulb, compact fluorescent lamps give out five times more light than traditional ones, so a 20W CFL replaces a traditional 100W bulb. Quality brands (Osram, Philips and Megaman) make CFLs that reach full brightness in a few seconds, and some can now be dimmed, too.

LED spotlights: LEDs, or light-emitting diodes, are even more energy-efficient, but expensive. Yet bulbs can last for up to 100,000 hours, so in effect never need replacing. However, as ambient lighting for the home, LEDs have a long way to go.

Halogen energy-savers: These bulbs' lifetime is two-thirds that of CFLs, but the quality of light is warmer and brighter – and they are dimmable. If you are replacing a 50W bulb, choose a 35W halogen energy-saver.

Fluorescent tubes: The old-fashioned strip light is energy-efficient, if ugly, but can be fitted along the top of cupboards, with a small facing to hide it. They will push a bright light up to the ceiling which will softly light the rest of the room.

(Source: the *Independent*)

How did Star Trek
conquer
the universe ?

As a multimedia, *pop-culture phenomenon, it's in the rarefied company of mega-franchises like* Superman, James Bond *and* Star Wars. *There have been 716 episodes of* Star Trek*'s various TV incarnations, along with eleven feature-length movies that have grossed some £800m. Merchandising, including home videos, action figures, computer games, toy laser guns, and other interstellar bric-a-brac, has pulled in another £2.6bn and, somewhere on Earth, a* Star Trek *book is sold every six seconds.* Star Trek *has also spawned an entire language, Klingon, and more websites than the US government, while many of the series' catchphrases – 'Resistance is futile' and 'Live long and prosper', for example – have joined the popular idiom.*

Why the enduring fascination?

Star Trek's simple but thought-provoking premise has proved to be irresistible. In virtually every *Star Trek* format, a crew of humans and aliens sets off in a giant spaceship to explore strange new worlds and advance the frontiers of knowledge, while getting in and out of trouble. Devotees say the flexible structure offers a convenient vehicle for delving into such universal themes as war, prejudice, power and love. It's also a lot of fun, with state-of-the-art special effects used to create a galaxy in which Earthlings, having invented such useful tools as teleporting and warp drive, interact with the cybernetic Borg, telepathic Betazoids, and countless other exotic species.

Who likes this stuff?

Forty-year-old nerds who still live with their parents, for a start. But beyond them, the ranks of Trekkies (or 'Trekkers', as many prefer to be called) include the Dalai Lama, *New York Times* publisher Arthur O. Sulzberger Jr, Bill Gates, and King Abdullah of Jordan, who made a guest appearance on a segment of *Star Trek: Voyager*. People who love *Star Trek*, says *Washington Post* writer Frank Ahrens, are 'perhaps the oddest, smartest, and most intense' on the planet. The most devoted of them are compelled to decorate their homes in *Star Trek* motifs, dress up in exact replicas of Starfleet uniforms, attempt to reconcile inconsistencies between episodes, and assimilate hoards of trivia questions, e.g.: 'What is the Vulcan time of mating called?' (*Pon farr* is the answer.)

Was Star Trek always this big?

Hardly. The original series, which ran from 1966 to 1969 on NBC, was a money-loser that never attracted a large audience. While some critics liked it, many didn't; *Variety* magazine called it a 'dreary mess of confusion'. The show was cancelled after 79 episodes, forcing the creator, Gene Roddenberry (a former bomber pilot and motorcycle cop) to make ends meet by selling *Star Trek* scripts, film clips and other memorabilia. William Shatner, who played the heroic Captain James T. Kirk, was reduced to living out of a camper van and appearing in B-movies like *Kingdom of the Spiders*.

So what turned it around?

Reruns, and fans. Syndicated in the early 1970s, *Star Trek* gradually accumulated a devoted following on local American TV channels. 'Thank God college kids discovered the show,' Roddenberry once said. By January 1972, the fans were motivated enough to organise the first *Star Trek* convention in New York, complete with panel discussions, a costume show and appearances by the cast. Conventions grew throughout the decade and in 1977 the explosive success of *Star Wars* helped revive the series. In 1979 *Star Trek: The Motion Picture* was released to mediocre reviews (some called it 'Star Trek: The Motion Sickness'), but the critical and box-office success of its sequel, *Star Trek II: The Wrath of Khan* (1982), assured the future of the franchise. Four television series followed, and new *Star Trek* episodes were made continually from 1987 to 2005. With an eleventh film in 2009, a prequel to the original show, the saga came full circle.

Is Star Trek good science fiction?

Many purists don't think so. Detractors criticise, among other things, its wooden storytelling, clunky moralising and implausible use of time travel. Even those who have worked on the show have got sick of it. David Gerrold, one of 55 writers on the original series, wrote in 1996: '*Star Trek* is the McDonald's of science fiction; it's fast-food storytelling. Every problem is like every other problem. They all get solved in an hour. Nobody ever gets hurt, and nobody needs to care. You give up an hour of your time, and you don't really have to get involved. It's all plastic.'

So why hasn't the series faded?

Once you get past the cheesy dialogue and dodgy acting, *Star Trek* offers an immensely comforting view of the universe to

---

William Shatner, who played the heroic Captain James T. Kirk, was reduced to living out of a camper van and appearing in B-movies like *Kingdom of the Spiders.*

---

come: after war, disease and other scourges have been conquered by benevolent science, mankind will unite and go forth to carry its collective destiny into the final frontier of space. Conceived during the Cold War, culture wars and racial antagonism of the 1960s, the series has always portrayed an unlikely, civilised future, in which all races and creeds will get along on the deck of the USS Enterprise. *Star Trek* showed American television's first interracial kiss, for instance, in 1968, when its cast included Africans, Chinese, Russians, Americans and half-aliens (Spock) all working together. And then, of course, there are the gadgets (see box).

A WINDOW INTO THE FUTURE

Much of *Star Trek*'s futuristic technology – faster-than-light travel, the transporter room – is purely speculative and will never come about, scientists say.

But the show has also been uncannily prescient about the development of other high-tech gizmos – sometimes actually shaping their invention. Martin Cooper, the Motorola engineer considered the father of the mobile phone, for instance, has said that early flip-top 'communicators' used in the show helped inspire him.

Likewise, Stephen Wozniak, the co-founder of computer firm Apple, used to watch the programme before sketching out ideas late at night, and Rob Haitani, the designer of PalmOne handheld computers, says he was inspired by the USS Enterprise's bridge panels.

A less direct path can also be traced from the 'library-computer' (used by Spock to research everything from personal histories to dead civilisations) to the internet, and the earpiece worn by Lt Uhura to today's Bluetooth wireless headsets. The 'holodeck' in *Star Trek: The Next Generation*, meanwhile, could conjure up entire worlds within the confines of a room, and offered an early glimpse of virtual reality.

What does officially being a pest mean?

You can be shot. *In 2009, the ring-necked parakeet, the world's most successful émigré parrot, joined the small club of British birds that can be killed without a special licence. Just forty years after they were first recorded breeding in the wild in Britain, parakeets were assigned the same status as magpies, feral pigeons and crows. That is to say, any landowner or other 'authorised person' can kill the birds as long as he or she has a good reason to believe they are a threat to crops or other wildlife. This 'general licence' applies only to common birds, such as wood pigeons and rooks, that can disrupt farming, or troublesome alien species. The South American monk parakeet and the Egyptian goose were added to the list in the same year.*

What problems do parakeets cause?

They oust natives from their roosts. Aggressive to other birds and highly sociable among their own kind, parakeets live in large flocks and, because they nest early in the year, they often beat woodpeckers and nuthatches to the best trees and nesting holes. Starlings, whose numbers fell by 60 per cent in 25 years, are also thought to be a victim. Once in place, the mid-sized, bright green parakeets have few predators and outcompete local rivals for berries and seeds. This led to fears that they could become 'the grey squirrel of the skies' – a marauding invader that threatens traditional British wildlife. Farmers don't like them either. As in other countries, parakeets are blamed for feasting on crops, especially fruit trees. Painshill Park vineyard, near Cobham in Surrey, claimed to have lost enough grapes in a single day of parakeet attacks to make 3,000 bottles of wine.

Where did they come from?

The Indian ring-necked parakeet (*Psittacula krameri*) is from the Himalayas. Spotted in the UK as early as 1855 – when sailors used to bring them back from Asia as pets – the parrots are known to have been breeding in the wild since 1969 and there have been plenty of escapes before and since to boost the population: parakeets got out during the filming of *The African Queen* at Shepperton Studios in 1951; Jimi Hendrix lost a pair on Carnaby Street; and aviaries were wrecked by the 1987 hurricane. Whatever the source, by 2009 there were 44,000 parakeets in Britain. They outnumbered kingfishers, barn owls and nightingales and their numbers were growing by 30 per cent a year. In the 2006 Big Garden Birdwatch, the parrots were seen in all thirty-three London boroughs.

Why were there so many?

They are brilliant migrants. Originally from a cold habitat, parakeets cope easily with British weather, but the climate hasn't stopped them settling in warmer European countries as well as in Iran, South Africa and Japan, and also in Florida. In the UK, they also benefit from the absence of predators – at 16 inches long they are a tough proposition for a house cat. Meanwhile, their diet of berries, nuts and seeds is plentifully supplied by the gardens and parks of London and the Southeast, where nine out of ten parakeets live. The environment has proved so hospitable that one colony is now thousands strong and lives in the trees of Esher Rugby Club in Surrey, whose women's rugby team is known as 'The Parakeets' and plays in green.

So they were all killed?

Hardly. 'General licence' does not

mean open season against the parakeets. To kill a bird or destroy its eggs you must give a legitimate reason: to conserve habitats, crops, timber or fisheries, or to prevent the spread of disease. Anyone killing birds without a reason faces a £5,000 fine or a six-month jail sentence. Natural England, the body responsible for designating pests, said the parakeet problem was not yet serious but warned that if the

---

Parakeets got out during the filming of *The African Queen* at Shepperton Studios in 1951; Jimi Hendrix lost a pair on Carnaby Street; and aviaries were wrecked by the 1987 hurricane.

---

birds got out of the Southeast, the problems would multiply.

Does everyone agree that they are 'pests'?

No. The London Wildlife Trust argues that parakeets are 'as British as curry' and maintains that there is little evidence the birds are pests. The Trust thinks that their negative impact have been exaggerated, and fears for the safety of similar-looking birds like the green woodpecker, which could be shot by mistake. Ian Rotherham, of Sheffield Hallam University, meanwhile, questions the merit of controlling invasive species at all.

But why shouldn't we try to limit their numbers?

Because, so the argument goes, we've been introducing non-native species, like cats (the Romans), rabbits (the Normans) and potatoes (Sir Francis Drake) for hundreds of years. 'British' wildlife is a mix of the indigenous and the newly arrived. Rotherham sees culls of alien species as 'eco-xenophobia', a prejudice that ignores the equally severe problems caused by native wildlife. Japanese knotweed, for example, receives publicity, public funding and tax breaks to help control its spread, while the equally pesky British buddleia and clematis do not. Likewise, bracken destroys heathland and badgers spread disease among cattle, but it is the 'foreign' grey squirrels and muntjac deer that get killed.

Rotherham highlights the positive contributions that invasive species like the rhododendron and Corsican pine have made, and argues that conservation efforts should focus on 'problem' species, not simply hitting those from overseas.

And is Rotherham right?

He has natural history on his side. As researchers from the Botanical Society of the British Isles noted in 2007: 'Many of our rarest and most treasured plants are recent arrivals, brought here by people in the last 2,000 years or so, or as natural immigrants as the climate became increasingly temperate.' In fact, almost the entire flora and fauna of the UK has arrived since the last Ice Age, 10,000 years ago. Fixation with alien species, says the Society, can distract us from larger challenges, such as the destruction of habitats. On a different note, the pressure group Animal Aid say that invasive species are used as scapegoats for the failings of humans; the real ecological dangers are modern farming, urban sprawl and industrial pollution.

THE UK: A SOFT TOUCH FOR IMMIGRANTS?

According to DAISIE (Delivering Alien Invasive Species Inventory for Europe), a three-year research project funded by the EU, more alien species live in Britain than in any other country in Europe. Of the 100 most problematic species found in Europe, 62 have reached Britain. The North American grey squirrel, Japanese knotweed and the Harlequin ladybird are all examples.

The main culprit is the free movement of people and goods. 'Trade is the biggest source of movement of species, and new transport routes are being opened up all the time,' says David Roy, from the Nerc Centre for Ecology and Hydrology, who coordinated the research. The government responded by launching the UK's first 'non-native species strategy' to deal with invasive pests like the Floating Pennywort, North American Signal Crayfish and American Mink.

Circumcision:
to cut
or **not to cut** ?

Since 1911, citizens *of California have been able to introduce new laws by collecting signatures on a petition and then putting the proposal to a referendum. The system also works for city government, and in May 2011 a group of activists opposed to male circumcision managed to collect the requisite 7,000 signatures for a 'San Francisco Male Genital Mutilation bill' to be placed before the city's voters six months later. The draft law proposed a ban on circumcising males under the age of 18, except for medical reasons. Breaking the law would incur a jail sentence of up to a year and a $1,000 fine. Unsurprisingly, the idea caused outrage among religious groups, and left doctors fielding awkward questions about the merits and disadvantages of this ancient medical procedure.*

What are the origins of circumcision?

Early Egyptian illustrations show how a baby boy's foreskin should be removed, and the practice became common among followers of the Abrahamic faiths – Christianity, Judaism and Islam. 'The uncircumcised man child whose flesh of his foreskin is not circumcised, that soul shall be cut off from his people; he hath broken my covenant,' Abraham chides in Genesis, and the ritual of circumcision, central to Judaism, remains an expression of Jewish identity. The ceremony, held eight days after a son's birth, is performed at home or in a synagogue by a *mohel*, who uses a scalpel or knife exclusively reserved for circumcision. Islam is the largest religious community to follow the practice – though it is not compulsory for Muslims.

Why isn't it universally practised among Christians?

St Paul, who – like Jesus and the early Christians – was himself circumcised, turned against the practice, hoping to make Christianity more palatable to Greeks and Romans. Hellenistic and Roman societies widely practised public nakedness, but regarded the idea of baring the tip of the penis as abhorrent. However, circumcision remains customary in some Christian churches in Africa and in some Oriental Orthodox churches. It is also practised in many other areas of the world, from Korea to Africa, where it is a coming-of-age ceremony in some tribes. The World Health Organisation (WHO) estimates that 30 per cent of males in the world are circumcised, of whom 68 per cent are Muslim.

Are there non-religious reasons to justify the practice?

Yes. In nineteenth-century Britain, it was prescribed to discourage masturbation and ward off sexually transmitted infections (STIs) in adulthood. 'The prepuce [foreskin] is a frequent source of disease, often requiring its removal,' wrote London physician Dr M. Clifford in 1893. And there's good evidence that circumcision reduces the risk of STIs, including syphilis and herpes, as well as of cervical cancer in women – one cause of which is the human papillomavirus, which thrives under the foreskin. In 2007, WHO announced that three separate trials had shown a 60 per cent reduction in the risk of contracting HIV among circumcised men in Africa. Circumcision, along with measures such as abstinence and condom use, is now part of the WHO's 'HIV prevention package'.

So why doesn't everyone support it?

Because many feel the benefits identified by research are insufficient to justify a procedure that's unnecessary and painful.

Campaigners in the USA ('intactivists', they call themselves) point out that the WHO's findings on HIV infection rates don't stack up in America, which is ravaged by HIV despite having had high rates of male circumcision until recently. A 2003 study conducted in the UK reported 'no significant differences' in the proportion of circumcised or uncircumcised men reporting an STI diagnosis. Such doubts, combined with the small but real risk of

---

Many feel the benefits are insufficient to justify a procedure that's painful. 'Intactivists' point out that findings on HIV infection rates don't stack up despite high rates of male circumcision.

---

infection or accident resulting from the procedure, has meant that few if any professional associations of physicians take a line on whether or not children should have it.

But why are US campaigners so opposed to it?

Groups such as Intact America,

from upstate New York, and California's MGM.org – the initials stand for Male Genital Mutilation – say it's a question of rights. 'Nobody has a right to perform unnecessary surgery on another human being,' argues Lloyd Schofield, who led the San Francisco campaign; until boys reach the age of consent, they should, just like girls under 18, be protected by law from having circumcision inflicted on them. However, the comparison with female circumcision is wide of the mark. Female circumcision is far more dangerous, involves the removal of the clitoris, has no health benefits and makes childbearing much more risky. The Intactivists' real agenda, say the critics, is ill-disguised anti-Semitism (see box). 'This is the most direct assault on Jewish religious practice in the US,' said Marc Stern, a lawyer for the American Jewish Committee, when election officials revealed there would be a referendum. 'It's unprecedented.'

So what's likely to happen?

Nothing. A plan was drawn up to challenge the ban on grounds of freedom of religion, but in the end it wasn't necessary. In late July 2011, a judge ruled that medical procedures are regulated by the state of California, rather than its cities, and scrapped the proposal. But the intactivists may yet have the last laugh.

And why is that?

Because circumcision is rapidly declining in the USA, which until recently had one of the highest rates of circumcision in the developed world, at around 80 per cent. Since the late 1990s, however, the proportion has fallen to 32 per cent – partly as a result of America's growing Hispanic population, which does not favour the practice, but also because the state-run Medicaid healthcare provider has stopped paying for the procedure, and private insurers in 23 states have followed its lead. In the UK, too, the popularity of the procedure waned after the establishment of the NHS, which does not carry out routine circumcisions. In this country, around three per cent of boys up to age 16 are circumcised, mainly for medical reasons (although, by a quirk, all the men in the Royal Family are circumcised).

FORESKIN MAN AND ANTI-SEMITISM

The campaign against circumcision is largely the brainchild of San Diego activist Matthew Hess, who sought to boost support for the MGM bill by creating an internet comic series. Its central character is 'Foreskin Man'– a blonde, blue-eyed superhero whose adversaries include doctors who practise circumcision and Orthodox Jews.

One character, 'Monster Mohel', is a bearded, black-hatted Jew who clutches bloody scissors while leering at his infant victims: in one episode, the *mohel* barges into a San Diego home, snatches a baby boy from his mother, and attempts to circumcise the infant on a pool table before being stopped by Foreskin Man.

'Nothing excites Monster Mohel more,' the Foreskin Man trading cards announce, 'than cutting into the penile flesh of an eight-day-old infant boy.' Jewish groups have likened the comic strip to the grotesque Jewish stereotypes that appeared in Nazi propaganda.

What's the point of the
European
Central **Bank**

?

It came into being with the euro. In 1992, when the Maastricht Treaty set the EU on the path to the single currency, it was agreed that the new Eurozone would need a single, central bank to look after it. Based in its own skyscraper in Frankfurt, Germany's financial capital, it would control the amount of euros in circulation and set interest rates, much as national central banks do. It began operations on 1 January 1999, with deposits of €4bn contributed by all EU members, Britain included. Three years later, it supervised the introduction of euro banknotes (euro members were allowed to mint their own coins). Yet from the start the ECB has been a very different animal from other central banks.

How does it differ from them?

In its official duties, for a start. A central bank like the US Federal Reserve has three legal duties: to help grow the economy, to boost employment and to control inflation. With such broad obligations, such a bank will often – especially during financial crises – take a range of actions to prop up the economy, from directly buying up its government's bonds to buying up troubled banks. By contrast, the ECB is expressly forbidden by Article 104 of the Maastricht Treaty (the 'no bailout clause') to finance any state in the Eurozone: it is explicitly prohibited, for example, from buying government bonds in the primary market (i.e. when first issued). In fact, it only has one mission, what it calls 'price stability' – that is, keeping inflation at or around 2 per cent.

Why was it limited in this way?

In part because eurozone countries still have their own central banks devoted to supporting their own economies. They may share the same currency, but they retain the freedom to trade in foreign currencies, buy and sell bonds, encourage private banks to lend money and so on. The ECB, sitting in the centre of these 17 national banks in a web known as the Eurosystem, is supposed to coordinate their activities but not get directly involved itself. Almost the only way the ECB is meant to intervene in the economy is to control inflation by altering the flow of billions of euros of short-term loans (from one week to three months) that it makes to fellow banks across the EU – in short, turning the euro tap on and off.

And has it been good at that job?

The ECB website shows a graph of inflation in the EU since 1990. From 1998, when the bank assumed its responsibility for 'price stability', there is a level blue line, at just above 2 per cent. To its supporters, this is the mark of its success. Despite the economic turmoil in Europe, it has tamed inflation and proved the ultimate haven for worried banks and investors. Since 2007, the ECB's balance sheet has tripled to almost €3trn. In December, it had overnight deposits of almost €500bn, as banks and big companies flocked to store their money. To its critics, however, the sheer size, credibility and power of the ECB (its assets are ten times larger than the Greek economy and it has enough deposits to pay off the Irish budget deficit 20 times over) mean that it should be doing far more to save the euro.

What could it do in principle?

Many economists (and European politicians) have argued for the bank to go beyond its historic brief and guarantee its members' sovereign debts – either by direct bailouts (so far the ECB hasn't contributed to any bailout) or by buying up unpopular assets (e.g. Greek or Italian government bonds) and replacing them with its own Eurobonds. Even with no change in its brief, they'd still like the ECB to be far more aggressive in buying up sovereign bonds in the secondary market, rather than pursue its present piecemeal, panicky bond buying. Some argue that had the ECB imposed a yield cap and undertaken to buy up troubled sovereign bonds as soon as yields hit, say, 6.5 per cent, it could have put a lid on the debt crisis. 'There's no solution to it without the ECB,' says Charles Wyplosz of the Graduate Institute in Geneva. 'The amounts we're talking about are too big for anyone but the ECB.'

How does the ECB respond?

It says it's doing more than people give it credit for: in 2011, it bought around €250bn of unwanted Spanish and Italian government bonds in the secondary market. Its main strategy, however, has been to work through Europe's banks. Days before Christmas

2011, it lent them €489bn at 1 per cent for an unprecedented three years (as opposed to the usual three months). The hope was that this cheap cash would encourage European banks – enticed by the prospect of a massive 'carry' profit – to buy unpopular sovereign bonds paying 5–7 per cent. To some this seemed absurd. 'Italian banks are now issuing state-guaranteed paper to obtain funds from the ECB and

---

From 1998, when the bank assumed its responsibility for 'price stability', there is a level blue line, at just above 2 per cent. To its supporters, this is the mark of its success.

---

then reinvesting the proceeds in Italian bonds,' said Bill Gross of Pimco. 'This is quantitative easing by any definition and near Ponzi by another.' But the bank's famously conservative officials insist that ECB bailouts, even if made legal, would make governments less inclined to tackle the basic problems of their economies, a view that happens to be exactly Germany's position.

So how 'German' is the ECB?

As well as being based in Frankfurt, the bank's overriding mission – to control inflation – was transplanted directly from Germany's central bank, where fear of the hyperinflation that gripped Germany in the 1920s is near-pathological. The Bundesbank is also the ECB's largest depositor and by far the most powerful of the 17 national banks in the Eurosystem (see box). But, to German eyes at least, the country's control seems under threat. The appointment of Mario Draghi, an Italian, as president was controversial, and in January 2012 a Belgian was named as the ECB's new chief economist. Yet money still talks, and German Chancellor Angela Merkel has made her feelings clear. 'If politicians believe the ECB can solve the problem of the euro's weakness,' she said, 'then they're trying to convince themselves of something that won't happen.'

THE GERMAN EAR OF THE PRESIDENT

There has never been a German president of the ECB – the first was Dutch economist Wim Duisenberg and the second Jean-Claude Trichet, governor of the bank of France – but that hasn't stopped Germany controlling the bank's inner workings.

In negotiations for the Maastricht Treaty, Germany won the argument to have the bank in Frankfurt. Otmar Issing, a German economics professor, became the ECB's first chief economist, designing its operations and the way it uses the money supply to control inflation.

In 2006, Issing was replaced by another German economist, Jürgen Stark, who used his influential position on the bank's 23-member governing council (each Eurozone member has a member, and there are six political appointees) to preserve the bank's conservative focus on inflation throughout the financial crisis. In September 2011, Stark announced his resignation after the ECB began buying Spanish and Italian sovereign bonds, a move he saw as a breach of its independence.

Yet Germany still has the president's ear: the ECB's governing council sits in a circle alphabetically, so the new German members, Jens Weidmann and Jörg Asmussen, sit on either side of the president and vice-president at every meeting.

What is the 'natural' gender ratio ?

Humankind seems to *have evolved in such a way that a few more male babies are born than females. Over centuries, demographers have discerned a ratio of 105 (sometimes 106) boys for every 100 girls – a ratio that still applies to babies born in the UK. Boy babies are frailer, and men tend to take more risks and die earlier than women, so over time the ratio equalises, until women outnumber men in old age. However, today's global sex ratio at birth is not in step with nature. It is running at 107 male births to 100 females, and in some countries, such as China, it is as high as 120:100. The reason is the strong preference, especially in Asia, for a son rather than a daughter. This is enacted in the form of millions of abortions every year and – somewhat unexpectedly – the problem is getting worse.*

Why is that unexpected?

It is no great secret that families in traditional patriarchal societies want a male heir. For centuries, many parts of the world have been blighted by the infanticide of baby girls. The economist Amartya Sen drew attention to the impact of this gender preference in India in his 1980s study of India's 'missing women'. What has surprised demographers is the discovery that economic development has not eased the problem. Increasingly prosperous and urbanised populations are actually more likely to get rid of females, albeit as foetuses rather than as full-term babies. India's 2011 census showed the lowest ratio of girls to boys under the age of six since 1947, with discrepancies even showing in parts of the country where the sex ratio had been balanced. In 2000, Vietnam had a nearly normal sex ratio; by 2010, it was 111:100. Increasing gender imbalances have also been recorded in Central Asia, and among immigrant populations in the USA.

Why are they increasing?

Technology. Since the 1970s, tests such as amniocentesis and ultrasound, developed to check foetuses for signs of ill health, have been co-opted for gender selection. These tests tend to be available first to the richer and more urbanised parts of society, which also have access to clinics willing to carry out abortions. In India, an ultrasound scan, commonly known as 'the sex test', costs about 600 rupees (just under £8). Female births have also been jeopardised by the tendency, as societies industrialise, for parents to have smaller families, thus curtailing their chances to have a boy. In China, the one-child policy has made this especially stark: in places where a second child is allowed if the first is a girl, the sex ratio for the second is 143:100.

What are the consequences?

'If you're going to wipe out 20 per cent of your population, nature is not going to sit by and watch,' says Dr Puneet Bedi, a doctor in the maternity ward of the Apollo Hospital in Delhi. The most obvious result of not having enough women in a society is that fewer babies are born. (Indeed, in the 1960s, demographers recommended sex selection as a means of population control.) But that brings with it many sorts of social collateral damage – most resulting from having too many single young men around. In 2007, researchers in the USA and Hong Kong noticed a clear correlation between Chinese crime rates and parts of the country with the steepest gender imbalance. Societies with surplus males, or 'bare branches', as they are known in China, have been linked with violence and lawlessness from ancient Athens to the Wild West: the sex ratio in California in 1850 was 1,228:100.

Won't scarcity raise women's stock?

Yes, but not necessarily in ways that benefit them. In China, bidding for wives is already common, with families saving up

---

Societies with surplus males, or 'bare branches', have been linked with violence and lawlessness from ancient Athens to the Wild West: the sex ratio in California in 1850 was 1,228:100.

---

to £10,000 to attract a woman for their son. But leaving aside the emotional ramifications of all this, the economic logic of such a market is that while wealthy men will always be able to find women, the gender imbalance will become even more marked and damaging in poorer sections

of society. Sex trafficking, mail-order brides and prostitution are already known consequences of the shortage of women in parts of India and China. 'The greatest danger associated with prenatal sex determination is the propagation of a female underclass,' says Lena Edlund of Columbia University.

Can anything be done about this?

In many countries, laws and public-information campaigns are already in place. Abortion on the grounds of sex is now illegal in India and China. Since 1994, doctors in India have been barred from revealing the sex of a foetus during a scan (although a friendly slap on the father's back is still common). The problem is that real financial incentives to favour sons remain: in societies with no welfare state, parents feel that a son is more likely to be able to support them in old age. At the other end of the spectrum, in rich countries improvements in fertility technology and the mantra of choice in all things suggest that selecting a baby's sex may even become more common (see box).

Is there any reason for hope?

China, whose gender imbalance has consequences for the rest of the planet, has promised to take the matter in hand. In 2011, Luo Mai, director of China's National Population and Family Planning Commission, said that redressing the sex ratio of its babies was one of the country's national priorities, with welfare reform a possible tool. In India, meanwhile, recent surveys of births have shown a more mixed picture than the 2011 census, suggesting that the country's gender imbalance may be getting worse at a slower rate than demographers had previously expected. A consolation, but only a small one in the circumstances. As Dr Bedi, the obstetrician, says: 'We are [still] dealing with genocide.'

SEX SELECTION: CALIFORNIA-STYLE

'Be certain your next child will be the gender you're hoping for,' says the website of the Fertility Institutes in Los Angeles. The clinic has been offering in-vitro fertilisation since 1986, and nowadays 70 per cent of its patients make use of it to choose the sex of their baby.

In the research for her book *Unnatural Selection*, US science writer Mara Hvistendahl travelled the world investigating the propensity of parents to select foetuses on the grounds of sex, and found plenty of enthusiasts in one of the world's most sophisticated and 'progressive' communities.

'Americans don't talk about gender preference,' writes Hvistendahl. 'We say "family balancing", a term that implies couples have an inherent right to an equal number of boys and girls. And we talk of "gender disappointment", a deep grief arising from not getting what we want.'

In the USA and Europe, the ethics of choosing a baby's sex comes up in the debate over 'designer babies' and how best to balance the forces of medical technology, our personal whims and the natural world. In California, the main difference from the rest of the world is that gender preference has been reversed: in IVF clinics at least, Californians prefer girls.

What motivated General Mladic?

The war crimes trial *in The Hague of the former military leader of the Bosnian Serb forces began in June 2011. Devoted to the cause of Greater Serbia, General Mladic liked to refer to himself as 'the Serbian God'. He was obsessed, said Gordon Rayner in the* Daily Telegraph, *with the idea of 'exterminating or driving out every Muslim, Croat and non-Serb from Bosnia' in his quest to carve a Greater Serbia out of the ruins of Bosnia, Croatia and Kosovo. And during the Bosnian War of 1992–1995 – the bloodiest conflict in Europe since the Second World War, in which at least 110,000 of Bosnia's four million people were killed – that is precisely what he tried to do.*

Was he the mastermind of that war?

No. As its ruthless and omnipresent military leader, he worked in tandem with the political leader of the Bosnian Serbs, Radovan Karadzic, also indicted for war crimes in The Hague. But both men – dubbed 'the psychopath' and 'the psychiatrist' (Karadzic's former profession) – were creatures, at least at the start, of the man who was president both of Serbia and of the disintegrating, Serb-dominated Yugoslav federation: Slobodan Milosevic. A former communist apparatchik, Milosevic exploited the rising tide of nationalism that accompanied the collapse of the Yugoslav Communist Party in 1990 in order to cement his power.

How did Milosevic exploit it?

As Yugoslavia fell apart, he stepped up the Serbian nationalist rhetoric, recognised the legitimacy of Serb breakaway entities in Croatia and Bosnia, and purged the Yugoslav army of non-Serbs. And when Croatia and Slovenia declared independence in 1991, he encouraged Serbs in Croatia to take up arms and sent in the Yugoslav army to help them seize control of some 25 per cent of Croatia. Among their number was the man who was to become the embodiment of Balkan terror: Colonel Ratko Mladic. The reputation he quickly acquired for efficient brutality (a senior UN official described him even then as 'a psychopath: highly intelligent and profoundly violent') recommended him to Milosevic. So when Bosnia in turn declared independence in 1992, the Serbian president sent his henchman Mladic back to his native Bosnia, promoted him to

general and made him head of the Bosnian Serb military. It was under Mladic's military leadership that Bosnia became, in the next three years, the scene of the worst bloodshed in the breakup of Yugoslavia: 'a whirlwind,' said Ian Traynor in the *Guardian*, 'of murder, pogrom, siege and destruction, giving birth to the term "ethnic cleansing".'

Why Bosnia?

A patchwork of nationalities – Serbs, Croats and Muslims (Bosniaks), none constituting a majority – Bosnia-Herzegovina was always a fragile entity: coveted by, and at one time or another controlled by, neighbouring Croatia or Serbia. Thus when Mladic was born in 1942, Bosnia was under the control of the pro-Nazi Croatian regime: Mladic's father, a Serb partisan, was killed by Croat soldiers. The deep antagonism many Bosnian Serbs felt for their fellow Muslim and Croat Bosnians meant that the vast majority boycotted the referendum on independence: instead, with the backing of Milosevic's forces, they set up their own Bosnian

Serb republic – Republika Srpska – under Karadzic. Within a few months, the Bosnian Serb army under Mladic had taken over 70 per cent of Bosnia, putting millions of Bosniaks to flight, killing thousands, and laying siege to the capital, Sarajevo, a largely Muslim city – famed, said *The Times*, 'for its sophistication and multi-ethnic tolerance'.

What happened in Sarajevo?

For the next 43 months, the city endured the longest siege in modern warfare. Some 10,000 of its citizens were killed. Scurrying through the streets in a desperate search for food and water, they were picked off by Serb snipers or blown up by field guns. Mladic took personal charge of the siege: according to Gordon Rayner, he could be heard bellowing 'Burn their brains' as he urged his troops to bombard the city. Sporadic humanitarian aid was provided by UN peacekeeping forces, sent in to monitor the conflict in February 1992, but they were a feeble presence.

Why couldn't they stop the bloodshed?

Partly because the British government, led by John Major, played a key role in persuading the international community not to intervene: foreign secretary Douglas Hurd's refusal to lift the international arms embargo also ensured that, throughout the war, the lightly armed Bosniaks had no real chance of fighting back. (They came to rely, increasingly,

---

Mladic took personal charge of the siege of Sarajevo: he could be heard bellowing 'Burn their brains' as he urged his troops to bombard the city.

---

on a combined force of 'Afghan' volunteers – mainly Arab 'Afghans' – and Bosnian Islamists.) But it was also because Mladic was so adept at schmoozing, tricking and bullying UN, Nato, British and French officials into doing things his way. As a result, instead of forestalling attacks, the peacekeepers were often reduced to supplying the victims with food. Such was Mladic's contempt for the UN that he went on to attack UN safe havens at Gorazde, Bihac (where he took 200 UN soldiers hostage) and Srebrenica – scene of the worst atrocity on European soil since the Holocaust (see box).

Were Serbs always the culprits?

By no means. Atrocities committed by Croats against Serbs and against Muslims (Croatia was just as keen as Serbia to grab bits of Bosnia for itself) are well documented. And as Mladic's defenders like to argue, his attacks were often in response to the murder of Serb civilians by Muslims: they cite the attack on Orthodox Christmas Day on the village of Kravica, near Srebrenica, where one of Srebrenica's worst massacres later took place. But it was Mladic's forces who committed the most heinous crimes, if only by virtue of the fact that they had far greater military strength.

THE MASSACRES AT SREBRENICA

Even before Ratko Mladic led his forces to the eastern Bosnian town of Srebrenica in July 1995, the townsfolk, cut off from the outside world for three-and-a-half years, had endured terrible suffering. 'It was like a big concentration camp,' one survivor told *The Times*. When Nato aircraft dropped food, 'people would run towards it, but there were so many some would suffocate.'

It was designated a UN 'safe haven' and 'protected' by 600 Dutch peacekeepers, who requested an air strike to prevent Mladic's forces from shelling the town. But the French commander of the UN Protection Force, General Bertrand Janvier, who had dined with Mladic days before, declined the request on the grounds that the wrong form had been filled in. After entering the bombarded town, Mladic then quaffed champagne with the Dutch UN commander and got him to deliver an ultimatum for its terrified citizens to surrender. 'You don't have to be afraid. Nobody will harm you,' Mladic reassured them.

But even as his soldiers handed out sweets to the children, said Jon Swain in the *Sunday Times*, the children's fathers and brothers were being led away to be killed. Some were mown down in the town square, or herded into warehouses and slaughtered. Others were clubbed to death or had their throats slit as they tried to escape through the forests to safety. In all, some 8,000 Muslim men and boys are thought to have been killed. Bulldozers were later brought in to bury many of them in mass graves.

What is a solar storm?

Three large eruptions *took place on the surface of the Sun on 2 and 3 August 2011, gouging huge amounts of gas, energy and radiation (literally pieces of the Sun) out into space. These eruptions, known as solar flares, combined to make the most powerful solar storm for five years. Fortunately for us, the bulk of the 'coronal mass ejection', as scientists call it, did not come anywhere near Earth – but a shower of radiation arrived about five days later, with enough force to disrupt satellites, pose a threat to astronauts and trigger the Aurora Borealis (Northern Lights) as far south as Germany and Poland. The largest solar storm on record took place in 1859, bringing enough energy to start fires, short-circuit the newfangled telegraph system, and display the Northern Lights in Cuba.*

What causes these storms?

The precise mechanics of the Sun are still not understood. (It is easy to forget what a staggering object it is: containing 99.86 per cent of the mass of the solar system, it's bigger than a million Earths.) But it is known that solar flares erupt near patches of the surface known as sunspots. Sunspots appear to the naked eye as tiny darkenings (some are 80,000km wide), and they are considerably cooler than the rest of the Sun's surface. They are caused when the star's complex magnetic fields become twisted and contorted. Crudely speaking, the more sunspots there are at a given time, the more active is the Sun. Since 1843, astronomers have noticed that solar activity ebbs and flows in cycles that last about 11 years. The current cycle is due to reach its 'solar maximum' in 2013, hence the increase in solar activity and storms at the moment.

So these storms are not unusual?

Not at this stage of the solar cycle. There were other large flares in 2011, and NASA issued a solar storm warning in early 2012. Just because they are common, though, that does not mean they are unimportant, and scientists warn that we are becoming increasingly vulnerable to solar storms (see box). However, what has really grabbed astronomers' attention has not been these bursts of activity from the Sun – but the prospect that it may be about to go dim for a long while. The Sun might be cranking up for the busiest phase of its current solar cycle, but plenty

of observers believe that – for the first time in 200 years – there may not be another cycle to follow.

Why do they think that?

Because the usual early indicators of the next solar cycle are simply not there. Since the mid-1990s, scientists have observed that each cycle is presaged by the growth of a huge jet stream that carries energy and magnetic activity towards the Sun's north pole. They expected the jet stream for the next solar cycle, due to begin in 2020, to start forming in 2008 or 2009, but as yet there's no sign of it. What's more, despite the recent storms, the current solar cycle (the 24th since records began) has only manifested half as many sunspots as the one before, suggesting an overall weakening in the Sun's activity. 'The next one, Cycle 25, may not happen,' says Dr Frank Hill of the National Solar Observatory in Tucson, Arizona. 'The solar cycle may be going into hiatus, like a TV show.'

Has this happened before?

Yes. Records of solar activity only go back as far as 1610, but since then there have been two periods of diminished solar activity (both named after scientists): the 'Maunder Minimum' (1645–1715) and the 'Dalton Minimum' (1790–1830). Between them, they lasted just over a century – coinciding with a period of global cooling known as the Little Ice Age. The Thames froze for months of the year and there were ice floes in the North Sea. During the winter of 1684, at the depths of

There's no obvious link between activity on the Sun and how hot it is on Earth. A skipped solar cycle could lead to a decrease in average temperatures, but only a fraction of the predicted rise.

the Maunder Minimum, diarist John Evelyn described 'streets of booths set up upon the Thames' in London. One of the reasons Stradivarius violins sound so fine is thought to be because they date from this period, when the cold slowed tree growth, causing wood to become more dense.

So is the world about to get cooler once again?

Climate-change sceptics have certainly leapt on the idea. For those who point out that the Earth has long experienced variations in climate, news that the Sun may be entering a dull phase after decades of relatively high activity provides a welcome alternative to the narrative of global warming, and suggests there is more to the story than manmade carbon emissions. 'A new Ice Age is on its way,' writes James Delingpole in his blog for the *Daily Telegraph*. 'This makes global cooling a much more plausible prospect in the next few decades than global warming.'

Do most scientists and astronomers think so, too?

They're not so sure. Counter-intuitive as it may sound, there's no obvious link between activity on the Sun and how hot it is on Earth. Scientists agree that a skipped solar cycle could lead to a decrease in average temperatures, but most seem to feel it would probably only be between 0.1°C and 0.3°C, a fraction of the 3.7°C and 4.5°C rise that the Intergovernmental Panel on Climate Change now predicts for the end of this century. They also point out that the Little Ice Age lasted more than 300 years, far longer than the Maunder and Dalton Minimums, and its worst effects were mostly restricted to Europe: across the world as a whole, temperatures dipped by less than half a degree. The truth is we don't know what will happen, but that has not stopped Sun-watchers seeing what they want to see. 'It is unfortunate,' says Dr Hill, 'that global warming/cooling studies have become so politically polarising.'

TSUNAMIS IN SPACE

Scientists charged with monitoring solar activity have two fears relating to solar storms, which have been likened to 'tsunamis in space'. The first concerns humanity's reliance on satellite and communication systems that can be disrupted by solar storms. That dependence has increased enormously since the last solar maximum ten years ago: GPS technology, smart electricity grids, oil pipelines, power and other electronic infrastructure are all vulnerable. The UK government's chief scientific adviser, Sir John Beddington, has warned that a solar storm could cause as much as £1tn of damage worldwide.

The second fear is to do with prediction. According to Thomas Bogdan, director of the Space Weather Prediction Centre in Boulder, Colorado, there is just one satellite positioned between the Sun and the Earth to warn us of the approach of billions of tonnes of energy and charged particles hitting the atmosphere. The satellite gives a 20-minute warning and a good description of 'how big, how strong, how nasty that storm might be', said Bogdan in 2011. 'The trouble is, it's 14 years old, and what keeps me awake at night is worrying about whether that satellite would be running the next morning when I get up.'

Is cryonics the path to immortality?

Cryonicists believe *that, in the nearish future, medicine will have advanced so far that disease, ageing and death will all be reversible. But until that point arrives, the important thing is to arrest biological time by keeping the body as well preserved as possible. And the best way to do that is by freezing it.*

Why freezing?

There are well-attested cases of people being revivified after being clinically dead in sub-zero temperatures. In the 18th century a Swedish peasant was found 'frozen stiff' in the snow, apparently dead. As his friends conducted a raucous wake, a physician passing by the coffin noticed faint signs of life. The man was warmed and recovered. In 2001 a Canadian toddler wandered into the snow and 'died' of hypothermia, but was revived an hour later none the worse for her ordeal.

Who first thought of cryonics?

It was the brainchild of Robert Ettinger, a Michigan chemistry teacher whose book *The Prospect of Immortality* launched the cryonics movement 50 years ago. Ettinger, who died in 2011, is viewed with almost religious awe by his followers. In his book he claimed that scientists were on the verge of finding a new method of freezing bodies without destroying cells, and speculated that dead neurons may one day be reparable. You could cheat death, he said, if you 'freeze, wait and reanimate'. The first ever cryonaut, 73-year-old academic James Bedford, was frozen in 1967.

How does one embark on immortality?

The most serious threat to everlasting life, say the cryonicists, is the point just after you deanimate (no one 'dies' in cryonics circles). In the minutes and hours after the blood stops circulating, irreversible structural damage is inflicted on the brain, so the main priority is to get hold of the body before its point of no return – what cryonicists call its biological death, as distinct from clinical death, which is seen as an unavoidable, inconvenient step on the road to your second life cycle. Thus, when a would-be cryonaut deanimates, his body is immediately chilled, often in an ice bath in an ambulance, and brought to a cryonics centre. Clients are advised to reserve a private jet in advance, to minimise delay.

What happens then?

The body undergoes perfusion, a process in which the blood is drained and replaced by a cryo-protective chemical solution that minimises the damage that freezing inflicts on body tissue. Next it is placed in an ice box where its temperature is reduced until it is deemed cold enough to be lowered head-first into a cryostat (a big white thermos-style flask) for long-term storage. The cryostats are kept topped up with liquid nitrogen and maintained at minus 196C. It costs $200,000 for a full-body suspension, but a company called Alcor (see below) offers a cheaper head-only alternative. For $80,000 it will sever your head from your body and freeze it until it becomes as brittle as glass. (This option assumes that it will one day be possible to graft a head onto a newly created body.)

Who on earth wants to be frozen?

There are some one hundred bodies

or heads, mostly female, frozen at centres across America. (As Robert Ettinger put it: 'there appear to be a lot of people, relatively speaking, anxious to freeze their mothers.' Sure enough, he froze his own.) By contrast, most of the 1,200 cryonauts-in-waiting are men. The late pop singer Michael Jackson was said to have considered it, but most would-be cryonauts are white, libertarian computer buffs living in California. Psychedelic guru Doctor Timothy Leary at one time intended to have his head frozen, but he changed his mind before he died in 1996, fearing cryonicists lacked a sense of humour. 'I worried I'd wake up in 50 years,' he said, 'surrounded by people with clipboards.'

Are all cryonicists cranks?

So most scientists would argue. Yet the movement has attracted support from some highly qualified minds. One is Professor Marvin Minsky of the Massachusetts Institute of Technology (MIT), generally regarded as the grandfather of Artificial Intelligence. Another convert is Doctor Eric Drexler,

also from MIT, whose specialist field of nanotechnology is the cryonicists' great white hope. Although only a fledgling science, nanotechnology promises one day to be able to construct machines (speculatively known as nanobots) smaller than cells, yet more complex than today's most powerful computers and capable of repairing damaged cellular tissue, molecule by molecule (see box).

As Robert Ettinger put it: 'there appear to be a lot of people, relatively speaking, anxious to freeze their mothers.' Sure enough, he froze his own.

Where can you sign up to become a cryonaut?

Several companies offer cryonic services, including the Cryonics Institute of Michigan which has 108 human cryonauts and 86 frozen dogs and cats. Alcor Life Extension Foundation is based in Scottsdale, Arizona and has 110 human cryonauts, 33 pets and

959 members-in-waiting. Housed in a pink building, its interior, with its huge white flasks, looks like a winery. Photos of the frozen clientele when they were alive adorn the walls. It's here that Ted Williams hangs upside down inside a nitrogen cylinder which he shares with three other bodies and five heads. Alcor also has a thriving British chapter which includes a stockbroker, a chef and a garden centre sales rep. Alcor's British centre is equipped to perform the process of perfusion and freezing, but for long-term storage the bodies are shipped to America.

How can cryonauts ensure they will be brought back to life?

They can't, since there's no guarantee a particular cryonics company will still be in business 200 years hence – or however long it takes. The industry has already had its share of scandal. The Cryonics Society of California, run by a TV repairman, went bust, leaving the bodies to thaw.

NANOBOTS: HOW TO RECOVER YOUR YOUTH

Cryonicists admit that the freezing process, not to mention the toxicity of the anti-freeze chemicals, will cause serious damage to organ tissue. But they are confident that advances in nanotechnology will soon enable us to release trillions of microscopic robotic surgeons (nanobots) into a frozen body where they will reverse the molecular damage caused by death, freezing and ageing.

Once cellular health has been restored, the patient's temperature will slowly be raised until a blood supply grown from the body's own tissues will begin to circulate. The metabolism will then be restarted and the cryonaut will wake to find himself in a completely youthful body.

That may sound far-fetched, but cryonicists point out that this rejuvenation process is what our body's cells do already; it's just that, at present, we have no control over how the process works.

The cryonics movement received a huge boost in 1997 when a rat heart was said to have been frozen to minus 196C, then thawed out and brought back to life. However, most scientists have since dismissed the finding.

What's **wrong** with the **Oscars**?

The results. *'The movie industry's most prestigious honour' somehow managed to elude Orson Welles, Alfred Hitchcock, Richard Burton, Cary Grant and Greta Garbo. This is the system that chose* How Green Was My Valley *over* Citizen Kane *in 1941, and* Rocky *ahead of* Taxi Driver *in 1977.* Oliver Twist *won Best Picture in 1969 when* 2001: A Space Odyssey *wasn't even nominated. Critics of the Oscars say they routinely discriminate against certain genres (comedies, science fiction and Westerns), and loathe any sort of controversy and 'brave' filmmaking (until recently, anything by Martin Scorsese) – instead favouring strong, simple storylines.*

When did the Oscars begin?

The first Academy Awards ceremony was held on 16 May 1929, over dinner in the Blossom Room of Hollywood's Roosevelt Hotel. It was attended by 270 people, each paying $5 to bring a guest, and was hosted by silent-movie actor Douglas Fairbanks, who handed out the awards in a few minutes. The 12 winners had been disclosed three months beforehand and the very first 'Oscar' – a 34-cm gold-plated statuette designed by MGM's art director, Cedric Gibbons – had already been handed to German actor Emil Jannings, who had sailed to Europe a few weeks before. Actually, Jannings was the runner-up in the leading-actor category, the real winner being Rin Tin Tin, a celebrity dog – but the new awards ceremony wanted to be taken seriously in its first year.

How did the Oscar get its name?

Legend has it that a librarian in the offices of the Academy of Motion Picture Arts and Sciences, which awards the prizes, took a peek at a statuette and said: 'Gee! He looks just like my Uncle Oscar.' The name stuck, and so did the 'Little Man', who remains the single most prized object in the entire, mad multi-billion-dollar movie business. And each year is much like the previous ones, with studio bosses, actors, directors, sound editors and make-up artists doing their utmost to be called up on stage before a worldwide audience of hundreds of millions on the night. Their fate rests entirely on the votes of the Academy members, whose numbers have risen from 36 in 1927 to 5,783 in 2012.

How does one get to be a member of the Academy?

You're either invited to join after being nominated for an Oscar, or you're elected by at least two other members for your services to the film industry. Members join for life, making the Academy a large and unwieldy band: characters range from major Hollywood figures like Tom Hanks to anonymous insiders and ageing outliers like Mother Dolores Hart, a 73-year-old Benedictine nun who once played opposite Elvis Presley in 1957's *Loving You*.

How does the Academy vote?

It has used the same Byzantine voting system (and the same accountants, PricewaterhouseCoopers, to do the counting) since 1936. In stage one – choosing the nominees – members of the 15 branches vote for nominations in their own specialism, though all can nominate for Best Picture. Thus actors nominate actors, make-up artists nominate make-up artists, etc. Each member makes five choices in preference order, and shortlists are compiled using the alternative vote system rejected for parliamentary elections by British voters in 2011 but used in Australia and Papua New Guinea. Stage two – choosing the winner – is simpler. All members are allowed to vote for a winner in every category, who is chosen on a first-past-the-post basis. (In some categories, e.g. Documentary Short Subject, they must promise that they've actually seen the film.)

> Academy members range from Tom Hanks to ageing outliers like Mother Dolores Hart, a 73-year-old Benedictine nun who once played opposite Elvis Presley in 1957's *Loving You*.

And does this system work?

Some say the voting system is so complicated that even the Academy members don't really understand it. To many, though, the real problem is that the average Academy member is 57, white, male and looking out for his next job in Hollywood. Only a minority (some 1,500) are actors or directors – the rest are the producers, set builders, visual-effects specialists, sound guys and PR execs that make the industry tick. They're known as the 'steak eaters', and when it comes to the decisive second round of voting, they are by far the Academy's largest voting bloc. 'Call it the steak-eater vote, call it the old geezer vote, call it the babe vote. They always vote for the babes,' says Jeffrey Wells, who runs the Hollywood Elsewhere website. They don't favour gay, lesbian or remotely foreign films; and in any given year, around 700 of them will be associated with an Oscar-nominated film, lobbying on its behalf.

Does much lobbying take place?

The Academy says it 'aggressively monitors award campaigning', but that doesn't stop the studios and nominees doing all they can to influence the process, from releasing major films just in time for the awards season (six of this year's nine Best Picture nominees were released in the last four months) to placing adverts in the Los Angeles press. In 1991, Diane Ladd, nominated for her role in *Wild at Heart*, distributed a video of herself saying that she wanted 'Oscar to come on home to Momma'; last year Melissa Leo, a nominee for best supporting actress in *The Fighter*, took out full-page adverts in the Hollywood trade press that just said: 'Consider...' Ladd lost. Leo won.

Does winning make a difference?

You bet. In crude financial terms, winning an Oscar, and even being nominated, can have a huge effect on a film's success. US ticket sales for *Slumdog Millionaire* jumped by almost 200 per cent when it was nominated in 2009. Studies have shown that nominations alone can extend a film's showing time in cinemas for weeks. At the real business end of Hollywood, however, Oscars are a bonus but don't affect the takings of a box-office smash. Of the top 50 grossing films of all time, just three have won Best Picture: *Titanic*, *Forrest Gump* and *Lord of the Rings: The Return of the King*.

HOW TO WIN AN OSCAR

The first hurdle is to apply for an Academy Award. To be eligible (with the exception of the foreign-language and short-film categories), films must be more than 40 minutes long, have shown at a cinema in the county of Los Angeles for at least one week during the previous calendar year, and have a minimum projector resolution of 2,048 x 1,080 pixels.

Sociologists from Harvard and UCLA have found that certain factors are crucial for nomination: you must be in a drama (nine times more likely than comedies to be nominated); be a woman (the smaller number of female actors and roles makes actresses twice as likely as men to be picked); be in a year with as few other eligible films as possible. In 2012, there were 265, up from 248 in 2011. To win, *Esquire* recommends a film should be long (more than two hours), American-made, and about crime or a socially important issue.

Another successful tactic is not to go to the ceremony. Marlon Brando didn't pick up his Oscar for *The Godfather* in 1973; Paul Newman stayed away in 1987, convinced he wouldn't win at his seventh attempt; and when Woody Allen's *Annie Hall* won Best Picture in 1978, he was 3,000 miles away, playing the saxophone in a New York bar.

How many
people
are **bipolar** ?

It is very hard to know *how many people are bipolar. The disorder, which used to be known as manic depression, has become much better – and more widely – understood in the last 20 years, but it is sometimes difficult to distinguish from other mental illnesses. Obtaining a diagnosis typically takes almost a decade. Nonetheless, surveys suggest that up to 2 per cent of the world's population suffers from the condition. In March, a study of 61,000 people across 11 countries found that around 1 per cent of adults have bipolar disorder and a further 1.4 per cent have 'sub-threshold' symptoms of the condition. In the UK, around one million people are thought to be bipolar. Everywhere, however, numbers are on the rise.*

Why is that?

In part because celebrities are helping to strip bipolar of the stigma that has accompanied mental illness in the past. As well as the actress Catherine Zeta-Jones, others who have 'come out' include pop stars (Sinéad O'Connor and Robbie Williams); comedians (Stephen Fry, Ben Stiller and Ruby Wax); and sportsmen (Frank Bruno and Paul Gascoigne). Their openness is thought to have encouraged more people to seek help and – say sceptics – more doctors to diagnose the disorder. In 2007, the Archives of General Psychiatry reported a 40-fold increase in the diagnosis of bipolar disorder among American children between 1994 and 2003. The number of adults diagnosed nearly doubled in the same period.

How can the numbers have grown so fast?

'We do not know how much of this increase reflects earlier under-diagnosis, current over-diagnosis, possibly a true increase in prevalence of this illness, or some combination of these factors,' said Dr Thomas Insel, director of the US National Institute of Mental Health in 2007. Bipolar disorder is a recently defined condition. Doctors began classifying 'manic depressive insanity' – in which patients suffered episodes of hyperactivity alternating with periods of crippling melancholy – in the late nineteenth century. But it was not until 1966 that two psychiatrists, Carlo Perris and Jules Angst, presented firm evidence that this disorder should be treated separately from 'unipolar' or clinical depression, which is characterised by lows alone. In 1980, 'bipolar disorder' replaced 'manic depression' in the American Psychiatric Association's *Diagnostic and Statistical Manual of Mental Disorders* (DSM) – the profession's standard reference book.

What are its symptoms?

There is no single definition of the disorder: instead, doctors place sufferers on the 'bipolar spectrum' according to the type and severity of their mood swings. Those diagnosed with Bipolar I suffer from full-blown manic episodes alongside depression, while those with Bipolar II tend to experience less intense bouts of 'hypomania' (this is the form Zeta-Jones suffers from). Further along the spectrum, doctors diagnose 'cyclothymia', a more extreme version of the variations in mood that we all experience in daily life. This 'subclinical' end of the spectrum is where critics believe most over-diagnosis of bipolar disorder takes place, particularly among the young. A study in 2001 found that almost half of bipolar diagnoses made in US adolescents were subsequently reclassified as other, frequently less serious, mental conditions.

How do bipolar sufferers behave?

During manic episodes, patients have racing thoughts and a grandiose sense of their importance. Their speech becomes rapid, they need only a few hours' sleep a night, feel euphoric and irritable, and have little insight about themselves or their actions. In extreme cases, they may wear weird clothes for days at a time, run up huge credit card bills, or sleep with strangers (heightened libido is a common symptom). The most severe attacks may include wild delusions, in which sufferers hear the voice of God or believe they are being persecuted. In their milder form, however, these spells can make people productive and inventive, and lend them 'enhanced access to vocabulary, memory and other cognitive resources', according to a study published in the *British Journal of Psychiatry* last year.

Do patients actually benefit from these moods?

The idea of a link between creative thinking and mania has been around for centuries, and there may be some proof that it exists (see box). But for most patients, these spells are part of a damaging cycle of mood swings that can, in the case of 'ultra-ultra rapid cycling', take place several times a day. Every patient has their own rhythm, but there are patterns to bipolar, and depressive moods dominate. A 12-year study of patients found that those with Bipolar I feel depressed around 32 per cent

> Patients' speech becomes rapid, they need only a few hours' sleep a night, feel euphoric and irritable, and have little insight about themselves or their actions.

of the time, and manic around 10 per cent of the time. Those with Bipolar II, by contrast, feel depressed around 50 per cent of the time, and manic just 1 per cent. Bipolar II sufferers are more likely to attempt suicide: 24 per cent of patients try to kill themselves at some point during their illness (versus 17 per cent with Bipolar I).

What is the treatment?

There is no known cure. Treatment focuses on trying to smooth out the most extreme mood swings, often with drugs, and long-term counselling from a psychotherapist or psychiatrist. With the right therapy, patients can spot patterns of behaviour and possible triggers for episodes of depression or mania – a technique known as 'mood monitoring'. Cocktails of drugs, often containing a stimulant to help ward off the lows and a stabiliser (such as lithium) to lessen symptoms of mania, have also been shown to be effective. However, many patients are wary of the side effects of such long-term pharmaceutical treatment – which can include weight gain and the increased risk of heart attack and stroke, as well as the sensation of being cut off from their actual emotional state, uncomfortable and bewildering as it may be.

TORTURED TALENTS

'There is no great genius without a mixture of madness,' said Aristotle. Researchers at King's College London and the Karolinska Institute in Stockholm, found evidence to support his idea: analysis of the exam results of 700,000 Swedish teenagers in the 1990s showed that those who scored top marks were four times more likely to be admitted to hospital with bipolar disorder by the age of 31. 'We found that achieving an A grade is associated with increased risk for bipolar disorder, particularly in humanities and, to a lesser extent, in science subjects,' said Dr James MacCabe, who led the study.

Music and literature were the subjects most likely to show a correlation between high marks and later mental illness, although the findings also showed that those with the lowest academic grades also had a slightly increased risk of developing bipolar disorder, suggesting that the condition is related to 'subtle neuro-developmental abnormalities'.

What use **is** Roget's **Thesaurus** ?

Plenty, *if sales of the book are anything to go by. Since it was first published in 1852, it has never been out of print and, with each succeeding edition, the popularity of the work has increased. Possessing the book came to be seen as a mark of civility ('The man is not wholly evil,' says J.M. Barrie of his villain, Captain Hook. 'He has a Thesaurus in his cabin.') The invention of the crossword puzzle in 1913 also gave it a huge boost – it has sold well over 32 million copies. 'The joy of Roget is that it's thematic,' said George Davidson, editor of the 150th Anniversary Edition in 2002. 'It can take you to places you hadn't even thought of when you began browsing or hunting for a particular word.'*

What kind of man was Roget?

Peter Mark Roget (1779–1869) was one of those intellectual giants of the Victorian era who seemed to know everything about everything. The son of a Genevan pastor, he was brought up in London's French Protestant community and was sent to study medicine at Edinburgh University. He graduated as a doctor at the age of 19 and went on to become a founder of Manchester Medical School. But his interests were by no means confined to the medical sphere.

What subjects interested him?

He wrote works on a huge range of topics including bees, Dante, the kaleidoscope and perception and feeling in animals. In 1814 he invented an early version of the slide rule. Ten years later, having proved that the image of an object is retained on the retina for about a 16th of a second after the object has gone out of view, he devised a shutter-and-aperture apparatus – the prototype for the cine camera. As the head of the commission investigating London's water supply, he developed a method of water filtration through sand that is still used in London today. He worked with Humphry Davy to examine the anaesthetic effects of laughing gas and with Jeremy Bentham on experiments in refrigeration. He was a chess master (and inventor of the travelling chess set), a Secretary of the Royal Society, and one of the founders of London University. It was only on retirement in his seventies that he decided to turn his attention to the classification of the English language.

What inspired him to write the Thesaurus?

He was obsessed with classification, an activity he felt reflected the orderliness of God's universe. Indeed, the book for which he was most respected in his lifetime, *Animal and Vegetable Physiology considered with reference to Natural Theology*, was an attempt to show how natural history, in all its variety, revealed the design of the creator. But Roget was also inspired by Jeremy Bentham's utilitarianism; he clung to the principle that he should help spread happiness and knowledge to the greatest possible number of people. He offered his medical services free to those who couldn't pay, set up a special clinic for the poor, and was a founding member of the short-lived Society for the Diffusion of Useful Knowledge. He wrote a series of sixpenny treatises on electricity, galvanism and magnetism, all intended to help poor and less-educated people learn. In the same vein his Thesaurus (from the Greek for 'treasure house') was designed to help those unpractised in writing. 'It is to those who are painfully groping their way and struggling with the difficulties of composition,' wrote the good doctor, 'that this work professes to hold out a helping hand.'

How did he compile it?

From his mid-twenties, Roget had carried a notebook around with him in which to catalogue words and their synonyms. His aim was to bestow on the kingdom of language the same taxonomic order that

Roget was inspired by Jeremy Bentham's utilitarianism: he clung to the principle that he should help spread happiness and knowledge to the greatest possible number of people.

Linnaeus had bestowed on the kingdom of animals. To this end he divided the entire linguistic world into six main classes, three to do with the external world –Abstract Relations, Space, Matter – and three the internal – Intellect, Volition, Sentient and Moral Powers. Each of these is then

subdivided into sections – under Intellect we find Materials for reasoning, Reasoning processes, Results of reasoning, etc – and these in turn are further subdivided (under Results of Reasoning comes Judgement, Credulity, Discovery, Assent, and many others). The result is that every word and idiom in the English language is corralled in less than 1,000 categories. The whole quaint system sounds engagingly archaic and arbitrary, yet many still swear by it.

Does it have its detractors?

A fair few. By uncritically offering up lists of alternative words, said author Simon Winchester, Roget helped transport us 'to our current state of linguistic and intellectual mediocrity'. Part of the blame, he said, must be laid at the door of Roget's son John, who developed the index (now 66 pages longer than the Thesaurus itself) at the back. As a result people no longer respond to Roget's thought-provoking categorisations; instead they use his book as a 'lexically lazy' way of finding an alternative word. Indeed, if Shakespeare had had Roget, said Robert McNeil in the *Scotsman*, he might have sounded thus: 'To vegetate or not to exist, that is the knotty point. Whether 'tis haughtier in the cerebellum to grin and bear the pea-shooters and harpoons of unmentionable serendipity...'

Is this being too snooty?

Undoubtedly. After all Sylvia Plath admitted that in writing the poems in her first volume, *The Colossus*, she had frequent recourse to Roget. The Thesaurus, she said, is a book that she would want instead of the Bible were she ever to be marooned on a desert island. 'Roget can harm your writing if you use it for elegant variation or showing off with sesquipedalian words,' said the writer Philip Howard. But his 'peculiar classification forces you to think of the precise meanings of the words you want to use... Not as a blunderbuss to pepper your writing or speeches with words to show off your verbal fecundity, but for retrieving a forgotten word or hitting the precise one.'

CAN ROGET KEEP UP WITH THE TIMES?

A new edition of Roget is routinely greeted by newspapers as a useful way of measuring the changes in society.

The 1980s gave us for the first time acid rain, creative accounting, insider trading, Cabbage Patch dolls and bag lady. And it was during that time that the then editor, Betty Kirkpatrick, provoked an enormous row by introducing four-letter words.

The 1990s added in-your-face, happy-clappy, alcopops, virtual reality, Millennium Bug, cyberpet, Tamagotchi, eating disorder, gesture politics, double whammy, care in the community, zero tolerance, Britpop, air-kissing, focus group, social exclusion, on-message, spin doctor, drug tsar, Prozac, keyhole surgery, ecowarrior, road rage, bad hair day, bit of rough and physician-assisted suicide.

Since 2000, we have had genetic map, frankenfood, Euroland, fusion cuisine, mouse potato, cybersex and m-commerce.

The encouraging thing is that all these new terms fit comfortably within the original classification structure that Roget created.

Could a
Robin Hood
tax **work** **?**

The proposal *to raise a tiny sliver of tax from every share, bond, derivatives and currency transaction was initially framed by Nobel prize-winning US economist James Tobin in 1972. Indeed, the Financial Transactions Tax (FTT), to give it its formal name, is often referred to as the Tobin tax – though having now been embraced by anti-poverty campaigners it's more popularly known as the Robin Hood tax. Oxfam reckons a global tax of just 0.05 per cent could raise $400bn a year. Billionaire philanthropist Bill Gates is pushing the G20 to adopt it, and now the EU is calling for it to be implemented by 2014 – reckoning it could raise €57bn a year with a 0.1 per cent tax on stock and bond trades, and 0.01 per cent on derivatives.*

What was the initial thinking behind the proposal?

Tobin first conceived of it as a brake against excessive currency speculation. A year earlier, the Nixon administration had taken the US dollar off the gold standard, effectively ending the existing Bretton Woods system of controlled currency exchange. Many saw this as liberating for international money markets, but Tobin worried things might get out of control, putting governments and central banks at the mercy of speculators. So he proposed a tax to 'throw some sand in the well-greased wheels' of foreign-exchange markets – any revenue raised being just a bonus.

Did his plan find favour?

No. Widely pooh-poohed by economists as impractical and over-interventionist, the generally held view was that Tobin's plan harked back to an age of Keynesian economics that had vanished for ever. Financiers, predictably, hated it. So did central bankers. The chief economist of the German Bundesbank, Otmar Issing, dismissed it as a 'Loch Ness monster'. Shortly before his death in 2002, even Tobin admitted his idea had 'sunk like a rock'.

So what brought it back into play?

The 2008 financial crisis. It shook the once unassailable belief that unregulated markets are always the most efficient allocators of resources, and made the idea of a tax on transactions less of a taboo. Indeed, Tobin's new fans argue that by deterring risky and unproductive high-frequency trading – if each trade bears a cost, you think twice

before making it – the tax would rein in the rogue elements of the financial sector and boost long-term investment. It would also ensure that financiers contributed their share to drawing down the debt. The IMF has pronounced it a 'highly progressive' tax: i.e. paid by those most able to afford it.

So why is the UK Government so against an FTT?

Ministers say they are 'in favour' – provided the tax is levied globally. If it isn't, they warn, a Europe-wide tax would lead to a disastrous exodus of business to international centres (e.g. Hong Kong and Singapore) with lighter regulation. Since London accounts for four out of five European financial trades (and so would stump up 80 to 85 per cent of the tax's yield), it would be hit disproportionately hard. A 'heat-seeking missile ... aimed at the City of London' is what former PM John Major calls the tax. And Britain, unlike many EU countries, already levies a 0.5 per cent tax on share trading, so introducing yet another transaction tax would be doubly vexatious, say the critics.

Are their criticisms persuasive?

Not to the British public, two-thirds of whom favour a Robin Hood tax. Nor to those who argue that if the City is able to maintain its ascendancy despite the burden of stamp duty, it should be able to accommodate an FTT without starting a stampede offshore. Yet the precedents aren't encouraging. In the very few cases where a Tobin tax has been imposed, real harm has ensued. Just ask the Swedes.

What went wrong in Sweden?

When Sweden tried a similar tax from 1984 to 1991 it raised only a 30th of the proceeds forecast, and nearly wiped out its national trading exchanges. By the time the tax was abandoned, half of Swedish equity trading had fled to London; bond-trading had slumped 85 per cent; and futures and options trading had virtually ceased. Meanwhile, the cost of government borrowing went through the roof. Tobin supporters insist this disaster was due to a specifically Swedish tax-design failure. But banking on that supposition would be quite a gamble – all the more so, given the tasty incentives already being dangled in front of financial firms by the proactive governments of Hong Kong and Singapore.

Any other reasons for cold feet?

Plenty. If, as is likely, financiers pass on the cost of the tax through higher charges, it will be ordinary businesses and pension-holders who get hit by it. Besides, nothing that Brussels has said bears out

---

The 2008 financial crisis shook the belief that markets are always the most efficient allocators of resources, and made the idea of a tax on transactions less of a taboo

---

the hope of the Robin Hoods that the cash would go either to fund overseas development, or to shore up Britain's poor. The suspicion – all the stronger given continued opposition to a global Tobin tax from China, Canada and the USA – is that the proceeds of an EU-wide tax would get sunk into Europe's debt swamp.

Any sign of Brussels taking account of the UK's concerns?

Zero. Euro politicians have publicly admonished the UK for being 'selfish' in refusing to sign up for it. (A UK veto would scupper an EU-wide Tobin tax, since EU tax changes must be agreed by all 27 national members.) But 'enhanced cooperation powers' would still allow France and Germany to levy the tax in the 17-bloc Eurozone... prompting Britain in turn to object that any Eurozone-registered bank operating in London would then fall foul of it. And so the wrangling continues. How could James Tobin ever have guessed that his once-obscure tax proposal has now become a litmus test of Britain's commitment to the EU?

WOULD A TOBIN TAX BE A FORCE FOR GOOD?

YES

1. What better way of pulling feathers from the goose with little pain than imposing a tiny percentage tax on financial transactions?

2. By deterring speculative trading, it would get financial markets to focus on their primary purpose of raising capital for companies.

3. The biggest threat to long-term growth is an unrestrained financial sector, not a minute tax on transactions.

NO

1. Chinese and American opposition makes a global tax impossible, while a unilateral EU levy would be a disaster for the City.

2. It's mad to impose a damaging levy when growth is needed.

3. Britain, unlike France and Germany, has kept up its foreign aid budget, yet is being asked to bear the brunt of a tax whose proceeds would most likely go to shore up the teetering Eurozone.

Is computer hacking getting more serious?

No question. *Sony suffered the largest theft of personal data in history in April 2011: the names, addresses, dates of birth and passwords of 77 million people (including 3 million Britons) were stolen from a network that allows Sony customers to play computer games against each other on the internet. This haul of information, which could theoretically be used to launch countless crimes, was the latest booty in an escalating conflict between hackers and some of the world's best-known companies and institutions. Since 2007, victims have included the Royal Bank of Scotland, Visa, Mastercard, Paypal, Google, Lockheed Martin, the CIA, the US Senate, the NHS and hence, by extension, millions of us.*

Why are these attacks on the increase?

In large part, the story of hacking is of a war between legitimate programmers and their bedroom-based foes – tricksters and vandals – that dates from the first days of the personal computer in the 1980s (see box). But in recent years, two important shifts have occurred. One is the increasing ability of hackers to make money through their crimes, either by stealing people's identity or by luring us to fraudulent schemes through emails and pop-up ads; the other is the involvement of state-sponsored hackers and new kinds of quasi-political, anarchic groups.

Which governments are involved?

A report just published by McAfee, the largest security technology company in the world, reveals that one country has systematically hacked its way into the computer systems of 72 corporations and government agencies in the USA, UK and elsewhere in just five years. These include the Olympics' anti-doping agency, which was targeted just before and after the 2008 Beijing games, confirming suspicions that the country in question was China. China was also found to have penetrated the British Foreign Office's internal communications system. But China is only the worst offender: a host of other countries and companies engage in similar enterprises. 'I divide the entire Fortune Global 2000 firms into two categories: those that know they've been compromised and those that don't know yet,' security analyst Rik Ferguson told the *Guardian*. Throw organised crime and industrial-scale production of viruses in

Russia and China into the mix, and it is no surprise that the UK classifies cybercrime as the nation's second-biggest national security threat after terrorism.

How do hackers operate?

Depends what they're after. One tool, though, is 'malware' – short for malicious software. These programs are often disguised as something useful (when they're known as 'Trojans') or as email attachments. In 2008, internet security company Symantec calculated that malware was now being produced in greater quantities than legitimate software. Some programs, like those that make a mess of your hard drive, are merely irritating – others are ominous. 'Screen-scrapers' and 'keystroke-loggers', for example, record everything you type and look at, and send it to a hacker. Other malware turns your PC into a 'zombie machine' entirely under the control of a fraudster, thousands of miles away.

What about anti-virus software?

Microsoft, Google and Apple

strive to keep ahead of the hackers, but the truth is that malware and 'phishing' (in which cleverly disguised emails try to coax personal information from you) are just part of the story. The cybercriminals are after your personal data (passwords, credit-card numbers, names, addresses – the building blocks of your online identity), and these details can be obtained in any number of ways. Last year

---

Malware and 'phishing' are just part of the story. The cybercriminals are after your personal data: passwords, credit-card numbers, names, addresses – the building blocks of your online identity.

---

a software developer in Seattle wrote a program called Firesheep to show how easy it is for hackers to sit in a café and steal personal information from the people around them surfing the net on their phones and laptops. We're all vulnerable. Last September, the head of Interpol, Ronald

Noble, realised hackers had stolen his identity to find out about an upcoming police operation.

What are hackers out to get?

Most want money. There's a huge black market for personal data, with higher prices for credit-card numbers or passwords known to work. In November 2008, hackers spent just over £5m in 12 hours with information stolen from RBS Worldpay, a payment system used by the Royal Bank of Scotland. But in truth there is a galaxy of motives for hackers: from the criminal, to the political (such as Google's repeated targeting by Chinese hackers) to the ideological. This last includes a mixture of anarchism and anti-capitalism, and drives groups from Julian Assange's WikiLeaks to the even more mysterious 'Anonymous'. Anonymous, and its splinter group, 'LulzSec', carried out sympathy attacks for WikiLeaks in 2011, as well as their own disruptions of Spain's electoral commission and the CIA, by directing millions of machines to their websites, crippling their servers.

How worried should we be by identity theft/cybercrime?

It cost Britain £27bn in a single year, so it's not a trivial matter. The UK has committed £650m to fight 'e-crime', and helped to set up the International Cybercrime Security Protection Alliance, which seeks to unify public and private-sector approaches to the problem. For individuals, however, the threat can be exaggerated. In the Sony case, customers' credit-card details were encrypted and kept separate from the rest of their data, making any direct identity theft hard to carry out. The greater danger posed by cybercrime is more subtle. The beauty and power of the internet lies in its ability to operate without restraints: its foundations are built on trust. Hackers undermine that trust, and the raft of security measures that may be set up in the war against them could start to block the free flow of information. 'The internet,' as the *New York Times* puts it, 'is getting scary.'

ORIGINS OF THE MALWARE PLAGUE

According to the *Observer*, the global malware epidemic began in 1971 in Boston, at the desk of a programmer called Bob Thomas, who was working on Arpanet, a prototype for the internet. Thomas released an experimental program that would replicate itself around the network, displaying a message as it went: 'I'm the creeper, catch me if you can!' Soon someone did, creating 'The Reaper', which chased and deleted it. But an idea was born.

In 1988, Robert Morris, a researcher at Cornell University, released a 'worm' that he hoped would tell him how many computers were connected to the internet. But the worm began reproducing and got out of control, and Morris was arrested.

The first common viruses were pranks spread by floppy disk. One, 'Melissa' (named after a stripper), caused $80m of damage. In the 1990s, the rise of the internet and the success of Windows 95 created overwhelming temptations for criminal hackers. Albert Gonzalez, an American fraudster, was sentenced to 20 years in prison in 2010 for stealing the details of 130 million credit cards.

Why should we
worry about
weapon dogs ?

Because the Dangerous Dogs Act *of 1991 – which made it illegal to own pit bull terriers, Japanese tosas and two other types of dog – failed to reduce attacks. The number of people in England hospitalised after a dog attack has risen from 4,328 in 1999 to 6,005 in 2011, with the number rising in five successive years. In several cases children have been killed. The number of dogs seized under the Act has also dramatically increased: 719 were impounded by the Metropolitan Police between April 2007 and 2008, compared to just 38 in 2005. Plans were even announced to teach magistrates in London how to distinguish between illegal pit bull breeds and 'legal' Staffordshire bull terriers. But since the latter is now the 'weapon dog' of choice, being able to make such a distinction has little effect in reducing attacks.*

And why are there so many attacks?

Because 'status dogs' or 'assault animals' are the 'must have' accessory for those craving power and respect in inner-city housing estates. The trend is said to have started around 2004 under the influence of US hip-hop videos by the likes of Lil' Bow Wow and DMX, featuring footage that glorifies pit bulls. (In America 'Bully pit bulls' are bred for their size and power.) But since pit bulls are illegal in the UK, the Staffordshire bull terrier has become the dog to own. Battersea Dogs Home now takes in more Staffordshires, or Staffordshire crosses, than mongrels. In 2007 it took in 2,677 of the dogs, a third of its annual intake.

What are the Staffordshires used for?

Most are loyal and friendly dogs, with strong protective instincts, and have long been popular as family pets. But a minority are trained to intimidate, and fight. Puppies are beaten and kicked to make them meaner, put on treadmills to strengthen their muscles and hung from tree branches to strengthen their bite. Dogs with 'game' – slang for aggression – are then set on other pets, or each other, in impromptu fights, known as 'rolling', or used as an accessory in robberies and other crime. Many are let loose in parks where they are encouraged to intimidate and attack other dogs and members of the public for their owners' entertainment. Nearly 70 per cent of all dog fights reported to the RSPCA involve youths using dogs as weapons

in streets and parks. In 2008, the *People* newspaper bought an illegal pit bull in London and was assured by the breeder: 'It's rough on this estate but you can walk in the middle of the road with that dog, no problem – it's like having a gun.' Although most dog fighting is casual, there is also a thriving underworld of organised contests.

Isn't that illegal?

Yes, since 1835. But it's on the rise. In 2004, 24 dog fights were reported to the police and the RSPCA; by 2007, the number was 358. Contests are well-organised and dogs are meticulously trained – often starved to increase their 'prey drive'. The rules are simple: the dogs take their positions behind two 'scratch lines' in opposite corners of a round pit. The first one to die or 'turn' and 'cur out' is the loser. Some fights last for hours and both dogs are often seriously wounded. It is common for them to be destroyed at the scene. Earlier this year, a Staffordshire bull terrier was found dead in Peckham after being thrown off a roof. The dog had recent facial injuries consistent with dog fighting.

Why do people do it?

For money and pride. Big contests, involving fight 'champions' (three wins) or 'grand champions' (five wins), can draw bets of several thousand pounds. Winning dogs also make money from breeding, with puppy prices rising from £150 to the thousands. Adverts for Staffordshire puppies often stress their 'game' bloodlines, or a breeder's 'ROM' ('Register of Merit'), which shows they have bred champion dogs – either fighters or legitimate competition winners – in the past. On a neighbourhood level, hastily arranged dog fights in parks, and even people's homes, have become a way of settling disputes between gangs. Less money is involved, but pride is at stake.

Who takes part?

There are thought to be around 200 'hardcore' dog fighters in Britain, many of whom are involved in other crime as well. In the past, most participants were white working class men, but now they have been joined by a new group: British-born Asians, many of Pakistani origin. Dog fighting is a popular past-time in Pakistan and there has been a rapid increase in fighting in regions such as the West Midlands where there are large British-Asian communities. The largest known British dog fight for 130 years was uncovered in 2007, when 26 men were arrested in the Alum Rock suburb of Birmingham as they watched two pit bulls, Elvis and Bullet, tear each other to death. The RSPCA's special

Puppies are beaten and kicked to make them meaner, put on treadmills to strengthen their muscles and hung from tree branches to strengthen their bite.

operations unit believes there is an illegal dog fight somewhere in the Midlands every week.

So what's the answer?

Animal protection groups say that the Dangerous Dogs Act has failed. Police do not have the resources to check the breed of every suspicious animal and breeders are crossbreeding dogs to give them physical features different from the banned dogs. One idea is to ban known gang members from taking their dogs into public places. The RSPCA, however, and some local authorities, say this is not enough and that it's time to reintroduce the mandatory dog licence – not the old version that could be bought for a few quid over the counter at the Post Office, but a licence that would involve a 'fit and proper person' test, as with gun ownership, and would require the payment of a substantial fee of perhaps £500, plus an annual sum to help pay for enforcement. The government announced a public consultation in mid-2010 and intends to publish its proposals during 2012.

SHOULD WE BRING BACK THE DOG LICENCE?

YES

1. The root of the problem is the dog owner not the dog. Licensing would subject them to a 'fit and proper person' test.

2. Licensing would allow local councils to scrutinise far more breeds than those covered by the Dangerous Dogs Act.

3. Most problems are caused by people aged 13 to 17. Licensing could set a minimum age for dog ownership.

NO

1. Ordinary law-abiding pet owners don't need another piece of expensive, intrusive bureaucracy in their lives.

2. The problem is enforcement: it is already illegal to have a dog out of control and dogfighting has been banned since 1835.

3. Aggressive dogs are just a symptom of deeper social problems. These cannot be patched up by a piece of paper.

Where has
China's soil
gone?

China has the most desertified land *in the world, and a growing population. According to its State Forestry Administration, around 2.6 million km² of China is now desertified: about 27 per cent of the country's land mass, or the equivalent of eight Germanys. While that is less than the global average – a third of the world's surface is desert – the rapid spread of arid and semi-arid conditions across China in recent decades is one of the most serious economic and environmental challenges facing the world's next superpower. Desertification already draws some $7bn from the Chinese economy each year; 80 per cent of the country's grasslands are degraded; and the government has had to resettle thousands of people from the country's north and west whose villages have been overrun by sand. The 'Yellow Dragon', a season of sandstorms that used to occur once a decade, is now an annual event in Beijing.*

What causes desertification?

There are various causes. Around 10 per cent of China's desertification is caused by water erosion along its major rivers (in which billions of tonnes of soil are washed into the water and become sediment), and 10 per cent is down to salination (where poor irrigation leads to the build-up of salt). But by far the most dominant cause – which drives

62 per cent of desertification – is the wind. Decades of increasing pressure on the land have driven farmers into precarious, semi-arid ecosystems where overgrazing and the demand for water have ended up drying out the land and removing the vegetation that held the soil together. China's livestock population tripled between 1950 and 2002: the trampling hooves break up the soil and the wind blows it away.

Is it only happening in China?

Not at all. Manmade desertification first captured the popular imagination in the 1930s, when overgrazing and poor irrigation led to America's Dust Bowl, and the westward migration of poor farm workers to California. The term 'desertification' was coined in 1949 by a French forester, and the phenomenon is now recognised as a threat to more than a quarter of the world's land and a fifth of its population. But China's problem is acute, as well as being on a vast scale: it already feeds 20 per cent of the world's population on just 7 per cent of its arable land (America feeds 5 per cent on 20 per cent of its arable land), and its increasing affluence and demand for meat and water will place ever-greater strains on that land. A recent Greenpeace report concluded that China's food supply would be inadequate by 2030. Its topography also makes it vulnerable to the effects of climate change.

Is climate change involved?

Yes, but not directly. The two great misconceptions about desertification are that it is either caused by existing deserts (it can happen far from any desert), or by shortage of water (dry but well-managed land can recover after drought). But of course climate change will affect China on all sides: from melting glaciers and the drying up of the northern arid regions of Tibet, Inner Mongolia and Xinjiang, to more frequent typhoons in the overpopulated, low-lying coastal regions of Guangdong in the southeast. At the very least, there is likely to be more pressure on the country's decent arable land, and the human habitats that have been fragile for decades will only get more so.

What is China doing about it?

Quite a lot. Desertification first caught the attention of China's leaders in the 1970s, when they ordered the creation of the 'Great Green Wall' – a barrier of millions of trees intended to stop the sand spreading from the country's north. In the last decade, the 'Desertification Control Office' in the State Forestry Administration has stepped up the effort: moving

China's problem is acute: it already feeds 20 per cent of the world's population on just 7 per cent of its arable land (America feeds 5 per cent on 20 per cent of its arable land).

hundreds of vulnerable villages; imposing a grazing ban on 71 million hectares of grassland (the size of two Germanys); and giving farmers and businesses tax breaks if they invest in desertification control methods such as laying straw to protect new grasses until their roots can hold the soil. More

radical schemes, such as piping seawater more than 1,000 miles inland to flood dried-up lakebeds, are still on the drawing board.

Are the techniques working?

Almost. China spent about £6bn in the last decade, and plans to spend another £20bn before 2020, and it is starting – slowly – to see results. A government survey of China's desertified lands between 2005 and 2010 showed, for the first time, that the deserts' spread has been halted. While noting that the 'desertification trend has not fundamentally reversed', it found that an average of 1,717km^2 of degraded land is being restored each year. At that rate, with a further 530,000 km^2 of land to recover, it will take China 300 years to roll back its manmade deserts, but its relative success has been enough to inspire similar efforts around the world. Last year, African leaders met in Chad to discuss planting their own continent's Great Green Wall – a bank of trees, nine miles wide and 5,000 miles long, stretching along the Sahara's southern edge.

What happens if they fail?

Beijing describes desertification as 'the most serious ecological problem facing the country', and a 'serious, hidden danger' to China's economic development and security. If it fails to control the spread of deserts, it will have to import more and more food – like the other 100 nations seen as vulnerable to the effects of desertification. And there will come a point where there is simply not enough soil to support us. A recent UN report concluded that Africa may only be able to feed 25 per cent of its population by 2025, if soil degradation on the continent continues at its current pace.

MUCKING AROUND WITH CLOUDS

For decades, one limited way of improving arid conditions has been 'cloud seeding' – introducing silver iodide crystals by rocket or aeroplane into the base of storm clouds to improve the chances of rain. China has been an enthusiastic participant, using the technique to clear the skies before the Beijing Olympics. But cloud seeding is expensive, depends on having some clouds in the sky and is not always reliable: in 2009, Chinese scientists were embarrassed after triggering a major snowfall in Beijing.

A year later, however, scientists working for the Abu Dhabi government managed to create more than 50 rainstorms using a secret – and apparently more reliable – new technique. The $11m Abu Dhabi project, performed by Swiss company Meteo Systems International, encouraged rain clouds to form by using large steel ionisers on the ground to charge air particles that in turn attracted dust, and then moisture, which then condensed to form rain. Out of the 74 times that the devices were used, rain fell 52 times – always on days when the weather forecasters were expecting no rain or clouds at all.

Are mega-farms
cruel
to animals ?

Although Britain already has huge farms, they are not as big as those planned. What Britain has are 'factory' or 'battery' farms that dominate parts of its livestock industry, though by no means all of it. Factory farming dates from the 1960s, when technological progress and the demand for cheap meat changed the way that we raise animals for food, milk and eggs. More than 80 per cent of British chickens are now kept in battery cages. In cow and pig farming, however, the picture is more mixed. Most dairy herds in the UK still number around 70 cows and graze outside; a third of pigs are raised outdoors. Such animals live in a different world to the 4,000-cow 'mega-dairy' recently planned for Lincolnshire, or the proposed farm of 2,500 'zero-grazing' pigs to be set up in Derbyshire.

What is the justification for these new farms?

Many scientists believe there must be a second agricultural revolution if we are to feed a global population of nine billion by 2050. Today's industrialised agriculture just about manages to feed the world, but only through a heavy – and frequently destructive – use of land, water and fertiliser. With decent farmland finite and the environment fragile, bodies such as the Royal Society have campaigned for the 'sustainable intensification' of agriculture. In crop farming, that means plants with higher yields and resistance to disease, and less need for water. In livestock farming, the same rules apply: maximum 'outputs' (eggs, meat and milk) for minimum 'inputs' (food, water and chemicals). And that points to bigger, more efficient farms.

How do mega-farms achieve this?

The UK government wants to find out. The Department for the Environment and Rural Affairs (Defra) asked researchers to explore 'the potential of mega-scale units to meet the challenge of improving productivity and efficiency, while minimising environmental impacts and maintaining animal health and welfare'. But there is also a more pressing, financial incentive: Britain's pig and dairy farmers are going out of business. Between 1998 and 2008, the relentless pressure of cheap imports and competing supermarkets caused more than 14,000 dairy farmers – around 45 per cent of the nation's total – to go to the wall. The

number of pigs raised in Britain also fell by more than 40 per cent in the same period. Mega-farms, with their massive economies of scale, uniform breeds and scientifically formulated feeding regimes, promise a return to profit for farmers as well as – their proponents contend – a reduced impact on the environment.

So the proposals have wide support?

Welfare campaigners are horrified by the plans. The plight of Britain's battery-raised chickens is well known. It was only in 2009 that Defra introduced a limit to how many birds could be kept in a certain area: 19 per square metre. Factory-farmed chickens grow so fast their legs can't carry them, and lay 16 times more eggs than they would in the wild; millions of useless cocks are gassed to death. Campaigners fear that pigs and cows 'continuously housed' in mega-farms would face similar problems. Anxiety for the welfare of the 3,770 cows that would live in Britain's first planned 'mega-dairy' in Nocton, Lincolnshire, was one reason the idea was shelved in 2011. Other fears included pollution of the local water table, and the increased risk of disease and infection among such closely packed herds.

What does the industry say?

Farmers, and the government, insist that mega-farms would have to comply with all of the UK's animal-welfare legislation. 'We have repeatedly stressed that animal welfare is our top priority,' says a spokesman for Midland Pig Producers, which hopes to build the farm in Derbyshire 'producing 1,000 pigs a week'. Companies planning mega-farms also claim there are environmental benefits that their opponents simply refuse to see: reductions in smells and noise, and crucially (thanks to increased yields in milk and meat per animal) reduced emissions of methane – a greenhouse gas far more harmful to the atmosphere than CO_2. The alternative, they say, is that mega-farms will be built elsewhere in Europe, where standards for both animal welfare and human health are far less stringent.

But surely there are EU regulations?

Yes, but they're nothing like as tough as UK ones. The EU didn't accept that animals should be regarded as 'sentient beings' rather than units of production until 1999. British niceties such as castrating pigs with anaesthetic don't apply across the bloc (the British Pig Executive claims that 70 per cent of the one million

---

Today's industrialised agriculture just about manages to feed the world, but only through a heavy – and destructive – use of land, water and fertiliser.

---

tonnes of pork products we import each year doesn't meet British welfare standards), and there's nothing to stop UK supermarkets buying the cheapest meat they can source. In Poland and Romania, EU funding has helped build precisely the kind of industrial pig farms people now fear will be set up here. And the fact that EU farm subsidies will be dismantled over the next decade will only make things worse: farmers, left to fend for themselves in the global food market, will increasingly convert to efficient mega-farms.

So what's the answer?

Britain's livestock farmers are in a bind. If councils refuse to grant planning permission for mega-farms, many farmers will go out of business – experiencing death by a thousand cuts at the hands of retailers and foreign competitors. But if mega-farms get the all-clear, smaller herds in the UK will be at a competitive disadvantage, and rural communities and millions of animals will have to ready themselves for a bleak future. In the end, continued existence of livestock outside the mega-farm will depend on consumers' readiness to pay more for their 'output'.

SHOULD MEGA-FARMS BE INTRODUCED IN BRITAIN?

YES

1. Unless farmers are allowed to invest in 'sustainable intensification', pig and dairy farms will go bust.
2. Mega-farms will be regulated by the UK's existing animal-welfare standards, which are tougher than most of Europe's.
3. The new farms bring important environmental benefits – such as the reduction of waste and greenhouse-gas emissions.

NO

1. In the USA, where mega-farms are common, they have wiped out small, traditionally run farms.
2. Mega-farms are incubators for disease and increase the risk of pollution to local water sources.
3. Factory farms are cruel to animals, preventing them from behaving naturally and causing disability and distress.

Did the Battle of Britain change the Second World War?

The summer of 1940 *saw an intense aerial conflict between the Royal Air Force and the Nazi Luftwaffe that turned, with the coming of autumn, into the Blitz and the bombardment of Britain's civilian population. 'The Battle of Britain' was coined as a phrase before it began, by Winston Churchill on 11 June 1940. Churchill had been Prime Minister for a month and had watched Germany's army overrun the Netherlands, Belgium and France in a few weeks. The Royal Navy had just spent nine days evacuating 338,000 Allied soldiers from the beaches at Dunkirk, and Germany's military planners were turning to Operation Sealion, the invasion of Britain. 'I look forward confidently to the exploits of our fighter pilots,' Churchill told the House of Commons, 'who will have the glory of saving their native land.'*

Was Churchill's confidence justified?

Only in retrospect. In France, the RAF had shot down 150 Nazi aircraft, showing that Britain's new fighter, the Hurricane, could match the German machines. But the RAF had also lost 100 planes and 80 pilots – a rate of attrition it could not sustain. In early July 1940, the Luftwaffe had 2,600 bombers and fighters under its command; the RAF had just 640 fighters. That month, the

German attacks began in earnest. In escalating phases that summer, the Luftwaffe sent wave after wave of bombers and fighters to destroy Britain's shipping and air defences, in some cases hitting the same airfields day after day, while the RAF scrambled patched-up planes and pilots to shoot them down.

How did the RAF keep up?

It was a close-run thing. By early August, Hermann Göring, the commander of the Luftwaffe, was convinced he was within days of destroying the RAF in southern England. The Nazis designated 13 August 'Adlertag', or Eagle Day, to land the knock-out blow. But the attack failed, and a week later, Churchill thanked the RAF on behalf of the country. 'British airmen are turning the tide of world war,' he said. 'Never in the field of human conflict was so much owed by so many to so few.' Hundreds of aircraft continued to clash in the skies each day. At the end of August, the RAF lost 248 pilots in ten days. But in late October the Luftwaffe switched its attention to bombing British cities by night, and the threat of invasion fell away.

How did the Few do it?

In part, by not being as few as they thought. The RAF was initially badly outnumbered by the Luftwaffe, but historians now know that rapid British aircraft production of the crucial Spitfires and Hurricanes kept the numbers of fighters roughly equal on each side. According to *The Battle of Britain* by Richard Overy, by 9 August the RAF had 1,032 fighters to the Luftwaffe's 1,011. Britain's factories out-produced Germany's from June to September, building 1,900 fighters to Germany's 775. The RAF was also helped by the short range of the Luftwaffe's dangerous Messerschmitt Bf 109, which could only fight over Britain for 30 minutes; and by Göring's crucial decision to stop bombing airfields, which gave them and their crews vital time to recover.

So Britain had gained the upper hand in the War?

It was not seen in that way at the time. By the end of 1940, Britain was as strategically weak as it had been in June. The Nazis controlled western Europe and the Luftwaffe regained its strength.

In terms of winning the War, the forgotten North African campaign of that winter (in which 36,000 British and Commonwealth soldiers defeated the Italians to hold onto the Suez Canal) was just as important. In early 1941, the factors crucial to Germany's success – the neutrality of America and Hitler's pact with Stalin – were still in place. Hitler still had no doubt that Britain would fall.

So was it significant, then?

No question. In the early summer of 1940, Home Intelligence was alarmed by the number of Britons who thought peace with Hitler would only hurt the rich. Churchill's wartime coalition was untried and, by many, untrusted. The Battle of Britain involved acts of exemplary courage and sacrifice (see box). It proved that the country's war effort was working, and galvanised its people to pull together. Of the 2,927 men who flew for the RAF and Fleet Air Arm that summer (574 of whom were from overseas), one in five lost their lives. Just over half survived the War. The Blitz, in which 43,000 civilians were killed and a million made homeless, strengthened the country's resolve. By the end of 1940, the War Office was being urged to change its slogan from 'Britain can take it' to 'Britain can give it'.

What was the German reaction?

Hitler and his generals thought the defeat was of limited significance. Their attention was turning to the

---

The Blitz strengthened the country's resolve. By the end of 1940, the War Office was being urged to change its slogan from 'Britain can take it' to 'Britain can give it'.

---

east. Britain was to be 'contained' by blockade while that larger objective was undertaken. In December 1940, Hitler signed Directive No. 21, authorising the invasion of the USSR. Germany's bombers were secretly transferred eastwards, and on 22 June Operation Barbarossa began.

And did that prove disastrous?

Yes. The invasion of the USSR was a massive and unsustainable expansion of Germany's war. As a campaign of extermination and enslavement against the Jews and Slavs of Eastern Europe, it also had a fundamentally different character to the earlier invasions. By December 1941, the German Army was calamitously bogged down in Russia, and the USA had joined the Allies. It was only then, and in the crucial reverses of late 1942, that the full importance of Britain's survival in 1940 became apparent. Had Hitler not embarked upon war with Russia, and had America stayed neutral, the Battle of Britain would probably not occupy the place in history it holds today.

'THE SKY SEEMED FULL OF THEM'

The following description of the approaching Luftwaffe was given by Pilot Officer John Beard, 21, of Squadron 249, in an account of the battle published in 1941. He survived the summer, and the War.

'Minutes went by. Green fields and roads were now beneath us. I scanned the sky and the horizon for the first glimpse of the Germans. A new vector came through on the RT [radio telephone] and we swung round with the sun behind us. Swift on the heels of this I heard Yellow flight leader call through the earphones. I looked quickly toward Yellow's position, and there they were!

'It was really a terrific sight and quite beautiful. First they seemed just a cloud of light as the sun caught the many glistening chromium parts of their engines, their windshields, and the spin of their airscrew discs. Then, as our squadron hurtled nearer, the details stood out. I could see the bright yellow noses of Messerschmitt fighters sandwiching the bombers, and could even pick out some of the types. The sky seemed full of them, packed in layers thousands of feet deep. They came on steadily, wavering up and down along the horizon. 'Oh, golly,' I thought, 'golly, golly...'

How
big is
cosmetic surgery ?

There are about *100,000 operations a year in the UK (not including non-surgical 'lunchtime' procedures, such as Botox injections). About 90 per cent are done on women, for whom the most common procedures are breast enlargement (there has been a 300 per cent increase since 2002) and blepharoplasty (eyelid surgery). But men are getting in on the act: in 2009, 7 per cent more men put themselves under the scalpel than in the previous year. The most popular operation for men is rhinoplasty (a nose job), followed by breast reduction. Reducing gynaecomastia or 'man-boobs' is increasingly popular, showing a 28 per cent rise in 2009. And cosmetic surgery is big business. Worth £143m in 2002, the UK industry had grown to £1.2bn by 2009. And that's a mere fraction of the US market – around 12 million cosmetic procedures are carried out in the country every year.*

How did it become such big business?

The starting-point was the First World War, when soldiers' facial wounds were so horrific that no one knew what to do with them. During the war, otolaryngologist Harold Gillies developed many of the techniques of modern plastic surgery on soldiers suffering from disfiguring facial injuries. His work was built on during the Second World War by his cousin and former student Archibald McIndoe, who pioneered treatments for RAF aircrew who had suffered severe burns. But what really kick-started the industry was the surplus of newly experienced US surgeons who found themselves with no one to cut, peel and stretch – by 1945 the country had 60 fully trained plastic surgeons, ten times as many as in Britain and twice the number in the rest of the world.

And how did they popularise their services?

By changing the focus from men to women (a man requiring a facelift, said an LA-based surgeon, is 'either an ageing actor, a homosexual, or both'). And in this they had some ground to build on. Back in 1923, when the stage actress Fanny Brice had a nose job, most people still thought it weird that she should seek to change what nature had ordained – 'she cut off her nose to spite her race,' quipped Dorothy Parker. Yet the *New York Times* celebrated it as a miracle of science that would help people get ahead, and soon the *New York Daily Mirror* was running a Homely Girl Contest: first prize was to be turned into 'a

beauty' by a plastic surgeon and given an opera audition. But the new surgeons wished to appeal to a woman's emotional fulfilment as much as to her vanity. If cosmetic surgery 'is to be elevated to its proper dignity in the [surgery] profession', noted surgeon Seymour Oppenheimer, it must be 'made available for the large number … who could be benefited in mind no less than in feature'.

How would 'the mind' benefit?

According to Elizabeth Haiken, author of *Venus Envy: A History of Cosmetic Surgery*, it was psychologist Alfred Adler who gave cosmetic surgery the theoretical boost that it needed to soothe anxieties about 'going against nature'. His 'inferiority complex' theory, popularised in the 1920s, gave Americans a reason to consider plastic surgery a form of therapy – 'psychiatry with a scalpel'.

Did it quickly become widespread?

No. Until the 1980s, cosmetic surgery was still the preserve of Hollywood celebrities and Manhattan socialites. But then new technology began to push prices down to a level accessible to most people. Soon cosmetic surgery became the subject of TV shows (*Nip/Tuck*, *Extreme Makeover*), while the industry started to adopt marketing ploys used by high-street stores and catalogue firms – interest-free loans, gift vouchers, loyalty cards and promotional discounts. 'If 2011 is the year you plan to really change how you feel about yourself,' said the Transform website, 'we're here to help you do just that.' It also ran a loyalty scheme for returning patients (buy four ops and get a voucher towards the fifth). This is just one of the practices that has earned the anger of medical groups, who worry that young people are being tempted to have operations that they don't need, and that can be dangerous.

So how safe is plastic surgery?

No operation involving surgery and anaesthetics is totally safe. Complications can include infection, bleeding and clotting (thrombosis). (A tummy-tuck tends to have higher complication rates because mobility is restricted after surgery.) But cosmetic surgery carries greater risk, because of the highly variable quality of the clinics that offer it – hence the renewed calls for closer regulation (see box). A report by an official review body found that patients were at risk from a culture in which inexperienced teams 'have a go' at operations they have rarely

In 1923, when the stage actress Fanny Brice had a nose job, most people still thought it weird – 'she cut off her nose to spite her race,' quipped Dorothy Parker.

performed. The rate at which clinics open and close was also found to be alarmingly high.

What are the consequences?

A significant rise in the number of negligence claims against doctors who harm and even kill patients during cosmetic surgery. Businesswoman Penny Johnson sued a cosmetic surgeon for £54m after her partial facelift in Leeds in 2003 allegedly left her with a facial twitch, pain around her right eye and grimacing. In the most high-profile case of alleged negligence, Denise Hendry, wife of ex-Blackburn Rovers footballer Colin Hendry, suffered multiple organ failure after a liposuction procedure at Broughton Park Private Hospital in Preston went badly wrong. She needed several corrective operations, and in 2009 she fell into a coma following surgery and later died. Further afield, a former Miss Argentina, Solange Magnano, died in Buenos Aires aged 38 after an operation involving buttock implants and injections. 'A woman who had everything lost her life to have a slightly firmer behind,' said her friend, fashion designer Roberto Piazza.

KEEPING THE CLINICS IN LINE

The Care Quality Commission (CQC) was put in charge of regulating the cosmetic surgery industry in England from October 2010. All independent clinics and hospitals that provide cosmetic surgery must be licensed with the CQC, which has powers to fine and prosecute below-standard cosmetic-surgery centres. Plastic surgeons should also be registered with the General Medical Council (GMC).

But some say more is needed. Fazel Fatah, president of the British Association of Aesthetic Plastic Surgeons (BAAPS), says the government should control advertising for the industry and ban all special offers and inducements. 'Companies see cosmetic surgery as a market to be exploited, and gimmicks like "recommend a friend" are stooping to the tactics of double-glazing salesmen,' he says. 'They're recruiting patients as agents to sell the treatments for a commission to friends who might never before have considered surgery.'

What exactly **is** a **bond** ?

It's simply a promise *to pay someone back and to keep paying interest until you do so. Debt of all kinds has been sold by merchants since antiquity, but not until the twelfth century, when the Venetian Republic promised to pay a fixed rate of interest to money-lenders from the proceeds of its salt monopoly, did governments come up with formal schemes to borrow against earnings. Bonds issued by Florence's Medici family helped fund the Renaissance. The British government issued its first bond, a 'tontine', in 1693 to fund a war against France.*

Why do governments favour bonds?

Because bonds enable them to turn short-term emergencies or costly building projects into a long series of predictable payments. The original Dutch 'consols' didn't even have a time limit: rich families bought them and lived off the interest for generations. The original 'tontine' paid out until the holder died and the government still pays 3.5 per cent on £1.9bn of War Bonds issued in 1917. The ability of bonds to raise vast sums of money quickly and spread repayment over long periods has made them vital in the financial crisis, as governments have struggled to make up budget shortfalls since 2008. The UK went from selling around £50bn a year in bonds before the crisis to £227bn in 2009–2010. Companies have also issued more and more corporate bonds as it has become harder to borrow from banks.

Who buys them?

As most bonds are issued by governments, which typically pay low rates of return, they've been seen as very safe investments. Two-thirds of bonds in the UK are held by pension funds and insurance companies, as they know exactly what they're getting with, say, a ten-year bond paying a 'coupon rate' of 4.25 per cent a year. The British government, whose bonds are known as 'gilts', prides itself on never having missed an interest payment in 300 years. Hence 'sovereign' bonds are often given the highest 'AAA' rating by the agencies that evaluate the safety of investments. It shouldn't always be applied. With the introduction of the euro in 1999, world financial regulators misguidedly deemed all Eurozone sovereign bonds to be 'risk free' while bond markets – overlooking the 'no bailout clause' in the treaty – began to price southern European debt at

if it were German debt. Hence the current crisis. But as a rule, the risk of default is not one of the main concerns of bondholders.

What are their main concerns?

Inflation and changes in interest rates. If inflation is 5 per cent and you're sitting on a ten-year gilt paying 3 per cent, your actual rate of return is a wretched -2 per cent. The same applies if government raises rates to 5 per cent. Such considerations, plus the unpredictable need for ready cash, has meant that bondholders are often keen to sell their bonds before they reach maturity, which is why, ever since the seventeenth century, there have been brokers willing to facilitate this desire.

So how does a bond market work?

It is actually made up of two types of markets: primary and secondary. Primary markets organise the sale of government or company bonds when issued for the first time. These normally take the form of auctions, with various types of bonds on offer: a 4 per cent bond for ten years, say, or 1.25 per cent over 50 years. The UK's Debt Management Office, the Treasury agency that runs Britain's bond sales, held 49 auctions in 2010 and pays interest on 48 types of gilt. Its auctions are only open to 20 pre-approved institutions called 'Gilt-edged Market Makers' or GEMMS: basically the big banks.

What do they do with them?

They buy billions of pounds' worth of bonds to trade them in the larger

---

The UK's Debt Management Office held 49 auctions in 2010, only open to 20 pre-approved institutions called 'Gilt-edged Market Makers' or GEMMS: basically the big banks.

---

secondary market, where ordinary investors (mostly via pension funds) take part. In the UK, this market trades about £20bn per day in gilts (40 times more than the primary). The government isn't involved, but how this secondary market behaves is critical to the government's ability to raise money in future auctions.

Why is that the case?

The key to a bond is its 'yield' – how much the buyer can expect to earn from it over its lifetime. Governments want to keep that yield – printed on in its new bonds as the 'coupon rate' – as low as possible, but will have to pay higher yields if interest rates rise or buyers start to doubt the government's ability to repay them on maturity. How this works in practice is that the price of bonds in the secondary market falls: if interest rates rise to 6 per cent, a £1,000 bond paying 5 per cent a year might now fetch only £800, because at that price the original coupon rate of 5 per cent, or £50 per year, will now offer a yield of more than 6 per cent. And that in turn means that when it comes to the next auction, the government will have to raise its coupon rates – and its cost of borrowing – accordingly.

Is that what's been occurring in Europe?

In a big way. Since members of the euro do not control their own currencies (see box) they can only make up their debt shortfall by selling yet more bonds: markets then demand ever higher yields, forcing governments to offer ever more extravagant coupon rates. Most economists believe this is unsustainable, as even small interest rate changes are hugely expensive. If the UK had to add just 0.5 per cent to its borrowing costs on the £170bn of bonds it plans to sell in 2012, it would cost it an extra £8.5bn – the same as its international aid budget.

Is that threat likely in the UK?

In 2010, when the euro debt crisis was building, Britain's bond yields were on a par with those of Spain – which had a similarly large budget deficit but smaller national debt. Since then, their paths have radically diverged. For all the country's economic woes, UK ten-year gilts were yielding a record low of 2.2 per cent towards the end of 2011. That the markets saw Britain as a safe haven was attributed to Osborne's get-tough-with-the-deficit rhetoric and to sterling being outside the euro. But mostly it was the result of faith that the Bank of England will intervene with quantitative easing (see box), as it did in February 2012 when it added £50bn to the £325bn it had already showered on secondary gilt markets.

LOSING CONTROL OF YOUR CURRENCY

Before monetary union, the southern nations of the Eurozone could have reduced their national debts via currency devaluation: either by slashing interest rates or, in extremis, by fixing the price of their currencies at a lower level and banning currency exchange at any other rate. With the euro, they can't do that. Nor can they employ a tactic, introduced in 2009, known as quantitative easing, whereby a government prints new money and then uses it to buy its own bonds in the secondary market. If all goes to plan, this drives the price of bonds up (and yields down), while putting money in the hands of former bondholders

(e.g. pension funds) who go off and spend it elsewhere. Instead, Europe's vulnerable economies have had to rely on the European Central Bank (ECB) to buy up bonds other investors don't want. In November 2011, with Spanish and Italian yields teetering at the 7 per cent mark, the ECB spent around €6bn buying their bonds. But critics say the ECB's bond-buying has been far too panicky and ad hoc, and thus has failed to reassure the markets. Had it been brave enough to impose a yield cap – making it clear it would flood the market with liquidity the moment yields hit, say 6.5 per cent – the crisis might have been brought under control.

How many
private eyes
are there?

Nobody knows for sure, *because the business of private investigating in the UK is completely unregulated. Most estimates, however, put the number at around 10,000. The industry runs the gamut from large firms specialising in entirely legal corporate investigations, debt collectors and tracing agents, to tiny, one-man bands that mostly help jealous spouses to spy on their partners. What all these private investigators have in common, though, is an ever-widening array of digitised personal data to go hunting for – by 2006, each working adult in the UK had given their details to around 700 databases on average – and increasingly high-tech ways to get hold of it.*

Aren't most of those ways illegal?

Plenty of personal information can be obtained perfectly legally, either from public documents such as the land registry and the electoral roll, or by reading what people broadcast about themselves online. But there is also a shadowy, vastly profitable, mostly illegal trade in confidential information, much of it controlled by unlicensed private detectives. The data mined by detectives is held by BT, the banks, the NHS and other organisations collectively known as 'data controllers'. But the problem is that the laws

passed to safeguard information
we give to data controllers –
the Regulation of Investigatory
Powers Act (RIPA), which forbids
the interception of phone calls
by anyone except the security
services, and the Data Protection
Act – aren't very effective.

Who is a major employer of these private eyes?

As the phone-hacking scandal
showed – newspapers. Fleet
Street's insatiable demand for
personal information, from ex-
directory phone numbers to car
registrations and mobile phone
records, has been a vital driver
in the market for confidential
data. In 2008, the Information
Commissioner's Office (ICO), set
up to police the Data Protection
Act, estimated that 25 per cent of
its cases stemmed from complaints
about private eyes, whose clients
were very often journalists. One
of the ICO's largest-ever cases,
'Operation Motorman', centred
on a private eye called Steve
Whittamore who, back in 2001,
was making more than £1,000 per
week from individual journalists.
In 2003, he was found to have

conducted searches for 13,343
pieces of data on behalf of 305
journalists, 85 per cent of which
were thought to have been illegal.

How did he go about them?

In myriad ways, that can be
grouped into three broad
categories. First, 'blagging': the
art of tricking data controllers – in
practice, their call-centre staff
– into disclosing data (see box).
Second, technology: using any one
of a vast range of easily obtained
gadgets to spy on a target's
computer or mobile phone – a
gadget such as the USB KeySafe
Pro, for example, that, for around
£30, can record any typed activity
on a target's computer, from
emails sent to websites visited.
Third, by corrupting staff at a
data centre and getting them to
hand over private data for a fee.
Much of the info that Whittamore
obtained for papers such as the
Daily Mail and the *News of the
World* was through a network of
skilled blaggers and contacts at BT,
the DVLA and the police. Among
his files, the ICO found the home
address and ex-directory number of
the then head of MI6, Sir Richard

Dearlove, and the addresses of eight England football stars which had been tricked out of BT while the players were out of the country. Allegations arising from the phone-hacking scandal suggested that a private eye only had to offer a few hundred pounds to get susceptible police officers to undertake highly sophisticated searches for him – locating a mobile phone through 'pinging', for example.

So is this all the journalists' fault?

No. The media certainly creates work for private eyes, but a much larger caseload comes from the meat and potatoes of PI work: relationship disputes, verifying insurance claims, tracing debtors. According to the ICO, PIs can make more than £100,000 a month for locating debt absconders, and not all will be following legal procedures. A journalist from the *Independent*, posing as a suspicious boyfriend, had no trouble finding PIs willing to place a GPS tracking device on his girlfriend's car or monitor her internet activity. It would be easy to hack her phone without even

getting hold of it, Paul Turner of WeTrackAnyCar.com explained, so that 'when she receives a text message, it'll send you a copy.' (Though not if she's 'got a BlackBerry or an iPhone – they're impossible to do because there's so many security settings there.') The danger posed by making this information available to criminals, violent former partners and even terrorists is obvious.

The industry runs from large firms specialising in entirely legal corporate investigations to tiny, one-man bands that mostly help jealous spouses to spy on their partners.

Isn't there a way of licensing private investigators?

There has been pressure on the UK government to do so for more than a decade, notably from the Association of British Investigators. 'We've done everything we possibly could to help,' says Tony Imossi, its president. But associations like his represent only five per cent of Britain's PIs. The creation of the Security Industry Authority in 2001 was a step in the right direction, but its powers have never been extended to cover PIs. So today anyone, as the Home Office notes, 'can undertake investigative activity regardless of skills, experience or criminality'. The *Independent* records the case of a man convicted of assaulting an 11-year-old girl working as a PI under an alias. The police lack the powers to stop him doing so.

So what should be done?

A new law to create licences for PIs was shelved after the coalition came to power in 2010, owing to the legislative logjam in Parliament. But in any case, as the phone-hacking scandal showed, regulations on their own don't stop abuse: what's required are penalties strong enough to deter the trade in illegally sourced private information. They do not exist at present. Whittamore, for instance, was given a conditional discharge at his trial in 2005. None of his clients was charged with a crime. The ICO has urged the government to punish breaches of the Data Protection Act with prison sentences, rather than the fines it currently levies – which amount to little more than a day's fee for a PI.

THE NOBLE ART OF 'BLAGGING'

'Blagging' is the stock-in-trade of private eyes and, unsurprisingly, many journalists. It involves talking personal information, through charm or subterfuge, out of people who know they're not supposed to give it. In the UK's multi-million-pound marketplace of confidential personal data, it is now a professionally taught discipline. 'It's all in the art of persuasion. You have to make that person want to tell you that address,' said a blagging 'manual' discovered by the ICO at the office of a PI in Middlesex. Blagged data can end up being used by legitimate clients, who have no idea how private investigators operate. In 2005, the ICO discovered that an unnamed council was the ultimate beneficiary of information illegally blagged on its behalf. An investigator tracing people who had not paid their council tax rang up a job centre in Hull, posing as a civil servant from the Department for Work and Pensions, and managed to obtain the current addresses and employment details of 140 people in a single call lasting 90 minutes.

Why did Britain deport **150,000** children to its **colonies**?

Appalling things *happened under a 'welfare' programme for thousands of poor children over the course of three centuries, right up until 1967. Taken from orphanages, care homes and families across the country, children from toddlers to teenagers were removed from everything they knew and placed on boats bound for Canada, Australia and southern Africa where they were promised a better, healthier life. Instead, they were either put to work – long after child labour had been banned in the UK – or handed to religious institutions where they received a meagre education and suffered physical and sexual abuse. 'We look back in shame,' said Paul Rudd, 'at how those with power were allowed to abuse those who had none.' Rudd, Australia's ex-Prime Minister, and Britain's then PM, Gordon Brown, apologised for the policy in 2009.*

How many British children were transported?

Around 150,000 were forcibly resettled across the Empire from 1618 to 1967. Records show that the average age of the children was eight years and nine months. Canada was the most common destination, receiving 100,000 'Home Children' between 1869 and 1939; Australia received no more than 10,000. The first known batch was of 100 children sent to Richmond, Virginia, in the early seventeenth century. And hundreds were sent to South Africa in the early nineteenth century to replace slave labour, which had been outlawed. It was not until 1850, however, that child emigration became a policy fully endorsed by the British government, which passed a series of laws – from the reformed Poor Laws of the 1850s to the Children's Act of 1948 – all of which provided funding to pay for the transport of children abroad.

Why did British governments do it?

The justifications changed over time. Until the mid-nineteenth century, it tended to be seen as an uncomplicated way of getting rid of undesirables: children were normally transported from prisons or homes for juvenile delinquents. But by 1850 it was being argued that it was actually in the best interest of orphans or children from 'immoral' families to be removed from the crowded slums of Great Britain and sent to Australia and Canada, which were crying out for cheap labour. By the 1920s, the rhetoric had changed again. With the passing

of the Empire Settlement Act in 1922, the children were rebranded as 'Empire Builders' charged with bringing 'good white stock' to the colonies. In Australia, the migrants became part of the government's fixation that the country must 'populate or perish' after the Second World War.

Did they keep links with Britain?

None whatsoever. The whole programme was predicated on separating the children from their past. In 1906, the children's charity, Barnardo's, which sent more than 30,000 children abroad from 1882 to 1967, made the position clear: 'For many of our children, emigration cuts the cord that in this country would bind them to degraded relatives and seriously handicap their futures.' Children were given new surnames and informed that their parents had died; siblings were split up and sent to different destinations. An investigation by the Australian Senate in 2001 described a deliberate 'process of depersonalisation'.

Who looked after the children?

In nineteenth-century Canada, children were typically handed over to farming families who agreed to pay their new charges $1 a year until the age of 18, and to give them food, shelter and a religious upbringing. A series of abuse cases led Canada, in 1925, to refuse to accept child migrants under the age of 14, so Australia became the country to which most of the

---

In 1906, Barnardo's said: 'For many of our children, emigration cuts the cord that in this country would bind them to degraded relatives and seriously handicap their futures.'

---

younger ones were sent, and by the first half of the twentieth century most were being placed in Christian farm schools, charities or church groups. Religiously inspired philanthropists – people such as Thomas Barnardo, Annie Macpherson and William Quarrier – all became convinced that

placing these children in Christian homes or schools abroad could be the basis of their salvation.

What were conditions like?

'Children were placed in large, isolated institutions and often subjected to harsh, sometimes intentionally brutal, regimes of work and discipline, unmodified by any real nurturing or encouragement,' the House of Commons Health Committee found in 1998. In 2001, the Catholic Church apologised to 1,300 migrant children who had endured slave labour, rape and whippings at farm schools in Australia from the 1930s to the 1960s. Abuses did not go entirely unnoticed at the time. An inspector at the St John Bosco Boys Town in Tasmania in 1951 was deeply unsettled by the absence of women at the institution and by the way the Salesian monks in charge did nothing but complain about the 'poor quality of migrants' they were receiving.

Why did Britain and Australia apologise after so long?

The child migration programme

was all but lost to history until the mid-1980s, when a social worker in Nottingham called Margaret Humphreys received a letter from a woman in Australia who had been transported at the age of four and was looking for relatives. Humphreys founded the Child Migrants Trust in 1987, and her research led to parliamentary investigations in both the UK and Australia, and in 1993 prompted the Christian Brothers to apologise for the abuses committed in the homes they ran in Western Australia (see box). The apology offered by the Australian government to the 'Lost Innocents' in 2009 was combined with an apology for the even greater scandals over the removal of Aboriginal children from their families and the 'Forgotten Australians' – the total of 500,000 children brought up in the country's inadequate care homes and orphanages between 1930 and 1970.

'FOURTEEN HOURS OF SUNSHINE A DAY'

Laurie Humphreys was living in an orphanage in Southampton in 1947. He was 13 years old when he was told that Australia needed new migrants. 'When the sisters asked who wanted to go to Australia, my hand was one of the first to go up,' he says. He was one of three orphans chosen to go, and was overjoyed. 'We were told that there would be fourteen hours of sunshine a day, and that we could ride a horse to school.'

But Bindoon Boys Town – a desolate abandoned farm sixty miles north of Perth in Western Australia – was a terrible shock. The institution had not even been built. Humphreys' education was over, as he and hundreds of other boys, some as young as ten, were put to work constructing dormitories and kitchens under the authority of the Christian Brothers, a Catholic order. Beaten heavily for wetting the bed and breaking minor rules, the boys suffered routine sexual abuse, calling their carers the 'Christian Buggers'. Humphreys worked as a truck driver from the age of 14. His only comfort were the other transported boys. 'We were all in the hardship game together,' he told the *Independent*. 'And you knew nothing better.'

 # Who
were
the **Mau Mau** ?

An incredibly violent insurgent movement *in British-controlled Kenya, consisting mainly of Kikuyu, members of the ethnic group worst-hit by the colonial government's land expropriation. Recruits had to swear the infamous Mau Mau oath, vowing to be united in their fight against the colonial enemy and sealing it, or so colonial officials maintained, by digging up a corpse, eating its flesh and drinking the 'Kaberichia cocktail': a mixture of semen and menstrual blood. Certainly anyone caught breaking the oath would face hideous reprisals. In response, the British authorities made it a capital offence to take the oath and forced many to take a 'cleansing oath' to reverse the original.*

And what kind of conflict ensued?

One of the nastiest in British colonial history: during the Mau Mau rebellion, which took place between 1952 and 1960, 79,000 Kenyans were detained, and some 12,000 were killed (officially – it may have been twice that), along with just 32 European settlers. The Mau Mau committed horrific sexual attacks and murders: their victims were overwhelmingly the anti-Mau Mau Kikuyu who wouldn't take the oath, typically those who had kept their land and made strong ties to the colonial administration. The response of the authorities was to declare a state of emergency, suspend the rule of law and institute mass detention without trial. Among those detained was Hussein Onyango Obama, the US President's grandfather, who, according to his family, was jailed for two years and tortured.

Has this only now come to light?

There was nothing secret about the atrocities committed on the colonialists' side: they were widely reported by the British press at the time. Tom Askwith, a former Kenyan official sacked for speaking out, witnessed, on a visit to the detention camp at Mwea, 'food denial with starvation for up to three days, and regular, brutal beatings'. John Nottingham, another ex-colonial official, recalls seeing patrols ambushing suspected Mau Mau by tossing grenades into huts. But such barbarity had always been dismissed as the action of a few 'bad apples' until five elderly Kenyans sued the British government for the brutal treatment inflicted on them by the British authorities in the 1950s.

What did the five Kenyans claim?

That they suffered 'unspeakable acts of brutality' in British-run detention camps. Wambugu Wa Nyingi, 83, alleged that he was detained without charge for nine years, subjected to forced labour and often suspended by his feet and severely beaten while cold water was poured onto his face to stop him breathing. Ndiku Mutwiwa Mutua, 79, a herdsman arrested for supplying food to the rebels, alleged that he was repeatedly beaten by European and African officers, and finally castrated. The only woman claimant says she was sexually violated using bottles filled with hot water. The essence of their case was that it was in fact a systematic policy organised and condoned by the British authorities, and sanctioned at the highest level of the British government. Following an order by the High Court judge that all relevant evidence be produced, files filling 110ft of shelves were discovered in a secret Foreign Office depository at Hanslope Park in Buckinghamshire, showing that this was indeed the case.

What are these documents?

When British colonies were granted independence, it was general practice not to hand over any files that – in the words of the Foreign and Commonwealth Office (FCO) – 'might embarrass HMG or other governments' or 'members of the police, military forces [or] public servants' (see box). So when the British left Kenya in 1963 they took away thousands of such documents. For many years afterwards, former Mau Mau detainees who sought the official records of their detention were told these had been lost: a rumour even circulated that they had been loaded into a Lancaster bomber and dropped in the Indian Ocean. Once they turned up, historian David Anderson was allowed to examine about 300 files relating to the Mau Mau period, and to provide written evidence about what he found to the High Court.

And what did he find?

Massive evidence of the scale of violence deployed against the rebels, including the sanctioning of torture – and of attempts to cover it up. 'If we are going to sin, we must sin quietly,' said Kenyan Attorney General Eric Griffiths-Jones, who also wrote to Secretary of State for Colonies Alan Lennox-Boyd, giving details of how detainees were to be treated. (Anyone protesting would have 'a foot placed on his throat and mud stuffed in his mouth … in the last resort knocked unconscious'.) The Governor of Kenya, Sir Evelyn Baring, also wrote to Lennox-Boyd, telling him that

'If we are going to sin, we must sin quietly,' said the Kenyan Attorney General Eric Griffiths-Jones, who also detailed how detainees were to be treated.

'violent shock' was the only way to deal with the insurgents, and later giving horrific details of cruelties inflicted by European officers – including one case of a district officer 'beating up and roasting alive' an African. Another file shows Baring discussing with Lennox-Boyd the 'political difficulties' that could arise from the use of torture.

What was the FCO's response?

Not to deny all this, but to rely on an obscure rule (derived from a case about licences to fish for Patagonian toothfish in South Georgia) which states that responsibility for acts committed by a colonial government passes to the successor government at independence. So government lawyers argue the Kenyans' suit should be dismissed, as the alleged abuse was carried out by the colonial government, which passed all rights and responsibilities to the independent Kenyan government in 1963. This has aroused much anger in Africa. 'The British government's attempt to pin liability on Kenya for British colonial torture represents an intolerable abdication of responsibility,' says Archbishop Desmond Tutu.

SKELETONS IN THE COLONIAL CLOSET

In April 2011, FCO Minister Lord Howell of Guildford conceded that thousands of files on the Kenyan uprising had been kept secret, along with copious material relating to 37 other British administrations in the days before independence (including the Bahamas, Ceylon, Cyprus, Jamaica, Malaya, Northern Rhodesia and Palestine). He said the government would make available to the wider public 'as much of this material as possible', but also noted that the files would be 'reviewed': the implication being that they could be selected or redacted before release, in a process that 'may take some years'. All of which, if the government loses this court case, could spell a multi-million-pound compensation bill for Britain.

It will come not just from the 1,400 other former Mau Mau detainees still alive, but from the nationals of other countries who claim to have been tortured and held without trial in the dying days of the British Empire. Other skeletons may rattle out of colonial closets in Cyprus, Palestine and above all Malaya, where 34,000 people were held without trial in the first eight years of the 'emergency' declared in 1948, and 500,000 were forcibly relocated into camps.

What
are 'rare earth'
minerals?

An elusive and, until recently, poorly understood family of 17 chemical elements. Discovered in quarries in the late eighteenth century, they were identified only as 'rare earths' – by-products occurring in exotic minerals. Only later did scientists realise that they were actually distinct, silvery metals. And they weren't even that rare. Cerium, the most common Rare Earth Element (REE), is the 25th most abundant element in the Earth's crust – more common than copper and lead. But since REEs are seldom found in large deposits, for more than a century they sat unnoticed at the foot of the periodic table until industrial engineers in the car and petrochemical industries began to experiment with them. Now they form part of an array of products, notably small electronic devices and green technologies, which are vital to modern life.

Why are rare earths so useful?

Because they readily shed and acquire electrons, thanks to their distinctive atomic structure. Excellent conductors of heat and electricity, some generate light, others store power, others – even when used in tiny quantities – make for the world's most efficient magnets. Their versatility, uniqueness and suitability for small devices mean that rare earths are now in everything from nuclear reactors to iPods. New cars have rare earths in their windscreens, headlights and catalytic converters. Each Toyota Prius contains about 15 kg of lanthanum in its battery alone. Neodymium makes the magnets essential to the engines that run laptop computers and wind turbines. America's main battle tank, the M1A2 Abrams, relies on samarium to run its navigation system.

Do they all come from China?

Yes and no. There are deposits of rare earths all over the world, but China – where rare earths are known as 'industrial vitamins' – is by far the largest producer. Of the 124,000 tons brought to market in 2009, 120,000 were mined there. Almost half are sifted from the tailings of a single massive iron ore mine in Baotou, in Inner Mongolia. But it's not just thanks to its large deposits that China dominates the trade – it's the result of deliberate policy. In the 1990s, China flooded the world with cheap exports, making rare-earth mines around the world uneconomical. Now it's raising taxes on those

exports and cutting back on them (by 70 per cent in the second half of last year), sending prices soaring. The cost of neodymium has tripled in 12 months.

Why is China doing this?

'They want it for themselves,' says Jack Lifton, a rare-earths specialist in the US. China's domestic needs for rare earths are vast – its factories consume 60 per cent of world production. Rare earths are crucial to the green technologies – such as electric vehicles and the gearless engines in wind turbines – that China is investing in heavily. By cutting exports, Beijing also hopes to entice more manufacturers to China and see the value added by rare earths benefit the domestic economy. There's an environmental motive, too. In many places, the landscape has been devastated as a result of the rapid increase in rare-earth exports in the 1990s (see box). Regulations to protect the environment have inevitably entailed a fall in production.

How is the West reacting?

It's beginning to panic, not least

because China is showing its determination to control all the world's rare earths – not simply those within its borders. Thus when a major Australian producer, Lynas, suffered credit problems in 2009, it was a Chinese mine that lobbied to buy the firm. Another Chinese company tried to buy Mountain Pass, the largest American rare-earths mine, which had been mothballed since 2002. The deal was blocked by Congress.

For more than a century they sat unnoticed at the foot of the periodic table. Now they form part of an array of products, notably green technologies, which are vital to modern life.

China is also starting to use its rare earths as a political pawn. After a shipping dispute, exports to Japan were halted for two months in 2010; a ten-day embargo was suddenly placed on Europe and the USA for no reason at all. US Secretary of State Hillary Clinton described China's actions as a 'wake-up call', and no fewer than five bills were prepared in Washington to boost America's domestic rare-earths production.

Can rare earths be mined elsewhere?

Most certainly. China only has about 36 per cent of the world's estimated deposits of rare earths, and there are significant reserves in the USA, Australia and the countries of the former Soviet Union. The problem is that extracting rare earths from the ground is a tricky business, since they normally occur in haphazard batches, hidden inside exotic and often radioactive minerals. 'No two REE ores are truly alike,' says the US Geological Survey. China has a huge cost advantage in being able to take most of its rare earths as a by-product from its Baotou iron mine. It has also used the last ten years to refine its extraction process, with the result that Chinese rare earths are the purest on the market. The US government audit office found that it would take America 15 years to develop a comparable rare-earths supply chain.

So has China won the battle?

It certainly has the rest of the world dancing to its tune at the moment, with industry experts predicting a 20,000-ton shortfall in the supply of rare earths by 2014. And rare earths will unquestionably become more significant to the world economy – a vital resource for the 21st century. But some analysts also believe that their increasing importance will reshape the entire industry. Right now the rare-earths market, while critical, is tiny – worth just $2bn a year, or the equivalent of one per cent of the iron ore industry. That's what has enabled China to corner it. But as soon as it becomes worthwhile for the rest of the world to develop other sources of supply, Australian and US mining entrepreneurs will step in to fill the gap. And then they'll probably be the ones making the killing.

SCORCHED EARTH

Rare earths may be the darlings of wind-farm engineers – and the magic ingredients inside solid-fuel cells, electric-car batteries, energy-efficient light bulbs and even the humble catalytic converter – but they don't come out of the ground easily. Part of the reason for China's monopoly of production is the lack of environmental safeguards covering the extraction of both its 'light' rare earths (which come predominantly from the Baotou mine in Inner Mongolia) and its 'heavy' rare earths – which are mostly dug up by unlicensed miners in the southern provinces of Jiangxi and Guangdong.

Both processes have caused terrible damage. At Baotou there is a five-mile 'tailing' lake, thick with dangerous chemicals from the mine, which has poisoned farmland for miles around. In southern China, where heavy rare earths are found in clays close to the surface, untrained miners drip a solution of sulphuric acid into the ground, leaching out the rare earths. The countryside in many areas is marked by pools of toxic residue, and the rain often sweeps the chemicals into the water supply, poisoning drinking water and killing crops and fish.

How did
Darwin
change **the world** ?

Religious fundamentalists *today rail against Darwin for challenging the account of the creation in Genesis, but this was not in fact a major issue at the time of his seminal work, On the Origin of Species, published in 1859. Long before Darwin, the Victorian geologist Charles Lyell had debunked the idea of seven days of creation; indeed, 19th-century scholarship encouraged Christians to see the early Bible stories as metaphors rather than literal accounts. Many theorists before Darwin had endorsed the idea of evolution – though to most it was a divinely ordained linear evolution, a march to ever greater perfection, with Man as the pinnacle. What was new and deeply unsettling about Darwin's idea was that it seemed to do away with the need to invoke divine authority or any sense of purpose or design.*

And what were the ingredients of Darwin's Big Idea?

It rests on three fundamentals: the observation that the offspring of plants and animals naturally vary from their parents by random mutation; the assumption that those variations are passed down through the generations; and the hypothesis that in a world where population growth outstrips the increase in available resources, any individual with a genetic variation that confers a competitive advantage in the struggle for resources is more likely to survive to breed and pass that variation on – eventually leading to the creation of a new species. Darwin referred to this process as 'natural selection', though even that was not entirely novel.

Who else had speculated on those lines?

His grandfather, Erasmus Darwin, among others. Long before his grandson, the noted polymath and free thinker had outlined his view – in works such as *The Origin of Society* (1803) – that life had evolved as a result of natural variation influenced by the 'three great objects of desire': sex, sustenance and security. Long before his grandson, he had earned the wrath of conventional thinkers. The idea that 'the whole human species is accidentally descended from a remarkable family of monkeys' is absurd, said the author of *Rip van Winkle*, Washington Irving, while Samuel Taylor Coleridge scoffed at the idea that man had descended 'from some lucky species of baboon'.

Was Darwin an infant prodigy?

Far from it. He was kicked out of school in Shrewsbury; he dropped out of medical studies in Edinburgh; and when sent up to Cambridge to study for Holy Orders – to prepare him for the Anglican priesthood – he spent his time on shooting trips and foraging for beetles. 'You care for nothing but shooting, dogs and rat-catching, and you will be a disgrace to yourself and your family,' said his exasperated father, a wealthy society doctor and financier. It was only because Darwin had befriended a botany professor at Cambridge that he was invited on a surveying trip to Tierra del Fuego on board the *Beagle*, as a gentleman naturalist and companion to the captain. And it was only after his uncle, Josiah Wedgwood, persuaded Darwin's reluctant father to pay for the jaunt, that he set off in 1831 on his five-year odyssey around the coasts of South America. Did he arrive at his theory on this trip? No, but the observations he made and specimens he collected set him on the path. The variations in the closely related species of finch he found on isolated islands in the Galapagos (notably their different-shaped beaks) would help show how animals evolved as they adapted to food sources and gave him the first inkling of his big idea. But the fully developed theory did not take its final shape for another quarter of a century.

What took him so long to publish?

Partly because he hated controversy (he once said that explaining his beliefs was like 'confessing to a murder') and was fearful about the effects on his devoutly Christian wife, Emma (daughter of Josiah Wedgwood). When he did publish, he confined his account of evolution to animals and plants, avoiding the tricky issue of human origins as 'surrounded with prejudices'. He also knew that if his ideas were to be accepted, he had to present a meticulously supported case. So he used the intervening years to add 'great quantities of facts' to his *Beagle* observations, turning his kitchen garden into a lab and developing a far-flung network

of correspondents – friends, pigeon fanciers, nurserymen, colonial officials, missionaries, gamekeepers, gardeners. He wrote out his theory in some detail in 1844, but was still hesitating to publish when, in June 1858, one of his correspondents, the explorer Alfred Russel Wallace, wrote to him outlining a mechanism for species change identical to his own. Ashamed of his 'trumpery

---

The idea that 'the whole human species is accidentally descended from a remarkable family of monkeys' is absurd, said the author of *Rip van Winkle*.

---

feelings' of disappointment that his 'priority' of discovery was compromised, Darwin went public with his big idea, in 1859.

So did his theory make Darwin an atheist?

Darwin claimed only to be agnostic, and it was personal tragedy rather than science that made him doubt – notably, the death of his beloved daughter Annie, at the age of ten. After her death, he no longer attended the village church and his failure to find spiritual comfort in his grief seems to have strengthened his trust in natural laws.

And his impact on science?

Origin gave to biology its key guiding principle. When Mendelian genetics, accompanied by the discovery of chromosomes, became established in the early 20th century, it explained many of Darwin's observations about heredity. When the DNA helix was unravelled 50 years later, it served to underpin the molecular basis of genetic variation on which the forces of natural selection act. Even the Pope had to declare in 1996 that Darwin's theory of evolution was now 'more than a hypothesis'. Even so, in a 2006 BBC poll, only 48 per cent of the British public accepted the theory of evolution as the best description for the development of life.

HOW THE PUBLIC REACTED TO ORIGIN

On the Origin of Species by Means of Natural Selection, or *The Preservation of Favoured Races in the Struggle for Life*, as the book was originally titled, was the first genuinely popular theoretical scientific work. Darwin was one of the first writers to negotiate an advance against royalties and *Origin*'s publication sparked huge international interest. The first print run sold out before it appeared and Darwin rewrote the work for a further five editions.

As he anticipated, it unleashed controversy, yet the scale of the uproar is often exaggerated. In 1860, only one year after publication, Frederick Temple, head of Rugby School and later Archbishop of Canterbury, gave a sermon praising Darwin for showing how God moves by natural processes. The same year, Darwin got a letter from novelist and cleric Charles Kingsley along the same lines. By the time Darwin himself addressed the debate about human origins directly in *The Descent of Man* (1871), most leading thinkers, including churchmen, had accepted his theory. A measure of his standing among the establishment came after his death in 1882, when he was one of only five 19th-century non-royals to be given a state funeral and buried in Westminster Abbey.

What was Japan doing in China in the 1930s?

It was the culmination *of a decades-long imperialist ambition to take over China and its abundant raw materials. Japan had occupied the northern province of Manchuria since 1931, but it wasn't until 1937 that the Imperial Japanese Army took Shanghai and moved inland to the then capital, Nanking. As the army drew near, China's nationalist leadership withdrew most troops, leaving 100,000 untrained soldiers and some 500,000 civilians. When the city fell on 13 December, the Japanese entered with orders to 'kill all captives'. There ensued a six-week orgy of rape and murder: at least 300,000 were killed, according to Chinese estimates, though others say it was more like 250,000. Either way, more died in the Rape of Nanking than in the attacks on Hiroshima and Nagasaki combined.*

What sort of things did the Japanese do?

The 90,000-odd Chinese soldiers who surrendered were herded into trucks to remote locations on the outskirts of Nanking where young Japanese conscripts were encouraged to torture them to death as a way of toughening themselves up. Film footage shows smiling soldiers conducting bayonet practice on prisoners, hanging people from their tongues, decapitating them and posing proudly among mutilated corpses. Some prisoners were slowly murdered with *zhuizi* (needles with handles), others were fed to dogs; more than 20,000 females were gang-raped, then killed – usually by having their breasts cut off or by disembowelling.

Why the extreme brutally?

Partly because the poor farmers, industrial workers and criminals who comprised the bulk of the frontline troops were themselves treated with intense harshness by their superiors. Regularly beaten, they treated all beneath them with the contempt they'd experienced. And partly out of vengeance: the Japanese had expected China to fall in weeks, but the siege of Shanghai had taken three months of bloody fighting: Nanking was a perfect opportunity for retribution. But then again, the culture of violence spread well beyond the military.

How did that manifest itself?

A striking aspect of the atrocity was the way the Japanese media gloated over it. There was a mentality, reflected in gleeful eyewitness reports, that brutality against 'inferior' peoples was no more than their due. The *Japan Advertiser* actually published a running count of the heads severed by two officers involved in a decapitation contest, as if it were a kind of a sporting match: 'Incredible record in contest to behead 100 people! Mukai 106, Noda 105. Second Lieutenant Mukai's blade was slightly damaged in the competition. He explained this was a result of cutting a Chinese head in half, helmet and all. The contest was "fun", he said.'

Is the atrocity remembered?

The surviving soldiers who took part in the 1937 assault on Nanking are now old men, and film-makers such as Japanese activist Tamaki Matsuoka have been anxious to record their memories of the atrocity before it's too late. In her documentary, *Torn Memories of Nanking* (2010), infantryman Sawamura (then just 21) recalls how he was ordered to bayonet a Chinese peasant, as taunting fellow soldiers looked on. 'We were told not to waste bullets,' he recalls. 'I stumbled forward and thrust the blade into his body until it came out the other side.' But while the Japanese perpetrators are on their way out, feelings about their crimes still run very high in China. Chinese director Lu Chuan has received death threats for trying – in his film *City of Life and Death* (2009) – to portray the Japanese as human. 'I want to kill you by dismemberment,' read one email.

The *Japan Advertiser* actually published a running count of the heads severed by two officers involved in a decapitation contest, as if it were a kind of a sporting match.

Why do we hear so little about it in the West?

Partly because the Western historical memory of the Second World War focuses on the struggle against Nazi Germany, and pays little heed to the war in Asia before Pearl Harbour. But there is another reason, too, argues Iris Chang in her book, *The Rape of Nanking* (1997). The Japanese still won't face up to what happened, and preserve a highly sanitised view of it. And after the War, she says, it suited the American and Chinese governments, keen to get along with post-war Tokyo, to connive in the 'conspiracy of silence'.

What, in her view, is the standard Japanese position?

Chang accuses Japan as a nation of trying to consign the victims of Nanking to 'historical oblivion', and undoubtedly conservative elements in Japan have always tried to downplay the 'Nanking incident', as they call it, insisting that casualty figures are wildly exaggerated and that the deaths were a legitimate consequence of what they regard as a just war. Until the 1970s, the massacre was not even mentioned in school textbooks. Now, however, the subject does get more of an airing: a translation of the diary of John Rabe (see box) became a bestseller; textbooks discuss the massacre, giving figures of between 150,000 and 300,000 killed; and Japanese scholars such as Hora Tomio and Yuki Tanaka have published significant studies about it. Even so, unlike Germans and the Holocaust, most Japanese people probably remain in steadfast ignorance.

What happened after it?

Initial reports of the atrocity were so full of horror they weren't believed in the West. But before long there was an international outcry, and the concern this created in Japanese diplomatic circles at last tempered the behaviour of the troops. But the occupiers remained until after the bombing of Hiroshima and Nagasaki in 1945 and, to pacify the population during the long occupation, they distributed opium, heroin and other narcotics. An estimated 50,000 people became addicted to heroin, while many others lost themselves in the city's opium dens. Rather than continue to rape Nanking's remaining female inhabitants, the Japanese brought in upwards of 100,000 women, mostly from Korea, for their troops, setting them up in 'comfort houses' as slave-prostitutes.

THE SCHINDLER OF NANKING

The improbable hero of Nanking in that terrible time was a German industrialist – and devout Nazi – called John Rabe (hero of an eponymous feature film, released in 2010). Rabe was so appalled by what he saw that he submitted a report to Hitler (whose response is not recorded), and, with Western missionaries, doctors and businessmen, set up a committee to form an International Safety Zone to protect the thousands of Chinese who had fled for safety into the part of the city where most foreigners lived.

Though Japan had just made the anti-Comintern pact with Germany, being German was no guarantee of safety and Rabe often risked his life challenging the Japanese soldiers. Catching one about to rape a woman, Rabe roared at him in German, flashed his swastika armband and drove him off.

He also negotiated with the Japanese, organised supplies of rice, and became de facto mayor of a ruined city. The 600 or so refugees ('my Chinese guests' as he called them) who took sanctuary in his house and garden, revered him as their 'living Buddha'. 'Around 30 people are asleep in my office, three in the coal bin, eight women and children in the servants' lavatory,' he notes in his diary. A total of 200,000 to 300,000 Chinese found refuge in the Safety Zone. Almost all those who did not make it into the Zone perished.

How
do
antidepressants **work** ?

As with all *mental health treatments, it is an opaque science, but the theory behind antidepressants is that they help moderate the flow of chemicals inside the brain. These neurotransmitters – the more familiar ones being serotonin and dopamine – are thought to have a connection with our moods and feelings of wellbeing, and pharmaceutical companies have been trying to isolate and control them since the 1950s. In the 1960s and 1970s, the best-known drug to do this was Valium, but a new generation of antidepressants, led by Prozac, have since proved much more popular. By 2010, nearly 23 million prescriptions for these selective serotonin reuptake inhibitors (SSRIs) were filled annually in the UK alone. In the USA, antidepressants are now the second most prescribed drug, after treatments for heart disease.*

So why are they now perceived to be a problem?

An increasing number of doctors and psychologists are wondering whether they actually do any good – except to the pharmaceutical companies that make an estimated £13bn a year from the global 'depression therapy' market. Some of the evidence that they do not comes from the drug companies themselves. In 2010, Irving Kirsch, a psychologist from Hull University, analysed data from clinical trials for the US Food and Drug Administration from 1987 to 1999 and found that, according to the drugs' own developers, antidepressants worked better than placebos less than half the time. Meanwhile, a study, published in *The Lancet* in 2011 on antidepressant use among people suffering from Alzheimer's (in which depression is a common co-ailment) showed no benefits at all – only side effects.

What side effects are these?

Prozac and other SSRIs, unlike Valium, have proved enormously popular because they enable people who take them to live a more or less normal life. But there are still side effects: patients report changes in their weight, how much they sleep – either too much, or too little – and their sex drive. These often diminish over time (many patients take SSRIs every day for years), but given how little we know about the interplay of the drugs and neurotransmitters in the brain, there is far greater uncertainty as to their long-term effects. Regulators in the USA and the UK maintain that antidepressants

are not addictive, but they do acknowledge that patients who stop taking them can suffer extremely disruptive withdrawal symptoms. Indeed, children under the age of 18 are banned from taking most SSRIs altogether.

So why does anyone take them?

Because millions of people around the world report that antidepressants have brought a meaningful improvement to their life – if not saved it completely. 'The professionally well might say I am deluded, that I am the victim of a medical conspiracy,' says John Crace, an author who believes that the drugs have saved his life several times. 'Possibly I am. But rather deluded than dead.' Much support for antidepressants comes from psychiatrists who have prescribed the drugs thousands of times, in different combinations, and seen patients improve before their eyes.

Is that not the placebo effect?

It might well be, but it's none the worse for that, argues Dr

Steven Reidbord, a psychiatrist from San Francisco. 'If a patient feels better, I don't worry too much about who or what gets the credit.' But plenty of other experts, led by Professor Peter Kramer of Brown University, feel this is to cede too much ground to the sceptics. There is plenty of hard evidence proving the benefits of antidepressants, he argues, but this is now being overlooked in a general shift of opinion against the drugs – particularly when prescribed by GPs to treat relatively mild cases. Writing in the *New York Times* in 2011, Kramer pointed out that there is no dispute about the beneficial effects of SSRIs in narrower studies focusing on treatment for specific conditions such as severe depression, strokes, epilepsy and multiple sclerosis. The argument should not be about whether the drugs themselves work, it is about when they should be prescribed in the first place.

And when is that?

Depression is an extremely varied condition, and Kramer argues that most criticisms of antidepressants are based around whether they help people who suffer from its milder strains. Not only are these the hardest symptoms to measure – during the course of a trial, sufferers may get better of their own accord – but those with moderate or mild depression are also likeliest to benefit from other forms of treatment, from psychotherapy to a better diet or more exercise. There might be plenty of doctors,

---

Doctors and psychologists are wondering whether they actually do any good – except to the pharmaceutical companies that make an estimated £13bn a year.

---

particularly those not trained in psychiatry, who are too quick to hand out pills to people who could tackle their depression by other means, but that doesn't make the drugs worthless. 'They've earned their place in the doctor's satchel,' says Kramer.

So how will this be resolved?

The UK government wants to provide patients with a range of treatments that include both antidepressants and talking cures. In 2011, it committed £400m to cognitive behavioural therapy, a form of short-term psychological therapy, aimed at changing people's patterns of behaviour, which it hoped would reduce the 1.1 million people then claiming long-term disability benefit for mental health problems. The NHS also hopes GPs will get better at recognising depression: 16 per cent of patients, it would appear, are misdiagnosed. However, crude economics may compromise that approach. As drug patents expire, SSRIs will become cheaper (when Prozac lost its patent in 2001, its price fell tenfold), and the cheaper they become, the more we're likely to take them.

ARE ANTIDEPRESSANTS BEST AVOIDED?

YES

1. According to drug companies' own data, antidepressants are no better than placebos more than 50 per cent of the time.
2. New antidepressants have reduced side effects, but they are side effects nonetheless, and people become dependent on them.
3. The connection between the chemicals in our brain and depression is not clearly understood. It is crazy to tinker.

NO

1. Antidepressants do not help everyone in the same way. Mass trials fail to show this variety.
2. Placebo effect or not, millions of patients around the world claim to have had their lives improved by SSRIs.
3. Mental health problems should never be treated with drugs alone, but that does not mean the drugs are worthless.

How did the
Six-Day War
change international politics?

Ever since Israel *came into existence in 1948 it had been in conflict with its Arab neighbours. Egypt's leader, Gamal Nasser (defeated by Israel in 1956), stirred up the Arab world with speeches about 'liberating' Palestinian lands and eliminating the 'alien' Israeli state. In the mid-1960s both Egypt and Jordan actively supported the Palestinian fedayeen (guerilla) attacks on Israeli civilians; and Syria regularly shelled Israeli farms. By early 1967 there were frequent skirmishes between Israeli and Syrian air forces, and by May 1967, after Syria appealed to Nasser for help, 100,000 Egyptian troops massed in the Sinai on Israel's southern border. It's not clear that either side truly wanted full-scale war but both became convinced the other did.*

How did the war begin?

With an Israeli air strike on Egypt that took the Arab nations totally by surprise. By the first day, the Israelis had destroyed Egypt's and Jordan's air forces and encircled Jerusalem. By the second, the Syrian air force had been crippled.

On the third, the Israelis pushed Jordan from the West Bank; on the fourth they reached the Suez Canal, having taken the Sinai and Gaza from Egypt. By the sixth, all combatant nations had signed ceasefires. In 132 hours, Israel had trebled its size and humiliated the Arab nations. The 'Six-Day War' is how General Moshe Dayan branded it: a deliberate echo of the six days of creation in Genesis.

And how did the war change Israel?

Before the war, it was a demoralised infant state massively outgunned by hostile neighbours. Its economy was in recession, there were rising tensions between the *Ashkenazim* (European-born Israelis) and the less educated, more religious *Mizrahim* (immigrants from north Africa and other Muslim nations) who were starting to eclipse them demographically. The socialist idealism that had inspired the pioneers was in decline. But victory had a galvanising effect, not least on the Jewish diaspora.

How did that manifest itself?

Until then the Jewish diaspora had had mixed feelings about Zionism. Now Jews worldwide celebrated a valiant little country that had proved, two decades after Auschwitz, that Jews were not fated to be history's victims.

The response ranged from the joyful to the Messianic as Israeli soldiers took possession of the totems of Biblical Israel: the Temple Mount, Jerusalem, Hebron and so on. Contributions poured in, strengthening Israel's economy. American Jewish groups lobbied for its defence, and for a short while after the war Israel enjoyed international support.

What kind of international support did it enjoy?

Pre-1967, Israel had faced a Soviet bloc that backed Egypt and Syria and a hostile China and India. Militarily it had had to rely on France, which, on the eve of war, decided to swap sides and impose an arms embargo on Israel instead. Israel's victory, however, hastened the collapse of the Kremlin's influence in the Middle East, won over the Indians and the Chinese, and forged a lasting alliance with the USA which, until then, had refused to sell arms to Israel.

So what went wrong?

Israel's leaders had initially assumed that most of the land they'd captured could be traded for peace. Indeed, the 'land for peace' formula of UN Resolution 242, passed at the end of 1967, envisaged just such a trade-off. And though the Palestinians and their Arab allies said they'd go on fighting, that formula did eventually work for areas that were essentially buffer zones (e.g. the Sinai, returned to Egypt in 1979). But it was a non-starter in areas of Palestinian concentration, notably the West Bank and East

---

Before the war, Israel was a demoralised infant state massively outgunned by hostile neighbours. The socialist idealism that had inspired the pioneers was in decline.

Jerusalem, not least because overnight these acquired a non-tradable status in the eyes of many Israelis. 'We have returned to the most holy of our places,' said General Dayan during the war, 'never to part from them again.' In the following months that wish was given solidity as Orthodox

settlers, the *Gush Emunim* (Bloc of the Faithful), established settlements in the West Bank.

Weren't the early settlements just 'temporary' outposts?

That's how they were originally designated, but the purpose of the settlers was to create a fait accompli that would undermine the principle of land for peace. In the decade following, mainstream Labour governments either feigned ignorance of the settlements or actively encouraged them, thus helping legitimise the ideology of their right-wing successors (Begin, Netanyahu and Sharon). Despite successive UN resolutions stating that the settlements are illegal, they and their 'jurisdictions' came effectively to control about 40 per cent of the West Bank, which is now home to a quarter of a million Israelis.

And did the Palestinians accept the occupation?

That was the hope of many Israelis who saw themselves as 'enlightened occupiers'. And for 20 years the Palestinians largely did acquiesce (40 per cent of those in work had jobs in Israel). But the effect of 1967 was to destroy the credibility of any Arab state to speak on behalf of the Palestinians, and to create a new militant brand of Palestinian nationalism under Yasser Arafat. When Arafat's Fatah group began carrying out raids in the occupied territories, the occupying Israeli forces cracked down hard, resorting to methods earlier used by the British: collective punishment, torture, demolition of Arab homes. Eventually Arafat and his notoriously corrupt entourage was eclipsed by more militant groups like Hamas and Islamic Jihad: Palestinians began to speak less of a battle against the Israelis for land and talk in the more apocalyptic terms of holy war. It was the 1967 conflict, says Michael Oren of the Shalem Centre in Jerusalem, that 'opened the doors to the new idea of Islamic radicalism'.

WAS THE SIX-DAY WAR A PYRRHIC VICTORY?

YES

1. The effects of Jewish occupation of Palestinian areas have turned Israel from international hero to international pariah.
2. The long-term effect of the war has been to radicalise Palestinian and Muslim opinion, undermining hopes of peace.
3. It turned Israel from idealistic democracy to ruthless coloniser that can only survive by repressing the Muslim majority.

NO

1. If Israel had not won the war, it would have been wiped off the map by its Arab neighbours.
2. It galvanised Jewish and world opinion behind the state of Israel, strengthening its economy, security and foreign standing.
3. The principle of land for peace gave Israel an invaluable bargaining chip in its search for peaceful co-existence.

Is it time to follow
Portugal
and decriminalise drugs ?

A decade ago, *the Portuguese government decided to stop treating the country's drug users like criminals. In 2001, it changed its laws so that possession of small amounts of drugs such as heroin, cocaine and cannabis became a civil rather than a criminal offence – not unlike a traffic violation. Instead of being arrested and prosecuted, drug users are brought before 'dissuasion boards' made up of social workers and psychologists, who interrogate them on their habit. Boards can impose sanctions – mainly fines – or recommend treatment. Regular offenders can be made to report to police stations or perform community service. The new regime, say the authorities, is actually tougher than the punitive one it replaced.*

In what way is it tougher?

Because the state intervenes in the lives of drug users more than it did before. Since 2001, the change in the law has been accompanied by investment in services for drug users (administered by the Ministry of Health), ranging from reducing HIV infections to rehab. There is more methadone treatment for heroin addicts and more medical support, and there are more hospital beds. The police, too, have changed their approach. Before, they often ignored casual drug users to focus on the dealers and traffickers. Now anyone caught with drugs must go before one of the 20 dissuasion boards to be categorised as a recreational user, a person with a developing problem, or an addict. Portugal now levies more fines as a percentage of population for drug possession than the UK does.

But has drug use increased or decreased?

It depends which drugs you refer to. An evaluation of Portugal's decade of decriminalisation, published by the European Monitoring Centre for Drugs and Drug Addiction (EMCDDA), found that rates of cannabis and cocaine use fell below the rest of Europe, but that the proportion of heroin users remained above average, as did the rate of drug-related HIV infection. It's a mixed picture, in other words: as the EMCDDA concludes, Portugal 'does not show specific developments in its drug situation that would clearly distinguish it from other European countries'. Counter-intuitively, this is why campaigners feel confident its example should

be followed around the world.

Why is that?

Precisely because nothing dramatic has happened. Drug use has been decriminalised, and the sky has not fallen in. The country isn't a holiday destination for junkies, and neither is it overrun by organised crime. In the UK, one million people have acquired criminal records because of their drug use since 2001; in Portugal, they have become supervised patients in the public health system. That is the shift in thinking that the Global Commission on Drug Policy – a panel of experts and presidents that includes former secretary-general of the UN Kofi Annan – want other governments to adopt. By imagining a 'war on drugs', in which success is measured in drug seizures and arrests, we are missing the point. 'These indicators may tell us how tough we are being, but they don't say how successful we are in improving the "health and welfare of mankind",' says the Commission. When you focus on such goals, Portugal's policy makes sense.

How does it do that?

By tackling drug use as a destabilising influence on society, more like smoking or alcohol abuse. This prompts the authorities to zero-in on the drugs – such as heroin – that cause the most harm. Seen this way, Portugal's experiment has been a success. Even though it still has a higher rate of 'problematic' heroin use than the rest of the EU, this rate has fallen significantly since 2001, particularly among the young. Deaths attributable to the drug have also declined, while the number of addicts seeking medical treatment has doubled. The Global Commission on Drugs says there is evidence that other 'liberal' approaches (such as in the Netherlands, where doctors can prescribe heroin) also reduce the overall harm they cause. The Commission even recommends a more lenient approach to drug dealers and growers.

Why should they not be punished?

Because there's no point. According to the Commission, the vast majority of the world's drug suppliers are 'little fish', forced into the drugs trade by poverty and replaced when they're arrested. 'Governments are filling jails with minor offenders serving long sentences, at great cost, and with no impact on the scale or profitability of the market,' it says. Countries should focus their efforts on reducing demand for the most dangerous substances and on breaking up

---

Cameron said the 'war on drugs… has been tried and we all know it does not work'. Obama called the policy 'an utter failure'. But that was before they came to power.

---

the big cartels that dominate the world's $300bn drug trade. And that process will only begin, say César Gaviria and Ernesto Zedillo, former presidents of Colombia and Mexico, when addicts are no longer seen as 'buyers in the illegal market [but as] patients cared for by the public-health system'.

How likely is this to happen?

Acknowledging that the war on drugs has failed is now fairly common among politicians. The US Senate concluded in 2011 that it had nothing to show for more than $3bn spent on trying to reduce the volume of drugs coming into the USA. In 2002, David Cameron said the 'war on drugs... has been tried and we all know it does not work'. In 2004, Barack Obama called the policy 'an utter failure'. But that was before they came to power. Now it is business as usual. In response to the Global Commission on Drug Policy campaign, a Home Office spokesman said: 'We have no intention of liberalising our drugs laws. Drugs are illegal because they are harmful... Giving people a green light to possess drugs through decriminalisation is clearly not the answer.'

IS IT TIME TO DECRIMINALISE DRUGS?

YES

1. Portugal's case shows that liberalising drug laws does not make drug use more prevalent in society.

2. Treating drug users as criminals separates them from the rest of society, making them more vulnerable to violence and disease.

3. Drugs constitute a highly complex challenge to society: it is folly to pretend we can arrest and jail our way out of the problem.

NO

1. Drugs cause terrible harm to society. We need the strongest deterrents to stop people using them, not greater leniency.

2. It simply is not true to say that fighting drugs doesn't work: 41 per cent of the world's cocaine is now seized before it reaches users.

3. Decriminalisation will make it easier for the criminals of the global drugs trade to sell their product.

What was
the origin
of the Quakers
?

A religious sect, *numbering around 200,000 worldwide, it emerged from the great crowd of radical and egalitarian movements that sprouted after the English Civil War. The Religious Society of Friends, as it is formally known, traces its beginnings to a sermon given by George Fox, a travelling preacher, on 13 June 1652. Speaking from a hillside near the Cumbrian town of Sedbergh, Fox told the thousand people gathered beneath of an 'inward light' he had received from God. Unlike those who believed that only the predestined can find salvation, Fox stressed the importance of good works, and taught that God is present in everyone. His ideas have sustained the movement for the last 350 years and have given Quakers, also known as Friends, their qualities of tolerance, pacifism and hard work.*

And how did they come to be such good businessmen?

Lack of other options, for a start. Being outside the Anglican church, the Quakers were banned from universities until the mid-nineteenth century, and so were effectively barred from careers in the law, science or medicine. Pacifism put soldiering out of bounds. So, like the Jews, Huguenots and other excluded communities, the Quakers poured their energy into trade and industry. At first their distinctive ways and the tight bonds between members of the sect – until 1860 it was forbidden to marry outside it – made them social outcasts (see box). But that togetherness also ensured a strong basis of support for Quaker firms, and meant that any hint of bankruptcy or shady practice was heavily censured. As a result, Quaker firms became a byword for reliability. In 1877, two US millers patented the name 'Quaker Oats', even though they themselves were not Quakers at all.

What else made the Quaker brand so attractive?

With their simple clothes (Quakers wore only black, grey and white) and straightforward ways, the Quakers personified the qualities of trust and stability essential to the growth of market capitalism. Quaker businesses were among the first to use fixed prices, for example, and their honesty was legendary. 'Let your yea be yea, and your nay be nay' were the words that helped launch great British Quaker businesses such as the Barclays and Lloyds banking groups, Clarks shoes, the biscuit-makers Huntley & Palmers, Reckitt Benckiser (now the world's largest cleaning products company) – not to mention the great Quaker chocolate dynasties: the Cadburys of Birmingham, the Frys of Bristol, the Rowntrees and Terrys of York.

Why the fixation with chocolate?

Because it was a product that enabled them to combine commercial success with social improvement. Quakers were at the forefront of the temperance movement, which sought to curtail the wrecking effects of alcohol on the working poor – and cocoa, made with boiled water, was promoted as a healthy and virtuous alternative. Quaker firms, led by John Cadbury in Birmingham, also made technological advances to remove impurities from cocoa and develop the first chocolate bars. As the Quaker companies grew, so did their opportunities for philanthropy – particularly in the case of Cadbury.

How did that manifest itself?

John Cadbury, who founded the company in 1824, was a

serial social reformer. He set up a forerunner of the RSPCA, and campaigned against the employment of children by chimney sweeps. With his sons, Richard and George, he ensured that Cadbury workers – who were often from the Birmingham slums – had better lives. In 1879, the Cadburys moved their factory to the banks of the River Bourn, on the southern edge of Birmingham, and built 'Bournville' to house

---

'Let your yea be yea, and your nay be nay' helped launch great British Quaker businesses such as Barclays and Lloyds, Huntley & Palmers – not to mention Cadburys, Frys and Terrys.

---

their employees. Sports pitches, a swimming pool, a theatre and a concert hall were all constructed; pensions became standard; young employees went to night school; and the working day began with prayers. True to its founding ethos, Bournville is still owned by a trust set up by George Cadbury, and it remains one of the last places in Britain where you cannot buy a drink. Even the local Tesco was refused a licence.

Did other Quaker tycoons make their mark as reformers?

Very much so. They were conspicuous campaigners in Victorian Britain despite there being so few of them. (Friends accounted for just 0.1 per cent of the population in 1851.) Quaker businessmen helped end the slave trade. Edward Pease, a wool merchant, was the first Quaker MP, a position he made use of to support the prison reformer – and fellow Quaker – Elizabeth Fry. The Darbys of Coalbrookdale, pioneers of ironworking, refused to make cannons during the Napoleonic wars, while the building of Bournville helped inspire the 'garden city' movement, and the construction of Welwyn and Letchworth in Hertfordshire. Yet Quakers weren't entirely divorced from their time: John Cadbury refused to employ married women, and chocolate-makers relied on sugar grown on slave plantations – at one time there was even a Quaker slave ship called *The Society*. Nor did their good intentions always catch on. The Cadburys' 'temperance pub' in Bournville closed for lack of interest.

What Quaker companies survive?

There are around 100, mostly small, in the UK. Large Quaker businesses have been moving away from their roots since the Second World War. Barclays, formed in 1690, expanded with the merger of 20 Quaker banks in 1896, and only appointed its second chairman from outside the founding families in 1987. Rowntree's was bought by Nestlé in 1988, and Reckitt (makers of Brasso) merged with the Dutch chemical company Benckiser in 1999. Cadbury became a public company in 1962 and started acting like a multinational corporation years ago. Despite improving its dealings with farmers and suppliers in developing countries, Cadbury, like Kraft, cut thousands of jobs as it moved production overseas.

HOW THE FRIENDS BECAME POPULAR

Unlike modern Friends, known for their quietude and tolerance, early Quakers were radical, sometimes violent and opposed to the customs of polite society. They refused to swear oaths, doff their hats or use formal titles. In his journal, George Fox, the preacher, described how 'people were shy of them, and would not trade with them; so that for a time some Friends could hardly get money enough to buy bread.

'But afterwards, when people came to have experience of Friends' honesty and faithfulness, and found that their yea was yea, and their nay was nay; that they kept to a word in their dealings, and would not cozen and cheat, but that if a child were sent to their shops for anything, he was as well used as his parents would have been; then the lives and conversation of Friends did preach, and reached to the witness of God in the people.

'Then things altered so, that all the inquiry was, "Where is there a draper, or shop-keeper, or tailor, or shoemaker, or any other tradesman, that is a Quaker?" Insomuch that Friends had more trade than many of their neighbours, and if there was any trading, they had a great part of it.'

Why has hostage-taking become big business?

Taking hostages *has always been a central part of warfare. After conquering a territory, the Romans would seek to capture a young prince and educate him – both to ensure the subjugation of his people, and with a view to installing a more moderate ruler when he came of age. In the Middle Ages, the Irish king Niall of the Nine Hostages got his name from capturing his rivals, while England's seizure of King John II of France at Poitiers, and his subsequent ransom of three million crowns, helped shape the Hundred Years War. The use of civilian hostages in war was common as late as the Franco-Prussian War in 1870, when the Germans held mayors of French towns to force their residents to house and feed the invading forces. But only in the last 50 years or so has hostage-taking become widespread for all sorts of political and financial motives.*

Who was responsible for popularising that sort of kidnap?

Latin American guerrilla groups of the 1960s, who seized on it as a means to increase their notoriety and fund their campaigns. Taking hostages deep into the jungle instilled fear and made for dramatic publicity. The four-day kidnap of the US Ambassador to Brazil in 1969 by MR-8, a group of Marxist revolutionaries, caught worldwide attention, and inspired Palestinian terrorists and European groups (such as the Red Army Faction) to do likewise. By the 1970s and 1980s, taking hostages – normally Western civilians – and using them as bargaining chips for captured terrorists or political prisoners became a standard tactic for militants across the Middle East. Iranian students held 52 US citizens hostage for 444 days in Tehran between 1979 and 1981, while Lebanese factions used Terry Waite and Brian Keenan to call attention to their causes during the country's civil war.

Did money change hands?

Ransoms were certainly paid but, as in the case of the Democratic Revolutionary Movement for the Liberation of Arabistan (the Iranian separatists who captured the Iranian embassy in London in 1980), the kidnaps normally had the political goal of getting an unknown group attention. It wasn't until the 1990s that hostages started to be taken for mainly financial reasons: and again the innovators were Latin American. The Revolutionary Armed Forces of Colombia (Farc) began seizing local politicians

and businessmen on an industrial scale to fund their war against the state. Blurring the line between terrorism and ordinary violent crime, such 'express kidnappings' – in which victims were marched to their banks and forced to empty their accounts – spread across the continent from Mexico to Argentina. Until 2004, 65 per cent of the world's kidnapping cases took place in Latin America.

What changed that?

The war in Iraq. In the insurgency, hostages became a commodity, with low-level criminals promised fortunes by militant groups such as al-Qaeda for the delivery of Western hostages, while day-to-day kidnaps of Iraqi professionals created a steady stream of income. The willingness of Western governments and companies to pay ransoms meant prices rose from around $25,000 per hostage in 2004 to several million dollars by 2007. In 2006, Italy, Germany and France paid a total of $45m to free nine hostages in Iraq. The effectiveness of such hostage-taking – both as a moneymaking and as a publicity-seeking venture

– led to the practice spreading to all unstable corners of the world.

How big a problem is it now?

Impossible to say. There are no accurate statistics from places such as Mexico, Nigeria and Iraq where kidnapping is endemic, and even high-profile international cases such as the ransom of Paul and Rachel Chandler by Somali pirates or Peter Moore (a British IT consultant held in Iraq for three years) are normally shrouded in secrecy. Estimates of the number taken hostage globally range from 12,000 to 20,000 a year, with around 2,000 thought to be in captivity at any one time. Criminals and rebel groups earn hundreds of millions of pounds a year from taking hostages, and the industry that has sprung up around their activities – 'K&R' (kidnap and ransom) insurance, highly paid negotiators, security personnel, even aircraft chartered to deliver ransom money – is thought to be worth a similar amount.

What are the social effects of all these kidnappings?

The taking of Westerners grabs press attention, but it's the churn of thousands of unknown hostages, for relatively small ransoms, that inflicts the most harm on societies. In Nigeria, where around $100m in ransoms was paid between 2006 and 2008, hostage-taking evolved several years ago from the occasional foreign oil executive to the families and children of Nigerian businessmen – worth around $30,000 each

---

Estimates of the number taken hostage globally range from 12,000 to 20,000 a year, with around 2,000 thought to be in captivity at any one time.

---

to kidnappers. The same goes for Iraq, where the owner of a sweet shop in Baghdad recently paid $10,000 to free his son. In Somalia ransom payments have been so great as to disrupt local economies, with the millions of dollars paid for captured ships causing runaway inflation in coastal towns, where ordinary people are now unable to buy basic goods. But in some Somali towns there's opportunity too: locals can invest in a sort of kidnapping stock exchange, hoping for big dividends when a big ransom comes through.

What can be done about all this?

A first step would be to get a more coordinated response to hostage taking. Currently, some governments pay ransoms, while others do not – and all suffer. Japan, which has paid some of the highest ransoms in recent years, has made its citizens targets for exactly that reason. By contrast, the UK's refusal to negotiate is thought to have contributed to the death of Edwin Dyer, a British tourist in Mali, who was killed last year after other Western hostages had been let go following prisoner exchanges. Several former hostages, including Terry Waite, have called for an international non-profit body – such as the UN or the Red Cross – to handle hostage negotiations, taking them out of the hands of national governments.

IN CASE OF KIDNAPPING (THE MANUAL)

With ships attacked every few days off the coast of Somalia – 128 were boarded by pirates in the first nine months of 2010 alone, with 773 hostages taken – the European Union Naval Force, which patrols the Gulf of Aden, has published a leaflet offering advice to those kidnapped.

'Piracy is a business,' it begins, before going on to tell sailors that most hostage detentions last between 6 and 12 weeks and are resolved without violence. Sailors should be aware, it says, that up to 50 Somali pirates may stay on board a ship throughout the kidnapping, and they should not seek relief in *khat* (a mild stimulant often chewed by Somalis), because cravings for it only 'increase tension'.

Most of all, a hostage must be patient. 'Be aware that the ransom payment process is very stressful for the pirates and they may be more agitated than normal. Try to avoid contact with them at this time. Confine yourself to established routines and behaviour patterns so as not to attract unnecessary attention on you. It may be some days after payment before your release. Do not expect to be released immediately.'

What was the
legacy
of the Iran-Iraq war

?

The Iran-Iraq war *of 1980–1988 was a brutal conflict between two nations – one Arab, one not, but both with large Shia Muslim majorities – in which around a million people on both sides were killed or wounded. From 1982, the USA backed Saddam Hussein, figuring it couldn't let Iraq fall into the hands of Iran's radical clerical regime. But after years of stalemate and billions of dollars spent on both sides, the conflict ended in a ceasefire, neither side gaining territorial advantage. Yet final victory could be said to have gone to Tehran: it has skilfully played kingmaker in post-Saddam Iraqi politics, ultimately paving the way for a pro-Iran, Shia-led government (see box). 'It's nothing less than a strategic defeat,' as a Western diplomat told the* Guardian.

What was the catalyst for the Iran-Iraq conflict?

The Iranian revolution of 1979 that swept the Shah of Iran from power and ushered in the theocratic regime of Ayatollah Khomeini. From the outset, Khomeini called on 'true' Muslims to overthrow corrupt governments in the region, and Saddam's Ba'athist regime – its support based on Iraq's Sunni minority – became his first target. But it was Saddam who initiated hostilities by renouncing a border treaty, agreed in 1975, in which he had ceded half of the

Shatt al-Arab waterway (Iraq's only outlet to the Persian Gulf) to Iran. On 22 September 1980, Saddam launched a full-scale attack, his aim being not just to improve Iraq's access to the Gulf but to assert his reputation as the region's strongman and to humble the Ayatollahs. He was confident of a quick victory.

And did his gamble backfire?

Yes. Initially, Iraq scored impressive gains: the city of Khorramshahr fell and the industrial cities of Abadan and Ahvaz were isolated. But his forces ran into unexpectedly stiff resistance from an enemy convinced it had God on its side. As Khomeini proclaimed to his people: 'You are fighting to protect Islam and he [Saddam] is fighting to destroy it.' Iranian women took up arms to liberate Khorramshahr, which they renamed Khuninshahr, City of Blood. So by the summer of 1982 Iran had regained all its territory and prepared to go on the offensive, convinced the Shias of Iraq would welcome its troops as liberators from their Sunni oppressors.

Instead, they too met stout resistance, and the war descended into a stalemate based on two distinct, equally vile, strategies.

What were those strategies?

The Khomeini regime launched vast suicidal 'human-wave' assaults against enemy lines. Boys as young as 12, often roped together to stop them deserting, were sent into battle, each armed with a plastic key (made in Taiwan) to unlock the gates of Paradise. 'They chant "Allahu Akbar" and they keep coming, and we keep shooting,' one Iraqi officer recalled. Iraq responded by breaking the laws of war with poison-gas attacks. As early as 1983, it began using chemical agents as a key part of its war strategy, with the aim not just of countering Iran's human-wave assaults, but of terrorising the enemy and sapping its morale. Some 20,000 Iranians are thought to have been killed by mustard gas and the nerve agents tabun and sarin. Talk of using pesticide to exterminate the 'swarms of mosquitoes' became common among the Iraqi leadership.

What was the West's role in this?

Initially, it was neutral ('It's a pity they both can't lose,' said Henry Kissinger). But the USA, alarmed both by the regime in Tehran and by Saddam's threatened disruption of the oil trade, was soon providing Baghdad with intelligence and commercial credits ($652m by 1987), even while publicly denouncing Saddam's use of chemical weapons. Iraq's allies in

---

Initially, the West was neutral But the USA was soon providing Baghdad with intelligence and commercial credits, even while publicly denouncing Saddam's use of chemical weapons.

Europe also proved generous arms merchants. However, confusingly, in 1985, the CIA also began selling missiles to Iran in return for its help in freeing US hostages held in Beirut. (The revelation that the profits from this trade had been channelled to Nicaraguan rebels – 'the Iran-Contra affair' – threatened to bring down the Reagan administration.) This web of dealing and double-dealing led to a succession of dubious incidents – an Iraqi attack on the USS *Stark* in 1987 that killed 37 American sailors; the USA shooting down an Iranian airliner in July 1988, killing almost 300 passengers – that have scarred relationships among all three countries.

So what was the legacy of the Iran-Iraq war?

In the view of Nigel Ashton, Professor of International History at the LSE, it dramatically altered the shape of Middle Eastern politics. The war bankrupted Iraq, prompting Saddam, two years after it ended, to recoup his losses by invading Kuwait and seizing its oilfields – a move that led to a new era of US hegemony in the Gulf and his eventual downfall. The war also gave critical early legitimacy to Iran's Islamic revolution, and helped frame its strongly anti-American foreign policy. It also brought to prominence within Tehran's establishment institutions such as the Basij militia and the Revolutionary Guard. The strong bond between Iran and Syria – crucial to the recent deal in Iraq – also dates from the conflict, when Syria's President Assad broke with the rest of the Arab world and supported Iran.

So has Iran won in the end?

Analysts stress that nothing is ever as simple as it seems between the two countries, but Iran has not held such a strong hand for decades. Militarily, Iraq is no longer a threat, and the Nouri al-Maliki administration is widely viewed as pro-Iran, especially by Saudi Arabia. As Ashton puts it: 'The US intervened in the Iran-Iraq war to stop Iranian expansionism. In a fit of historical amnesia, it is now leaving behind a political system in Baghdad through which Iran exerts the greatest political influence. What Khomeini could not achieve through war has been delivered through the ballot box.'

IRAN: THE THIEF OF BAGHDAD?

Iraqi politics was deadlocked after elections in March 2010 produced an almost perfect draw between two former prime ministers: the secular Iyad Allawi and the Shia-backed Nouri al-Maliki. With the stalemate unresolved, the USA pulled out its combat troops in August.

Then, in September, Tehran started to make its move. Through a series of meetings between presidents, generals and ayatollahs, it managed, according to the *Guardian*, to break the stalemate and deliver a new pro-Iran government. In order to deliver a parliamentary majority to al-Maliki, its preferred candidate, Tehran needed the influential anti-Western cleric Moqtada al-Sadr to declare his support. Al-Sadr and his allies control ten per cent of Iraq's parliament and hold the balance of power – but they loathed al-Maliki, who in 2008 built a reputation as a strong PM by attacking al-Sadr's militia, the Mahdi Army. But Tehran persuaded al-Sadr to overcome his loathing by enlisting two influential Shia ayatollahs, Hassan Nasrallah of Hezbollah in Lebanon and Kazem al-Haeri in Iran, to bend his ear.

Al-Sadr gave his blessing on 1 October, and within three weeks al-Maliki was visiting President Ahmadinejad in Tehran. 'We've gone from being under US occupation to Iranian occupation,' lamented Allawi's deputy, Osama al-Nujaifi at the time.

What
do we know
about Mercury
?

A 1.2-tonne robotic probe the size of a fridge, the MErcury Surface,
Space ENvironment, GEochemistry and Ranging orbiter – better known
as Messenger – was launched from Cape Canaveral on its $446m mission
back in August 2004. It completed an Earth 'flyby' a year later and then
pursued a meandering path, orbiting the Sun 15 times, completing
'flybys' of Venus in 2006 and 2007, and of Mercury three times in 2008
and 2009. It then settled into orbit round the planet after a journey of
4.9 billion miles.

Why couldn't it just go straight to Mercury?

Because it would have simply
sailed past it into the Sun: gravity
accelerates spacecraft as they
fall towards the Sun. Without
its six flybys – which used the
gravitational pull of the planets
involved to counter that effect
– it couldn't have slowed down
sufficiently to enable it to drop
into its intended orbit. This is the
opposite process to that employed
when sending space probes – like
the two Voyagers – away from the
Sun into the outer solar system: in
that case the gravitational pull of
the planets is used to speed them
up. Messenger could have made
a slightly more direct approach,
but only by using far more fuel
to help it apply the brakes.

And how does Messenger avoid getting burned up?

It protects itself from the Sun, which is up to 11 times brighter on Mercury than on Earth, by extending a sort of heat-proof ceramic parasol – a shade that stands between the spacecraft and the Sun. The other source of heat is Mercury, where surface temperatures can reach 450°C. For that reason Messenger's orbit is highly elliptical: it swoops in, then swings out into space to cool down.

How much did we know about Mercury before this?

What makes the planet special is that it is a 'terrestrial' – rocky like Earth, not gassy like Jupiter. Though Venus and Mars are also terrestrials, Mercury is especially interesting to scientists because of its extremes: it's the smallest, the densest, the planet with the oldest surface, the one with the largest daily variations in surface temperature, and the least explored. Before this, most of what we knew about Mercury came from Mariner 10, which flew past it three times in 1974–1975. Mariner gave no information

about the composition of the planet's surface, though it did establish, to everyone's surprise, that Mercury has a weak magnetic field, suggesting the core must be partly molten – it was previously thought to be solid. And in the past two decades, ground-based astronomy has discovered elements in its atmosphere (including sodium, potassium and calcium) that undoubtedly derive from the surface. Radar astronomy has also discovered bright-looking deposits at the poles. The leading hypothesis is that they consist of water ice in permanently shadowed areas within impact craters.

What else do we already know?

Data sent from Messenger's first flybys showed a jumble of craters, plains and immense, cliff-like scarps, hundreds of kilometres long. This was in line with the prevailing view of scientists that Mercury 'cooled off' a billion years after the solar system formed 4.5 billion years ago, leaving it relatively dormant in geological terms. The scarps, like wrinkles on a raisin, would have formed as Mercury's surface cooled and shrank. However, data sent back during Messenger's third flyby suggests that the planet may be more active than first thought. It revealed an unexpectedly young lava plain; rapid fluctuations in the planet's weak magnetic field (fluctuations around Earth occur over hours – around Mercury, in a matter of minutes); and an unanticipated 'dance of elements' within the thin atmosphere.

How long will Messenger orbit?

It was planned to orbit Mercury for one Earth year – which equals just two of Mercury's solar days (covering two sunrises and sunsets) – completing an orbit every 12 hours; that was later extended by another year. During its orbit, it has scrutinised Mercury's surface in extreme close-up. X-ray, gamma-ray neutron spectrometers have measured the elements present in rocks, while an infrared spectrometer has been used to create a mineralogical map of the planet's surface. Other instruments have probed the planet's internal workings. Once

the mission ends, the craft will drop to the surface of the planet.

What questions will Messenger help to answer?

With an uncompressed density of 5.3g/cm^3, Mercury is by far the densest planet in the solar system – and the question is, why? Scientists presume its density indicates a metal core, mostly of iron, that must take up around 60 per cent

---

Mercury is the smallest, the densest, the planet with the oldest surface, the one with the largest daily variations in surface temperature, and the least explored.

---

of the planet's mass – far more than the 15–30 per cent taken up by the cores of Venus, Earth and Mars, the solar system's other rocky planets. How this has come about is the subject of intense debate. One school holds that much of the planet's surface was either vaporised by the young, hot Sun or blasted into space after an asteroid collision; another that 'drag' in the nebula – the huge swirling cloud of gas and dust from which the solar system formed – would have herded its heavier, metal-rich dust particles into orbits close to the Sun, and that Mercury eventually condensed from these. Each theory predicts a different mixture of surface rocks. Messenger's instruments should settle the matter.

What else might an orbiting Messenger tell us?

It could help explain how the core has remained molten over the billions of years since the planet was formed; determine whether the bright deposits detected at Mercury's poles are indeed ice (which would provide further evidence that water is fairly common in the solar system); and discover what Mercury's atmosphere consists of (it's already known to be highly volatile, containing substances 'exotic' compared with atmospheric constituents on other planets). It could also help elucidate the Sun's activities – a matter of ever more pressing concern, given anxieties about global warming. Since we can't send a probe directly into the Sun, studying the planet closest to it is the next best thing.

HOW FAR? HOW HOT? AND OTHER KEY FACTS

Mercury is on average 154.9 million kilometres (96.3 million miles) from Earth, but a mere 58 million kilometres (36 million miles) from the Sun, and so is about two-thirds closer to the Sun than the Earth. With a diameter of 4,878 kilometres, it is a bit larger than the Moon and about a third the size of the Earth.

It has a highly elliptical orbit, ranging from 46 million kilometres to 70 million kilometres from the Sun.

Temperatures on Mercury's surface vary from a broiling 450°C in the daytime to -180°C at night. It orbits the Sun once every 88 Earth days, moving at an average speed of 48 kilometres per second, making it the 'fastest' planet in the solar system. It rotates on its axis once every 59 Earth days, but because of its slow rotation and fast speed around the Sun, one solar day (from noon to noon at the same place) lasts 176 Earth days, or two Mercury years.

Can 'clean coal' save the world?

'Clean coal' *is not so much fact or fantasy as an oxymoron... for now. Coal is still what it always was: cheap and dirty. The most carbon-intensive fossil fuel, it accounts for nearly 40 per cent of the world's CO_2 emissions, yet its use is rising, not falling. Coal-fired power stations provide 41 per cent of the world's electricity, a proportion forecast to rise to 44 per cent by 2030. With the huge increase in energy demand, the amount of electricity generated from coal in that same period is expected to rise 23 per cent in the USA, 172 per cent in China and 258 per cent in India. If coal stays dirty, its CO_2 emissions will almost quadruple. That's why 'clean coal' technology has been embraced by governments around the world.*

What does the technology involve?

A process called 'carbon capture and storage', or CCS, under which a power plant's CO_2 emissions are chemically diverted (or 'scrubbed') before they have a chance to escape into the atmosphere, then stored as a liquid, out of harm's way. That, in theory, would reduce the quantity of CO_2 emitted by as much 90 per cent. But in practice that presupposes the solving of a huge problem associated with CCS – where to store all those emissions.

What are the storage options?

The two main contenders are injecting CO_2 into depleted oil and gas fields or burying it in saline aquifers – porous rocks full of salty water – deep below the surface. But whatever solutions are chosen, the scale of the storage problem is daunting. One estimate says that by 2030 the USA alone would have to drill more than 100,000 wells, perhaps as many as 300,000, to keep its CO_2 emissions at 2005 levels. And there are still questions about how stable the CO_2 would be underground. Any leakage – and green groups say that the gas would have to remain sealed for ever – would defeat the whole purpose of storage.

But is the process of CCS technically feasible?

Very much so. Each of the various stages has been successfully tried, just never put together. Energy companies have been transporting and pumping liquefied CO_2 into oil and gas fields for decades to help flush out precious fossil fuels. Norway's state oil company, meanwhile, has been storing CO_2 in deep, off-shore aquifers since 1996. And the key bit of the process – 'scrubbing' emissions from power stations – has been operating at the world's first CCS demonstration plant in Germany since 2008. 'There do not appear to be unresolvable open technical issues,' was the conclusion of a major study on the future of coal by the Massachusetts Institute of Technology in 2007. The big issues are time and cost: even proponents of CCS don't expect the process to be commercially viable until 2020.

What are the cost considerations?

Capturing carbon emissions is a process that itself requires energy: indeed, a quarter of the energy produced by CCS plants – first-generation ones, at any rate – will be used up in the process of scrubbing, compression and transport. So they'll be a lot less efficient than existing coal-fired stations, and their electricity that much more expensive. Besides, only a handful of old power stations in Europe and the USA can be retrofitted with the new technology (there's greater potential with

China's more modern fleet) and for those that can be, the bill will be huge. In short, it will cost billions to research, test, build and run CCS facilities – which is why both government and the private sector seemed, until recently, to be cooling on the whole idea. IN 2008, the Bush administration withdrew funding for the first US clean coal power station after costs rose to $1.8bn.

One estimate says that by 2030 the USA alone would have to drill more than 100,000 wells, perhaps as many as 300,000, to keep its CO_2 emissions at 2005 levels.

So why did 'clean coal' become hot again?

The politics of the recession. Several governments have put CCS at the centre of their plans to restart their economies via investment in green technologies. The EU pledged $1bn to help get 12 demonstration plants up and running, while the Obama administration resumed funding for FutureGen, America's clean coal initiative – the largest in the world.

And what about the UK?

Britain embraced clean coal in 2009 when the Labour government announced it would build four new CCS power stations, starting with the Kingsnorth plant in Kent, and that all new coal-fired power stations built in the UK would have to be fitted with the technology. At first, the equipment only had to cover 25 per cent of emissions produced, but that would rise to 100 per cent around 2020. The CO_2 is stored in empty oil and gas fields under the North Sea. The coalition government has committed itself to supporting CCS, and launched a Carbon Capture and Storage Delivery Competition in March 2012, with £20 million pounds of funding for companies developing cheaper and more efficient plants.

So is it full-steam ahead then?

Yes, though it isn't a smooth ride, not just for technical and financial reasons, but for political ones, too. In Germany, where CCS testing has been going on far longer than in the UK, a new law mapping out how the country will adopt the technology has been delayed because of widespread opposition, with local communities expressing fears about CO_2 leakage from potential storage sites. In the UK, similar tensions have surfaced, as business groups press the government to build more nuclear and CCS plants, while the green lobby worries that the hunt for clean coal will crowd out investment in truly renewable sources of energy, such as wind power. But as proponents of CCS see it, there is no choice but to invest in clean coal since whatever happens in the West, India and China are going to press ahead with building coal-fired power stations whether the technology is there or not. China, the world's largest polluter, is building one new coal-fired power station each week. So better ensure that the coal is 'clean'.

SHOULD WE PUT OUR FAITH IN 'CLEAN COAL'?

YES	NO
1. We know that CCS can work. All it needs is the political and financial commitment to make it commercially viable.	1. CCS is not a proven technology: for a start, the permanent storage of CO_2 has never been tried on the scale envisaged.
2. It's our only hope – coal is cheap, plentiful and its use is rising, especially in India and China.	2. CCS renews our dependence on the most carbon intensive type of energy: we should be relying on wind, solar and tidal power.
3. In the UK's case, CCS will create jobs, let us use our coal reserves and become a world leader in a new and vital technology.	3. It's too late. By the time it comes on stream in 2020, all the new coal-fired stations will have irrevocably harmed the environment.

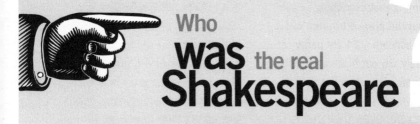

Who
was the real
Shakespeare **?**

Edward de Vere, *the 17th Earl of Oxford, was a scholar, philanderer, poet and lover of theatre, and a favourite of Queen Elizabeth I. He was born 14 years before a man called William Shakespeare. A glove-maker's son, Shakespeare left his young wife in Stratford-upon-Avon to try his hand as an actor in London. The Earl grew up in the house of William Cecil, the Queen's private secretary, and was educated at Cambridge, Oxford and the Inns of Court, with their famous companies of actors. During the 1570s he spent time in Italy before returning to court, where he was given a huge pension (£500,000 a year in today's money) for services that remain unclear. He died in 1604, five years before the publication of the sonnets, the most personal of Shakespeare's works.*

What evidence is there that he 'was' Shakespeare?

The Earl was first proposed as the true author of Shakepeare's works in 1920 by the unfortunately named J. Thomas Looney, an English teacher from Tyne and Wear. Looney's thesis was that the schooling received by the son of a merchant 'could never have provided Shakespeare with a vocabulary extensive enough to write the most talked-about literature in the world'. Oxford, by contrast, grew up among scholars: his uncle wrote translations of

Ovid; his tutor at Cambridge owned the country's only copy of *Beowulf*. Since Looney first aired his theory, a body of scholarship has sprung up in support of 'Oxfordism', claiming that everything about the plays attributed to Shakespeare – 14 are partly set in Italy, 36 out of 37 at court – indicate an aristocratic author.

Who believes this theory?

Roland Emmerich, for a start. The German director of *Independence Day* also made *Anonymous*, which advances the Oxfordist theory that the identity of England's greatest writer was accidentally slapped onto a moderately successful actor after the Earl's death. Emmerich's movie is part of a tradition dating back to the nineteenth century. Over the past 150 years, more than 70 'genuine' Bards have been touted: Sir Francis Bacon, Christopher Marlowe – even Queen Elizabeth I herself. Shakespeare doubters have included Sigmund Freud, Mark Twain, Orson Welles, Enoch Powell and two former members of the US Supreme Court. In 2007, the actors Derek Jacobi and Mark Rylance were among hundreds who signed the Declaration of Reasonable Doubt, intended to spark academic research into the subject.

Why does such doubt remain?

In part because of the sheer scale of Shakespeare's work: 37 plays in 23 years, with, in the years around 1600, masterpieces such as *Othello*, *Hamlet*, *King Lear*, *Measure for Measure* and *Twelfth Night* appearing every few months. The idea that a single actor could produce so much material, reinvent the English language and recast modern poetry is hard to countenance. A rival theory is that Shakespeare must have shared the writing with other members of his company (some later plays are now agreed to be collaborations). There is certainly scant written evidence from his own life that links him to the plays.

Is that really so surprising?

No. In Elizabethan England the playwright's name was often missing from published plays. Marlowe's never appeared on his plays during his lifetime. Yet there is a wealth of contemporary information placing a dramatist called William Shakespeare among the actors, theatres, patrons and audiences that performed, put on or saw the plays for the first time. Wills, entries in the royal accounts (from 1603, Shakespeare's company became the King's Men, James I's favourite), anecdotes, mortgage deeds and cast lists all speak of a 'William Shakespeare, Gent'. Shakespeare was first identified as the author of 12 plays in 1598 by Francis Meres, a cleric, who – awkwardly for the Oxfordists – also listed the Earl of Oxford as 'best for comedy'. If the Earl was happy to be known as a writer, why didn't he correct the record?

How do the Oxfordists handle that issue?

They argue that Meres, like almost everyone else, had no idea what was going on, and point to the inconsistencies between what we know of Shakespeare's life (see box) and his purported life of letters. The life of the Earl of Oxford, by contrast, is full of suggestive connections: his nickname, 'the Spear-shaker';

his experience of shipwreck (*The Tempest*); an affair which led to him being jailed (*Measure for Measure*) and then wounded by a member of the woman's family (*Romeo and Juliet*). Even the fact that the Earl died in 1604, before many of the plays were published, is not a killer, say the Oxfordists. After all, he had spent years in exile in Europe, when he'd have had time to

---

Over the past 150 years, more than 70 'genuine' Bards have been touted: Sir Francis Bacon, Christopher Marlowe – even Queen Elizabeth I herself.

---

amass a catalogue of work.

So is Anonymous credible?

Hardly. Shakespeare revisionism reaches new heights in this film: Elizabeth I is both mother and lover to the Bard. But then theories about the Bard's real identity seem to vary with the cultural concerns of the age in which they're proposed. It was the nineteenth-century preoccupation with the idea of the artist as Romantic genius – a Byron or a Keats – that kick-started the search for the 'real' Bard: the mundane facts of Shakespeare's life disqualified him. Preoccupation with social class may have been behind Looney's thinking in the 1920s. Modern doubts, as US scholar James Shapiro argues, reflect our current lack of faith in science and 'expert' authority: it no doubt grows out of a widely held modern view that claims 'based on conviction are as valid as those based on hard evidence'.

THE REAL, REAL SHAKESPEARE

William Shakespeare was born in April 1564, the eldest son of John Shakespeare, a glover and a trader who married Mary Arden, the daughter of a wealthy landowner. John Shakespeare was a prominent man in Stratford-upon-Avon. He filled several public offices, including that of bailiff (in which he gave licences to local companies of actors) and burgess: this gave him the right to send his son to the local grammar school, the King's New School. Although there is no written record, Shakespeare almost certainly attended this school.

In his teens, Shakespeare married Anne Hathaway, and had three children (including a son called Hamnet, named after a baker) before embarking on a parallel life that he maintained for the next 25 years. From 1587 to 1610, Shakespeare shuttled between London, the court, the stage (where he became a partner in the Globe) and Stratford, producing his first published poems in 1593 and becoming a player in the Lord Chamberlain's Men.

By 1596, he was wealthy enough to buy the second-largest house in Stratford, and by 1610 he had all but retired there. He died in April 1616, leaving no mention of any books in his will.

Who were the war heroes who never went to war?

In the late 1930s, *senior figures in the Secret Intelligence Service and the War Office grew convinced that appeasement would never prevent a Nazi invasion. So, defying high-level opposition, they quietly worked on a pre-emptive 'Last Ditch' survival strategy. But it was only after the fall of France in May 1940, with Britain isolated and its depleted forces in no state to repel an invasion by the German armies occupying northeast France, that Winston Churchill ordered those plans to be activated.*

What did the plans involve?

Churchill ordered Colonel Colin Gubbins (later to 'set Europe ablaze' in the Special Operations Executive) to create a secret network of civilian volunteers, known as GHQ Auxiliary Units. In the event of occupation, regular British forces would withdraw to the 'GHQ Line' just south of London, leaving behind the Aux Units who, from underground bases, would harry the enemy's supply lines in order to slow down advancing German troops and give the regular army time to mount a counterattack. The Units were divided into three sections: Special Duties – an intelligence-gathering service, spying on enemy troop movements;

Signals – a network of underground radio stations to transmit that intelligence back to GHQ; and the six-man Fighting Patrols – aka the Highworth's Fertilisers (see box).

What experience did Gubbins bring to the task ?

He had cut his teeth serving in Ireland during the Troubles and experienced at first hand the success of the irregular Irish Volunteers led by Michael Collins. They formed the model for Gubbins's Fighting Patrols, each led by a sergeant and coordinated in a given region by a local commander. Kent was the likeliest invasion area, and the first Aux Unit was established in a secluded farmhouse in Bilting by Peter Fleming, brother of Ian. By the end of August 1940 there were units as far north as Brechin on Scotland's east coast and as far south and west as Land's End and Pembrokeshire.

What kind of men were recruited?

Volunteers, mostly operating unpaid (for what seemed like a suicide mission), they were mainly selected for their knowledge of local geography, but also had to be physically tough. They could be anything from students to factory workers, but ideal recruits were foresters, farmers and gamekeepers (one Aux Unit had a poacher and a gamekeeper on the same patrol). Often farmers were chosen as patrol leaders and asked to select recruits from their labour force. At a time when motor vehicles were a novelty outside towns, it was often only farmers and their workers who had the mechanical knowledge to maintain (and sabotage) motor vehicles. Also, at a time of fuel rationing, farmers could be sure of extra coupons. And villagers would think nothing of tractors or farm lorries trundling back and forth.

How secret were their activities?

Auxiliers (motto: 'Be Like Dad – keep Mum') had to swear an oath of secrecy, and were told they'd be shot if they disclosed their role to outsiders. As cover, they were allocated to Home Guard battalions and given Home Guard uniforms. (Though to compare them to the Home Guard, as a senior officer put it, would be 'like comparing the Brigade of Guards to the Salvation Army'.) Difficulties arose when they were found not taking part in normal Home Guard exercises. Some were victimised by the local community, who thought they should be out fighting for King and Country. Others, unable to explain their absence at night, were accused of nefarious or extramarital activities.

Some were victimised by the local community, who thought they should be out fighting for King and Country. Others, unable to explain their absence at night, were accused of extramarital activities.

What were they to do once the Germans had invaded?

They had orders to leave their homes and move to pre-prepared Operational Bases underground, some in existing tunnels and mines, others (500 or so) constructed of corrugated iron sections sunk into the ground with escape tunnels and access via concrete pipes or grassed-over trap doors. Operational stores and rations were sufficient for 14 days only: Auxiliers who survived this period were to revert to their civilian occupations in the hope of a successful British counterattack. If discovered by the enemy, they were expected to shoot themselves rather than be taken alive.

What actions were they to take during the 14-day period?

Each patrol, operating within a 15-mile radius, was to emerge at night and carry out attacks, not just on aircraft, railway lines, fuel dumps, etc, but also on senior German officers. There were plans to booby-trap the smartest lavatories in the stately homes of Kent, on the basis that Nazi generals would be based in the grand houses and commandeer the finest facilities. Recruits were given sealed envelopes containing lists of potential collaborators – all to be shot if the Nazis landed. These included not just known fascist sympathisers but unsuspecting county chief constables who, it was reckoned, would have information the Germans would want.

Do these men deserve a medal?

They may not have seen action, but they were ready to make the ultimate sacrifice for their country. When stood down in late 1944, they were told their existence would never be acknowledged. In 1996, however, shortly after a group of ex-Auxiliers had staged their first-ever reunion, the Ministry of Defence agreed that some could apply for the 1939–1945 Defence Medal. But since not all were deemed to qualify, they have continued to demand recognition for their services. At the time of the 70th anniversary of their formation in July 2010, the MoD was urged to recognise their role before it was too late. All former Auxiliers have been invited to declare their involvement and contact the Coleshill Auxiliary Research Team via their website www.coleshillhouse.com.

THE NAMING OF HIGHWORTH'S FERTILISERS

The Fighting Patrols got their name from the Wiltshire village of Highworth, where selected recruits had to report to the village postmistress before being taken to nearby Coleshill House, the Aux Units' secret HQ, for a weekend's training in field-craft, sabotage and unarmed combat. Unarmed combat was taught by W.E. Fairbairn, founder of the Shanghai police Riot Squads, author of *All-in Fighting*, and co-inventor of the Fairbairn-Sykes fighting knife – a lethal dagger with which all Auxiliers were equipped. Recruits were taught deadly close-fighting techniques such as the 'sentry hold', the 'Japanese strangle' and 'drawing the smatchet' (a fearsome broad-bladed knife). They were shown the best places to stick a knife in, and trained in the use of the garrotte.

In July 1942, the Aux Units received their own Top Secret training manual disguised as an agricultural supplies diary – *The Countryman's Diary, 1939*. Its cover read: 'Highworth's Fertilisers. Do their stuff unseen until you see RESULTS!' The diary's 40-odd pages were crowded with examples of sabotage and demolition devices and booby traps that SOE agents used within occupied Europe. In the event, the Auxiliers only ever engaged in practice missions, but after the War the SAS recruited extensively from the Aux Units, so their training wasn't entirely in vain.

What is human growth hormone ?

Human growth hormone (HGH) *is a natural substance secreted by the pituitary gland at the base of the brain. Released into the body, it stimulates the growth of bones, cartilage and muscles. It is essential to the growth of children, and even though levels decline after adolescence it helps regulate our metabolism for the rest of our lives. From the 1950s to the 1980s, HGH was extracted from dead bodies and injected into children with stunted growth, often adding several inches to their height. However, after such transfers led to hundreds of cases of Creutzfeldt-Jakob disease (a brain degeneration similar to BSE, or 'mad cow' disease), synthetic HGH was developed in laboratories. Since synthetic HGH was cleared for use in 2003, its unlimited production has helped millions of children. But it has also spawned an entire 'off-label' industry, in which it is peddled as an anti-ageing drug and a way to boost athletic performance.*

So there could be another sporting scandal on the way?

It could have been the drug of choice at London's 2012 Olympics and we might never know. Although HGH is banned by the International Olympic Committee and most professional sports leagues, the current blood test can only detect illegal HGH use within 24 to 48 hours of it being injected – a tiny window of opportunity. Several drug cheats, such as Marion Jones, the former US sprinter, are said to have used HGH but never tested positive for it. Because it is the sort of drug that athletes use as part of their training regime, rather than a stimulant, they tend to be clean during events, when they are most likely to be tested. Terry Newton, a 31-year-old British rugby league player, became the world's first professional athlete to be found positive for HGH after being tested out of competition. Banned for two years, he hanged himself in 2010.

Does HGH give athletes an edge?

For years, doctors agreed that it helped add muscle mass, but that it didn't necessarily lead to better performance. However, a study funded by the World Anti-Doping Agency (WADA) claimed that it could improve a sprinter's time by as much as five per cent – the difference between coming first and last in the Olympic 100m final. Although limited to sprinting, the finding follows years of anecdotal evidence from users saying that HGH increased their strength and shortened their recovery time after training and injuries. (Newton began using HGH after noting how it helped him rehabilitate after a series of injuries.) Whatever the effect, it is likely to be subtle – but so are the margins between success and failure in elite sport. 'I don't blame the athletes for wanting it,' says Dr Stanley Korenman, an American endocrinologist. 'They operate under tiny percentage differences and worry about the consequences later.'

Can it make you look younger?

Because of its association with children, HGH is sometimes called the 'youth drug', but there is little scientific evidence to show that it delays the ageing process, and doctors in the UK are not allowed to prescribe it for cosmetic use. But that hasn't halted the development of a huge illegal market in HGH-based products, most of which are made in China and distributed over the internet. In the USA, where HGH is a $2bn industry, many people use it merely to stay trim and lean. Dawn Foley from Los Angeles, for instance, injects herself with HGH each night and says it has whittled away her belly fat, plumped wrinkles, boosted muscle tone and given her more energy – at a cost of $500 a month. 'I'm absolutely going to stay on it for ever,' she says. Doctors say the same results can be achieved with a healthy diet and regular exercise – without HGH's side effects.

What side effects are those?

Take your pick. Studies show that HGH injections can lead to headaches, and muscle and joint pain. More serious effects include high blood pressure, hardening of the arteries, arthritis and increased risk of diabetes. Because it is a growth hormone, HGH also simply grows things: users can develop spade-like hands, large brows and other deformities. Organs such as the liver and heart can also become dangerously enlarged. Finally, because it is a trigger for cell growth, HGH can initiate similar mechanisms to those that cause cancer. Several studies have linked high levels of HGH to increased risk of prostate and breast cancer.

Have the authorities cracked down?

They are trying to. On the sports side, scientists are developing a test that can detect HGH up to two weeks after it has been injected. There are also plans to develop a urine test for the hormone, because these tests are much

---

A study claimed that it could improve a sprinter's time by as much as five per cent – the difference between coming first and last in the Olympic 100m final.

---

more widely administered than blood tests (1,600 were carried out during the 2010 Vancouver Winter Games, against just 450 blood tests). But catching HGH cheats is never going to be easy. Natural levels can vary hugely – as much as 100-fold among young people – giving different results at different times of the day.

What about other users?

It is legal to own and to take HGH in the UK, so there is little that the government can do except remind doctors of their responsibilities and warn users of possible side effects. In the USA, however, the authorities are going after the sellers. Last week GeneScience, a Chinese company responsible for up to 90 per cent of imports of HGH to the country, had $7.2m of its assets seized and was ordered to pay a further $3m into a 'clean competition fund'. GeneScience pleaded guilty to the charges of distributing HGH, but continues to manufacture it in Changchun, northern China.

IS HEIGHT A MEDICAL CONDITION?

HGH is not just attracting controversy in sport and among those who dream of delaying the ravages of time – it is also at the centre of a debate over whether being unusually tall or short is a medical condition. When HGH was harvested from cadavers, the shortage of supply meant that it was rationed to children who couldn't produce normal levels of HGH. However, the potentially unlimited manufacture of synthetic HGH has opened the door to parents asking for the hormone simply because their children are not the size they want them to be.

At the age of 11, Jeffrey Stern was 4ft 1in, a foot shorter than most of his classmates in New York. With HGH, he grew to 5ft 7in by the age of 16. But his mother didn't think that was tall enough, and his family is now suing their insurance company to continue Jeffrey's £1,500-a-month injections. Doctors warn that the lifetime effects of such hormone treatments are still not properly understood, but for pharmaceutical companies, the medical definition of 'normal' height is now a commercial battleground. 'It is tremendously satisfying for physicians, as well as enormously profitable for drug manufacturers,' as Susan Cohen and Christine Cosgrove wrote in *The Lancet* this year, 'to make a child grow.'

Is Glencore
more than
just a trading house?

In the largest ever flotation *on the London Stock Exchange, a secretive Swiss commodities trader became the first company in 25 years to leap straight into the FTSE 100 on the first day of trading. Glencore's £37bn valuation left top employees with mind-boggling paper gains: 485 scooped $100m each; five became instant billionaires; and the estimated £7bn haul of its enigmatic chief, Ivan Glasenberg, rivals the GDP of the Democratic Republic of Congo. The real significance of the 2011 float, however, was the light it shone on the hidden workings of the global commodities trade, and the power of the shadowy Swiss firm at its heart. Even seasoned traders were shocked by the scale of its trading dominance.*

What does Glencore control?

From its modest base in the wealthy Swiss village of Baar, it controls around 60 per cent of the third-party global zinc market, 50 per cent of copper, 45 per cent of lead and almost a third of thermal coal. (Third-party trades, which affect prices more than any others, are those occurring outside long-term agreements between suppliers and consumers.) A growing player in energy, currently supplying 3 per cent of the world's daily oil needs, Glencore also has substantial interests in food – around 25 per cent of the global market for barley, sunflower and rape seed, and 10 per cent of the wheat market. In short, its money-making tentacles extend into almost every aspect of daily life, bringing in monster revenues of $145bn last year.

So Glencore is the giant of world trade?

Yes. Under Glasenberg's tenure, it has acquired physical assets, too: mines in Congo and Colombia, smelters in Bolivia, grain elevators in America's corn belt, a fleet of oil tankers… There are rival traders, miners and commodities transporters, but no other entity combines all three like Glencore. And going public will give it the financial heft to extend its interests much further.

What was the philosophy behind Glencore's success?

To follow the resources wherever they're located – even if that meant dealing with pariah regimes or, as some alleged, sanctions-busting. These days, the firm's top brass is keen to play down links with its infamous originator Marc Rich, who became America's Most Wanted white-collar fugitive

when he fled to Switzerland in 1983 after being indicted for 'trading with the enemy' in Iran, tax evasion and racketeering (see box). But Rich's influence is still apparent – and not just in the firm's gung-ho, secretive culture. He is said to have built a better intelligence network than many governments – a legacy his protégé, Ivan Glasenberg, has refined into a formidable data machine. Traders draw on real-time market intelligence (weather events, news of political coups, etc) to identify sudden dips and spikes they can profitably exploit ahead of rivals.

Are Glencore's deals ethical?

Making bets on grain prices while the developing world riots over food doesn't look attractive, though it's hardly the only big player to speculate in this way. NGOs argue that Glencore is 'still in the dark ages' when it comes to corporate governance and environmental responsibility. Among its many imbroglios are charges of tax avoidance in Zambia, a land dispute in Colombia, and an oil battle with the Namibian government. Most seriously, it is caught up in a criminal investigation in Belgium into the alleged bribery of EU officials. But beyond the question of its ethics lies the question of its size: what risk does a commodities behemoth dubbed 'too big to fail' pose for global financial stability?

Why is that an issue?

In a sector as prone to ruinous booms and busts as global commodities, which lacks

---

Concentration of so much power in the hands of one company has always posed a hazard – especially when the inner workings and global complexity of that company are so little understood.

---

any supranational regulation, concentration of so much power in the hands of one company has always posed a hazard – especially when the inner workings and global complexity of that company are so little understood. But the ante has been upped considerably now that the commodities trade (formerly a

risky market backwater, dominated by specialists and high-rolling speculators) has moved into the retail mainstream. Widespread take-up of Exchange Traded Funds (ETFs) – funds that allow ordinary punters to buy a share in the market in gold or wheat without buying the product itself – is a major factor in a roaring bull market that has pushed prices of everything from copper to coffee to record highs since the last big bust in 2008. Barclays Capital reckons the amount invested in commodities ETFs is 40 times higher than it was a decade ago. The Financial Stability Board (set up to monitor global risks after the 2007–2008 banking crash) has fingered the largely unregulated ETF market as a possible trigger for the next systemic global financial meltdown.

Is Britain particularly exposed?

Yes, because London has become the global centre for listed commodities and oil and gas firms which – even before Glencore's leap into the FTSE 100 – accounted for a much greater weighting on the FTSE All-Share index (around 30 per cent) than on any other major stock market. The arrival of the Swiss giant increases the exposure of ordinary savers considerably because Glencore's sheer size dictates that it will automatically be bought by most index-tracking funds, and thus find its way into the UK's pension pots.

Is a commodities bust likely?

A sign the market may have peaked was the sight of Glencore's savvy partners cashing out at the top of the market (its listing was accompanied by a mini price crash), in the same way as did the partners in Blackstone, the private equity giant, when it was floated at the height of the 2007 debt bubble. Yet the drivers underpinning long-term metal and crop prices (an industrially expanding and hungry developing world) remain sound, so the current commodities 'supercycle' could well continue. Britain's savers must certainly hope so.

INFAMOUS RICH: THE SMOOTH CRIMINAL

For a generation of investigative journalists, Marc Rich was the ultimate prize – one of the world's smoothest villains, in control of a shadowy trading empire that straddled the globe. A confidant of dictators and close associate of secret services from Mossad to the KGB, he was once described as 'the kind of guy James Bond would have pursued – if he hadn't already had Bond on the payroll'. He operated above the law, telling his biographer Daniel Ammann that he'd never met an incorruptible head of state.

The son of Jewish Belgians, Rich arrived in the USA as a child refugee in 1941 and made his name as a commodities trader at the Wall Street firm Phillipp Brothers. He scored a major coup in 1973–1974 by taking on the 'Seven Sisters' (the oil majors then controlling the oil trade), singlehandedly inventing the spot market for oil. Even after becoming a criminal fugitive in 1983, Rich continued breaking sanctions to ship Iranian oil to Israel and South Africa. But he came badly unstuck in 1994 when a giant bet on zinc turned sour, forcing him to sell Marc Rich & Company to partners. One half of the firm became Glencore; the other, Trafigura. Controversially pardoned by President Clinton in 2001, Rich remains in Switzerland – and continues to trade commodities.

How good
are our
children's skills **?**

Average – *and that's the problem. Despite the economic downturn, the UK still has the world's sixth largest economy and average incomes to match those of other big European economies. But the UK's wealth hides a lack of skills. For years now, Britain's workforce has lurked towards the bottom of the rankings of the OECD nations, the world's richest 30 countries – well below Germany, France and the USA. In 2009, 31.7 per cent of Britain's workforce had 'low skills' (compared with just 13.4 per cent of Canadians), putting the UK in 19th place; 36.5 per cent of the population had 'intermediate skills' (the equivalent of five good GCSEs), putting the country in 21st place (just below Greece). Fortunately, the UK does better on high skills (workers with a university degree or equivalent), but even that number, 31.8 per cent, is good enough only for 12th place.*

Does this unimpressive performance matter?

Yes. Chancellor George Osborne cited the UK's relatively poor skills as 'probably the biggest problem facing our economy in the future'. In the short term, it means that even when jobs are hard to come by, many employers cannot get suitably skilled workers. In 2009, the UK Commission for Employment and Skills found that 13 per cent of jobs remain unfilled for lack of qualified applicants. Poor skills also hamper productivity: British workers are about 20 per cent less productive per head than their French and American counterparts. In the long term, as the global economy becomes ever more competitive, Britain's wealth could sink to the level of its skills. A review by Lord Leitch for the last government concluded that it would take nothing less than a 'new shared national mission' to improve the skills of the British workforce.

What is the answer?

One solution being proposed by the coalition government is to develop a new kind of school, a university technical college (UTC) that would blend vocational and academic learning to produce the kind of young workers companies want to employ. Pioneered by Lord Baker of Dorking, a former Conservative education secretary, UTCs will teach students aged from 14 to 19, rather than following the current system (see box), and will in some ways be more like workplaces than schools, operating from 8.30am to 5.30pm with close involvement from local businesses.

Until the age of 16, students will spend 40 per cent of their time on vocational skills and 60 per cent on academic learning. After 16, the proportions will switch.

Hasn't this been tried before?

Sort of. To many, UTC's resemble the unpopular technical schools brought in by Rab Butler's 1944 Education Act. Children who did well on their 11-plus test got into their local grammar school, while the rest were sent either to secondary moderns or to technical schools to learn a trade. But a shortage of willing pupils meant that only 172 technical schools were ever set up, and most had disappeared by the 1950s. Critics of the government's proposal say that UTCs are in danger of resurrecting a 'two-tier' education system and pigeonholing children, placing some in vocational training too early. 'Attempting to separate technical or vocational education from mainstream schools is socially divisive,' says Christine Blower, general secretary of the National Union of Teachers.

How is this meant to be different?

By taking place on a much smaller scale, for a start. Initially, there was only one UTC, set up by the machinery firm JCB in Staffordshire in 2010. Even though the idea was lauded by Osborne, the government committed to only 24 more, providing a total of just under 20,000 school places. That's largely because a UTC can be set up only where employers are prepared to get involved, and the links between business and the education system are still rudimentary. As Minister for Universities and Science David Willetts puts it: 'We are running out of skills in the right places, and that tells me there is a market problem.'

How do they work?

More than anything, the UTCs are modelled on Germany's much-praised vocational schools. Germany has a diverse education system, with four different types of state secondary schools; the part the UK wants to import are Germany's 'dual schools'. At the age of 15 or 16, after ten years of compulsory schooling, two-thirds of German students begin up to three years of further education, spending two days a week at school and three days training at a local company and earning a small wage. In the UK, just one in ten companies provides apprenticeships; in Germany about 25 per cent of all companies and 93 per cent of large ones offer training to young people. Since 2005, students educated at dual schools

---

British workers are about 20 per cent less productive per head than their French and American counterparts. Britain's wealth could sink to the level of its skills.

---

have also been able to use their qualifications to enter university, a move aimed at removing any of the stigma that might be attached to vocational training.

So will the UTCs overcome Britain's skills deficit?

They will certainly help, but they won't succeed on their own. The challenge of matching workers to the demands of the economy is centuries old. 'The greater part of what is taught in schools and universities ... does not seem to be the proper preparation for that of business,' wrote Adam Smith in 1776. One striking conclusion of the Leitch review in 2006, however, was that the need to improve skills is most pressing for those who have already left school or university: more than 70 per cent of Britain's workforce in 2020 will be made up of people no longer in the education system today. Hence the main burden of improving the nation's skills lies with individuals and their employers rather than with the state, and here the UK falls down badly. A mere 19 per cent of adults in the UK pay something towards their further education and training, while across the rest of the OECD it is 37 per cent. The question for everyone is, how much do we want to learn?

THE CASE FOR DROPPING GCSES

An estimated 12 million people in Britain lack functional numeracy or literacy, and for many concerned about the skills level of the workforce, GCSEs are part of the problem, not the solution. Conceived at a time when young people left education at 16 – an increasingly rare occurrence – GCSEs have become a suite of qualifications that employers no longer respect, and which deter students who might be more motivated by practical or vocational learning. From 2015, young people will *have* to stay in some form of education until they are 18, 'so why are we still running a school-leaving exam at 16?' asks former Labour education secretary Estelle Morris. Her solution, which fits the target age range of the new UTCs, is non-selective exams that students sit at 14 as a guide to what they might study over the next four or five years. It's time to scrap GCSEs and let students aged 14 to 19 'take relevant exams and do extended projects at the times that suit them', argues Peter Hyman, Tony Blair's former education adviser who is now a deputy head teacher. 'The best schools are starting to offer this already.'

Are weather **forecasters** worth the **money**?

After a series *of errant weather forecasts, Britain's Met Office found itself in danger of being dumped by the BBC. The Corporation announced that it would invite competition to ensure it was getting the best possible value for licence-payers' money. So, although the Met Office has provided its weather forecasts since 1923, the broadcaster put out a tender for its weather bulletins and asked other companies to bid to supply them. The Met Office secured another five-year contract, but had to see off competition from Metra, the commercial arm of New Zealand's state weather forecaster, which developed the BBC's new weather graphics in 2005.*

Does the Met Office rely on the BBC?

The BBC forecasts are the organisation's most high-profile output, and thus vital for maintaining its relationship with the public. But they actually constitute only a fraction of its work. Since it was founded as part of the Board of Trade in 1854, the Met Office's primary duty has been to provide information about the weather for Britain's ships, aircraft and armed forces. Today, operating as a for-profit 'Trading Fund' within the Ministry of Defence (MoD), the Met Office has revenues of more than £180m a year, 85 per cent of which comes from contracts to supply various kinds of weather data across government. The rest comes from commercial contracts with utility companies, foreign weather services and media organisations – including the BBC.

Why do we need so many different forecasts?

There is a world of data beyond what we see on the evening news. The NHS, for instance, needs special warning for cold snaps (there are 25,000 extra deaths in winter compared to the rest of the year, and the cold contributes to 80 per cent of them); the Highways Agency needs to know about road temperatures; oil rigs want wave heights; and the MoD has uniformed Met Office staff helping plan operations in Afghanistan and elsewhere. Despite the variety of customers, however, the core of the Met Office's work remains its Public Weather Service – the constant monitoring of the UK's weather – which underpins all its national forecasts. That cost £86m last year and was funded almost entirely by the MoD, the Civil Aviation Authority and the Coastguard Agency.

Why does it 'sell' its data?

In 1988, Prime Minister Margaret Thatcher's efficiency adviser, Sir Robin Ibbs, identified dozens of public bodies that could become 'executive agencies' and act more like businesses with customers. In 1996, the Met Office was turned into a Trading Fund – there are now 36 such agencies in the MoD alone, and the Met Office is one of four expected to make a profit on public investment. It does this by selling data that has been beamed to its supercomputers, located in Exeter, from a network of ocean buoys, radars, oil rigs, helium balloons, aircraft and more than 6,000 land-based observation sites around the world. This has made the Met Office a global player in the supply of climate-change research and weather data (it licenses its software to India and Australia, among others) but also makes it vulnerable to competition from the private sector.

How do companies compete?

By offering better, cheaper weather forecasts. Since becoming a Trading Fund, the Met Office has been forced to sell its raw weather data to competitors at a reasonable rate. Private-sector meteorologists then compare the Met Office information with other sources and draw up their own analyses, which, they claim, benefit from a broader perspective. In recent years, the Met Office has watched as leaner, more entrepreneurial rivals like Metra have stolen customers such as Sainsbury's and Tesco (which need

---

There is a world of data beyond what we see on the evening news. The NHS needs special warning for cold snaps; the Highways Agency needs to know about road temperatures...

---

bespoke forecasts for their supply chains), while Dutch company MeteoGroup now provides forecasts to more than half of the UK's local authorities. The existence of competition also means that there is far more scrutiny every time the Met Office makes a mistake.

And does it make many mistakes?

The Met Office used its new IBM supercomputer to predict an 'odds-on barbecue summer' for 2009 – which turned out to be so wet and cold that the organisation later felt obliged to apologise. Undaunted, it then predicted a mild winter: cue the coldest January for 23 years and temperatures of -22C in Scotland. John Hirst, the Met Office chief executive, defended the forecasts, claiming they were exaggerated by the media (there was only a 65 per cent chance of a hot summer) but there is no doubt they have damaged the organisation. The close ties between the Met Office and the Climate Research Unit of the University of East Anglia – implicated in the 'climategate' scandal – did not help either. A YouGov poll recently claimed that 74 per cent of people believe the Met Office forecasts are generally inaccurate.

Are its rivals doing any better?

Some private companies did a better job of predicting the UK's colder-than-average winter in 2009. On Christmas Day, Joe Bastardi of US firm AccuWeather wrote: 'Cold of a variety not seen in over 25 years in a large scale is about to engulf the major energy-consuming areas of the northern hemisphere.' But most meteorologists agree that the Met Office's record stands up to scrutiny, suggesting that it should abandon the long-range forecasts that had caused it so much trouble. According to Michael Fish, the former BBC weatherman,

the Met Office didn't like issuing them anyway. 'The pressure to do so comes in large part from the very same parts of the media that now seek to discredit it,' he said. The Met Office abandoned long-range forecasts in 2010, forcing much of the media to turn to alternative forecasters. Their record turned out to be no better, and in early 2012 *Guardian* journalist George Monbiot questioned the credentials – and even the existence – of a couple of them.

THE MET OFFICE: AT SEA AND AT WAR

Robert FitzRoy, captain of HMS *Beagle*, who sailed with Darwin to the Galápagos Islands and became Governor of New Zealand, was also made Britain's first 'Meteorological Statist to the Board of Trade' in 1854. With a staff of three, FitzRoy began the task of recording the weather at sea. The loss of a passenger ship, the *Royal Charter*, and 459 lives in the Irish Sea in 1859 led to the first gale-warning service, and within two years there were 15 weather stations around the British coast. Barometers designed by FitzRoy with his interpretations – 'Sinks lowest of all for the great winds' – were installed in ports around the country.

Mariners remained in charge of weather forecasting – a term invented by FitzRoy – until the First World War, when the Air Ministry became involved. During the Second World War, meteorologists were asked to explain why so many Spitfires were running out of fuel and crashing into the sea on their return to Britain. The force of the jetstream, they realised, was to blame. But the Met Office's finest wartime moment came in June 1944, when it successfully predicted a 36-hour window of calm weather for the D-Day landings to go ahead – 'Probably the only day during the month of June on which the operations could have been launched,' President Truman later said.

Is Obama **serious about** cutting back **on nukes** ?

At a Prague summit *in April 2010, US President Barack Obama and his then Russian counterpart, Dmitry Medvedev, agreed to reduce their countries' nuclear arsenals by around a third: to 1,550 warheads each and 700 'delivery systems', such as missiles or bombers. The deal replaced the Strategic Arms Reduction Treaty of 1991, which expired in 2009, and was the first cut agreed since 2002, when George Bush and Vladimir Putin set limits of 2,200 warheads each by 2012 – a reduction of more than 60 per cent from their then stockpiles of 6,000 warheads each. This new treaty also marked the start of a crucial nuclear season for Obama, as he sought support for his goal of 'global zero', a world without nuclear weapons.*

Did he really mean it?

He seemed to. To coincide with the treaty, he announced a modest change in America's 'nuclear posture', further limiting the role of nuclear weapons in its defence planning. It included a commitment not to use nuclear weapons against attacks involving biological or chemical weapons or large-scale conventional forces. Obama was also keen for the Senate to ratify the Comprehensive Test Ban Treaty (which it has refused to do since 1999). In the wake of the Prague agreement, he hosted 47 heads of state in Washington for a summit aimed at preventing weapon materials getting into the hands of terrorists and rogue states, ahead of a five-year review of the Nuclear Non-Proliferation Treaty (NPT) at the UN. That summit produced a communique and a work plan. But politics around nuclear weapons is tense and baffling. As George W. Bush once scribbled on a briefing about America's nukes: 'But why do we still have to have so many?'

Was the deal with Russia significant?

Potentially, yes. Between them, Russia and the USA have 95 per cent of the world's nuclear weapons, even if their accounting is dodgy (see box); and when they make cuts, other countries tend to follow. So far, both France and the UK have phased out their nuclear bomber aircraft and offered to reduce the size of their submarine fleets. The Netherlands, Belgium and Germany, meanwhile, have all sought the removal of US weapons stationed there since the Cold War. But not everyone is guaranteed to

move in step. As the US 'nuclear umbrella' shrinks, those who feel insufficiently protected – allies such as Japan and South Korea – could well decide to develop their own weapons. Meanwhile, other states, such as China, do not seem to be paying any attention at all to the USA-Russia deal. That is why a functioning global regime – in the form of the NPT – is considered so important.

What does the NPT entail?

It was a deal struck in 1968 between the then five nuclear-armed powers (the USA, Russia, China, France and Britain) and the rest of the world, under which – in broad terms – these nuclear powers agreed to work towards disarmament as long as other nations promised not to develop their own weapons. The treaty allows every signatory to pursue nuclear technology for peaceful ends – as Iran says it is doing – but, as a condition of doing so, countries must allow international inspections. Almost the entire world has signed up to the NPT, yet that hasn't necessarily made the world any safer. In fact, Obama warned last year that 'in a strange turn of history, the threat of global war has gone down, but the risk of nuclear attack has gone up.'

Why are things more risky today?

Because the gloomy, but familiar, dynamics of the Cold War, exemplified by 'Mutually Assured Destruction', have been replaced by a much more unpredictable array of terrorists, failed states and technology smugglers. The priority for Obama's summit was to gain better control over the world's 'loose nukes' – poorly supervised pieces of fissile material, mostly emanating from the former USSR, that could end up in a terrorist's dirty bomb. Between 1993 and 2008, the International Atomic Energy Agency recorded 421 incidents of lost or stolen nuclear materials, with an average of 28 instances per year.

Hasn't the Non-Proliferation Treaty helped reduce the risk?

Not really. Adding to the uncertainty is the fact that countries on both sides of the NPT bargain

have been openly flouting their obligations. Forty-four years after promising to work 'in good faith' for disarmament, none of the world's five original nuclear powers has come close giving up the bomb – an inconsistency that undermines the NPT and makes it unconvincing in its dealings with countries that break its rules, or choose not to engage with them at all. The world's four other nuclear weapon states

Politics around nuclear weapons is baffling. As George W. Bush scribbled on a briefing about America's nukes: 'But why do we still have to have so many?'

(Israel, India, Pakistan and North Korea) are all outside the NPT and yet receive different treatment: an international embargo prevents Israel and Pakistan from trading in civilian nuclear technology, but not India. Meanwhile Iran, a founding signatory of the NPT, has been accused of repeatedly breaching its rules, and yet there is no formal way of punishing it. And when North Korea decided to go nuclear in 2003, it simply walked out of the NPT.

So how can the NPT be strengthened?

Obama's goals remain fairly modest: he wants to make it harder to withdraw from the NPT, and to draw up standard punishments for renegade nations. He also needs China to support the next round of sanctions against Iran. But, as always in non-proliferation, the first question is: how much are the most powerful countries prepared to sacrifice? And in America's case, the real battles are always fought in the Senate, which has shown no sign for more than a decade of agreeing to the Comprehensive Test Ban Treaty, widely seen as a crucial step towards non-proliferation. All the while, America's nuclear arsenal needs looking after. In 2010, Obama requested a $5bn increase in the US nuclear-weapons budget to look after its ageing bombs.

COUNTING THE BOMBS

Estimates of the world's nuclear weapons depends on who is doing the counting, and how they are doing it, said Julian Borger in the *Guardian*. The 2010 US-Russian disarmament treaty applies to 'deployed strategic warheads', but that leaves out most of the weapons both countries are sitting on. 'Deployed warheads' only refers to those ready to fire or load onto aircraft, whereas there are thousands more 'reserve' weapons and other warheads 'retired for dismantlement'. These are stored in bunkers and could, theoretically, be redeployed in a matter of days or weeks.

The USA has 4,200 'retired' warheads, and dismantles just 270 a year. Russia has about 8,000 reserve and retired warheads. Even though these stockpiles are the largest category of nuclear weapons in the world, and still useable, they are not counted as part of the total for treaty purposes. Neither are short-range, tactical weapons like nuclear artillery shells, depth charges and anti-ballistic missiles, of which the USA has an estimated 500 and Russia about 2,000.

What are
the impacts
of wind farms ?

About four per cent *of the UK's electricity is now provided by wind farms – enough to power all the homes in Scotland. The industry as a whole reached five gigawatts (GW) of generating capacity in September 2010, making wind by far the largest source of renewable energy connected to the National Grid. And wind power is going to become more important over the next decade. With another 3,000-plus turbines being built or having planning consent, it's scheduled to overtake nuclear power in its contribution to Britain's energy mix as soon as 2013.*

So will we see turbines on every hill?

No, because the UK's largest wind farms are being built in the sea. Until recently, the added expense and technical difficulties of maintaining offshore wind farms meant that almost all wind turbines were placed on land. Ninety-nine per cent) of the world's current wind power is onshore – but objections to the noise and ugliness of turbines, and improvements to offshore technology have persuaded energy companies to seek the windy quarters of Britain's 7,700 miles of coastline. The steady winds that buffet the UK are believed to be able to generate 2.2 terrawatts of electricity – ten times our present energy consumption.

And how many offshore wind farms are being planned?

Dozens. With 487 wind turbines operating across 13 sites off its coast, the UK is already the biggest producer of offshore electricity, generating more than the rest of the world combined. And several thousand more propellers are on the way. The Crown Estate, which owns the seabed to a distance of 12 nautical miles, began renting zones to energy companies in 2001, and completed its third round of allocations in 2010. The first 34 sites awarded had a total potential generating capacity of 45GW (equivalent to more than half the current capacity of the National Grid). The Thanet 'wind park', which powers homes from seven miles off the coast of Kent, offers a glimpse of the future: 100 giant turbines, each 380ft (115m) tall, turning slowly in the English Channel. These will become a familiar sight. Some of the zones allocated this year will stretch 100 miles. One day the Norfolk Heritage Coast will confront a horizon of turbines.

Won't that be an eyesore?

On a clear day, yes it will – but it will also represent money and jobs. According to the British Wind Energy Association, building 20GW worth of offshore wind farms by 2020 will pump billions of pounds into the UK's engineering and manufacturing sectors, and create 45,000 jobs. Building on such a scale is expected to bring costs down and give the UK a chance to become a centre of wind technology (currently most turbines are manufactured abroad), and then export its expertise. But in any case, unlike onshore wind turbines, the main objection to offshore turbines is not their visible impact, but all the things we can't see.

What are those invisible impacts?

For a start there are the 40 or 50 mangled seal carcasses that washed up on the Norfolk coast during 2010. Scientists claimed that the seals were caught in the ducted propellers of boats, most likely involved in the construction of the Sheringham Shoal offshore wind farm, which was being built by two Norwegian companies. Evidence from other projects suggests that a range of hard-to-predict environmental consequences could result from sinking hundreds of 500-tonne chunks of machinery into the sea floor. Under UK law, energy companies must produce a Strategic Environmental Assessment before they proceed, but the truth is that the available data on the interaction of turbines and marine life is thin and often contradictory.

The Thanet 'wind park', which powers homes from seven miles off the coast of Kent, offers a glimpse of the future: 100 giant turbines, turning slowly in the English Channel.

What sort of contradictions have emerged?

A study in Denmark found that ducks and geese successfully avoid flying into wind turbines, whereas a Belgian study claimed that many terns had been killed by the blades. The RSPB estimated that Norfolk could lose 50 per cent of its sandwich terns to the turbines. And while some scientists are convinced that fish will gather around the turbines – creating artificial reefs safe from fishing trawlers – others warn of a potentially devastating impact on whales and dolphins, which can get confused by the turbines' underwater vibrations. The main charge against wind turbines, however, relates not to what damage they do when they turn, but to their regular failure not to turn at all owing to lack of wind.

So how often does the wind fail to blow?

Wind turbines at sea deliver their maximum capacity about 35 per cent of the time (onshore ones 30 per cent), compared to 90 per cent for nuclear power, 75 per cent for coal and 50 per cent for hydro-electric. However, the industry claims that fears about reliability are overplayed. An Oxford University study found there wasn't a single moment in the last 35 years when the wind didn't blow somewhere in the UK: so with wider distribution and larger turbines, the amount of redundancy required to be built into the system is quite small. And considering the relative speed and political ease of building them, and the fact that each turbine can be added to the National Grid as soon as it's built, it's clear that wind farms have important advantages over big, single power stations, which often take several years to come on stream.

How about the cost?

That's a real problem. The rising cost of steel, exchange-rate fluctuations and the absence of a settled supply chain saw the cost of turbines double. That means each unit of electricity produced by wind still costs almost twice as much as a unit generated by a coal-fired power station – a source of annoyance for those who oppose the £1bn subsidy the industry receives each year. Such considerations have been enough for Shell to pull out of the vast London Array, scheduled to come on line in 2015, although Centrica has a number of ongoing projects.

SHOULD WE WELCOME OFFSHORE WIND FARMS?

YES	NO
1. With its varied climate and 7,700 miles of coastline, Britain is ideally placed to harness the power of offshore wind.	1. Even when they're out to sea, wind turbines are still an eyesore.
2. Unlike most other forms of electricity generation, wind power is clean and renewable.	2. Turbines can kill birds, and their low-frequency, underwater vibrations pose a potential threat to aquatic life.
3. Developing offshore wind farms will create thousands of engineering and manufacturing jobs, and could turn the UK into an industry leader, generating further income.	3. Offshore wind farms aren't reliable as they depend on the vagaries of the weather, and require lucrative government subsidies to make them economic.

Do planes still need pilots?

Perhaps not – *remote-controlled 'drones' have changed the face of modern warfare. They range in size from surveillance craft small enough to fit into your hand to Northrop Grumman's Global Hawk that has the wing-span of a Boeing 737 and is expected to replace America's U-2 spy plane. The best-known US military drone – or UAV ('Unmanned Aerial Vehicle') – is the Predator, a 27-foot-long aircraft made of lightweight graphite and carbon fibre, which was used extensively in Iraq and Afghanistan, and increasingly in Pakistan. 'The key thing in a UAV,' says Damian Kemp, a former editor at Jane's Defence Weekly, 'is that it does missions that are dull, dirty and dangerous.'*

Have drones proved to be effective?

Enormously so. In just six months in 2009, Predators operating in the tribal regions of Pakistan and Afghanistan helped capture or kill nearly half the terrorists on a list of 20 'high-value targets': some military analysts believed that al-Qaeda had been crippled as a result. US forces claimed to have killed Khalid Habib, al-Qaeda's third-ranking member, Abu Khabab al-Masri, its chemical and biological weapons chief, and Osama bin Laden's son, Saad. Thanks to drones, 'a significant fraction of the al-Qaeda leadership in that part of the world has been taken off the battlefield,' says CIA director Michael Hayden. After the 2011 Tohoku earthquake and tsunami, drones flew over the affected areas in Japan for 300 hours. In 2010, the US air force, for the first time, ordered more drones than manned aircraft, and in February 2012 the Pentagon announced plans to spend $1.2 billion for the first three NATO-version Global Hawks.

And how do drones operate?

Predators, each carrying two laser-guided Hellfire missiles, can stay aloft for up to 40 hours at a time and, having no pilot, require no rest. Flying at altitudes up to 25,000 feet, their quiet engines are very hard to detect from the ground. Using infrared sensors, radar and zoom cameras so powerful that they can distinguish a person's facial features from five miles up, a Predator can capture still and video images day or night, in any weather, and transmit them in real time to pilots thousands of miles away.

And where do the Predator pilots sit?

Mission control is at Creech air force base outside Las Vegas. The armchair pilots operate up to four drones at once, enabling them to 'fly' missions in Iraq and Afghanistan on the same day. Using video screens and computer consoles, 250 pilots work round the clock, guiding drones 7,000 miles away and scanning the ground for suspicious activity. When a target is identified, commanders on the ground in Iraq or Afghanistan decide whether to attack. 'When you're on the radio with a guy on the ground, and he is out of breath and you can hear the weapons fire in the background, you are every bit as engaged as if you were actually there,' Major Matthew Morrison, a drone pilot, told the *New York Times*.

Does only the USA use drones?

Far from it. Remote-controlled aircraft have existed since the First World War, and dozens of countries have drones of one sort or another. Israel, a leader in drone technology, has used them since the 1970s for surveillance and missile attacks in the Palestinian territories. The 32nd Regiment of the Royal

Artillery, the UK's specialised drone unit, has flown UAVs extensively since the 1999 Kosovo war. The UK uses Israeli-built Hermes drones in Afghanistan, but an unarmed joint French, British and Israeli model, the 'Watchkeeper', came into service in 2010. And drones are increasingly used for civilian purposes, too (see box).

Do drones have major drawbacks?

Yes. US air force officials admit that more than a third of their unmanned Predator spy planes have crashed, mostly in Iraq and Afghanistan. One reason for that, say the pilots who control them from afar, is that some of the controls are clunky, and the missile-firing button sits dangerously close to the switch that shuts off the plane's engines. Another problem is that good drone pilots are in such short supply that the air force recently put out a call for retirees to help. But their biggest drawback is that they often kill the wrong people.

Who are the casualties?

In 2008, Predator missiles hit a wedding party in Afghanistan, killing 30 civilians, including children. Dozens of Predator strikes in the Waziristan borderlands of Afghanistan and Pakistan killed or nearly killed those in the vicinity of the strike. No surprise then, that these attacks cause huge resentment among the local population. David Kilcullen, who helped design the Iraq 'surge' strategy, believed that Predators had made as many enemies as

---

'When you're on the radio with a guy on the ground, and you can hear the weapons fire in the background, you are every bit as engaged as if you were actually there.'

---

those they had killed off. 'We need to call off the drones,' he told the US Congress in May 2009.

What happens in a strike?

Silence… followed by a powerful explosion. 'It's not like any other plane,' an unnamed militant in Gaza told the Associated Press. 'You don't see the missile leaving. It's very quiet.' The prospect of drones hovering overhead so unnerved al-Qaeda and Taliban leaders in Afghanistan and Pakistan, according to one intelligence report, that some were sleeping under trees at night rather than risk an attack on their homes. Sara Carter, a reporter for the *Washington Times*, described a video of a drone attack on a group of men outside a large building as follows: 'In an instant, the men on the ground and the building disappeared in an explosion of brilliant white light.'

What is the future of drones?

Engineers are working to make drones self-sufficient, so they can repair themselves if disabled.

More are also now able to land themselves – reducing the number of crash landings – and the machines are becoming ever more deadly. Reapers, the successor to the Predator in the US air force, fly at 50,000 feet, carry not two but 14 Hellfire missiles, and can distinguish the 'heat signatures' of rocket launchers, anti-aircraft guns and other weapons on the ground. The US government envisions a future in which drones will remain aloft for months, if not years, at a time, using fuel cells or constantly refuelling while airborne. 'These systems today are very much Model T Fords,' said defence analyst P.W. Singer. 'These things will only get more advanced.'

WORKING OUTSIDE THE WAR ZONE

Drones aren't just a military tool. They're also used to monitor forest fires, volcanoes and the weather, and to watch America's borders with Canada and Mexico, where from 2005 to 2008, drones helped interdict 20,000 pounds of drugs, leading to 4,000 arrests. Police in Houston, Miami, and other cities have expressed interest in using drones for surveillance.

Police forces in Britain are keen on them, too – and in particular on the Microdrone, a toy-sized remote-control plane that can hover above crowds and takes pictures of them. They cost only £30,000 – a fraction of the price of a helicopter – and the police got a lot more of them since they were first used at rock festivals to take pictures of the fans. But aviation authorities are in no hurry to increase congestion in civilian airspace, especially with pilotless planes. Human pilots, as a US government report notes, have a distinct edge in 'seeing and avoiding other aircraft'.

Is our tabloid press really so awful?

'TWO SH*GS PRESCOTT: *There's hope for fat old gits everywhere' (the* Daily Star *on John Prescott's love life). 'ZIP ME UP BEFORE YOU GO GO' (the* Sun *on George Michael's indiscretion in an LA lavatory). 'WORLD WAR 2 BOMBER FOUND ON MOON' (the* Sunday Sport*). Tawdry though it is, there are many who find Britain's brash tabloid press, with its ribald, ingenious and often loopy headlines, an essential feature of our democracy and way of life. But others feel it is given far too much licence to destroy reputations and intrude on private life. Eighty years ago, Prime Minister Stanley Baldwin complained that, in the absence of proper regulation, the press wielded 'power without responsibility – the prerogative of the harlot through the ages'. The ongoing inquiry, under Lord Justice Leveson, is charged with recommending 'a new more effective... regulatory regime'.*

Don't other countries have a tabloid press?

They certainly do. Germany's most popular newspaper, *Bild*, is read by 12 million people a day and regularly featured nude women on its front page until an announcement in March 2012 that it was dropping its 'Page One Girls'. Italy's tabloids, for several years, were full of stories about former Prime Minister

Silvio Berlusconi's '*bunga-bunga*' parties, at least some of which came from questionably obtained transcripts of private telephone calls. And in the USA, celebrity news sells like nothing else. Yet that said, no other country's gutter press quite matches the ferocity of the British tabloid newspapers, or the lengths to which they have been willing to go.

Is that because other countries have tougher regulation?

Britain's much-derided Press Complaints Commission, a body funded by the newspaper industry and with no statutory powers, is often cited as a reason the tabloids run amok. France, in contrast, has long-standing privacy laws that bar newspapers and magazines from printing intrusive photographs of public figures in private moments. In 1997, these were extended to give individuals the 'right over one's image', a provision that, among other things, controls reporting of the early stages of criminal proceedings. (Photographs of the former IMF chief, Dominique Strauss-Kahn, in handcuffs in

New York were shown in his home country only by daring outlets.) But laws are not the only reason that reporting in France tends to stop at the bedroom door.

What else is going on?

Under French law, journalists – like their counterparts in the UK and elsewhere – have recourse to a public-interest defence if they choose to publish a story whose subject wants to keep it a secret. In practice, they rarely test their luck. During the 1980s, President François Mitterrand managed to keep out of the newspapers the fact that he had a second, secret family, and that he was suffering from cancer – despite there being a fair claim of public interest in each story. Experts in French media law put the reticence down to the close relations between newspaper proprietors and the political elite, who are, in some cases, one and the same: *Le Figaro*, the influential right-of-centre broadsheet, is owned by Serge Dassault, a businessman and senator for President Sarkozy's UMP party.

So money talks – or rather, stops talk?

Yes, though not always through political channels. In America, where tabloids derive the bulk of their income (up to 80 per cent) from advertising, there's a financial incentive for newspapers to provide a 'credible and respectable' platform for advertisers, says Tom Rosenstiel, director of the Pew Research Center's Project for Excellence in Journalism.

> In America, there's a financial incentive for newspapers to provide a 'credible and respectable' platform for advertisers, hence tabloids steer clear of the riskier, more salacious stories.

Hence tabloids steer clear of the riskier, more salacious stories. In the UK, where the *News of the World* generated two-thirds of its income from newsstand sales, the opposite pressure applies: cut-throat competition between titles pushes reporters to seek ever more sensational scoops. And that leads to what investigative journalist Nick Davies calls a 'regime of fear' in tabloid newsrooms, in which ethical niceties are given short shrift.

Don't a nation's history and culture also play a role?

Trite as it may sound, there is some truth in the adage that we get the press we deserve. Thus Germany's appetite for tabloid fodder stops way short of the British taste for intrusion (there was no mention in the German press that future chancellor Gerhard Schröder, a married man, was having a widely known affair with a female journalist) – a reticence at least in part explained by the legacy of the Gestapo and the Stasi, and the resulting respect for the right to privacy. 'In Germany, too drastic reporting, too much diving into people's private sphere, wouldn't be welcome,' says media analyst Jo Groebel. In Sweden, the press is governed by a system of self-regulation similar to the UK's, but this has more bite: the public is critical of the retractions and corrections that papers are forced to publish.

Swedish readers 'hate seeing such notices', says Ola Sigvardsson, Sweden's press ombudsman.

And how might we rein in the British tabloids?

There have been numerous suggestions: new privacy laws; new rules for meetings between politicians or police officers and journalists; reform of the Press Complaints Commission along the lines of the Advertising Standards Authority, which has a broader remit and can refer offenders to the Government for sterner punishment. But there has also been a quieter, more resistant body of opinion which insists that the excesses of the press revealed in 2011 have long been illegal, and that fresh curbs on press freedoms will, over time, be used to protect those who should be exposed. The day after the Leveson inquiry opened, the *Guardian* revealed that one of its reporters, Amelia Hill, had been held and questioned by police under caution for – of all things – receiving leaked information from detectives about tabloid misbehaviour.

TIME TO STRENGTHEN PRESS REGULATION?

YES

1. The *News of the World*'s hacking of the phones of Milly Dowler and 7/7 victims clearly shows the press is out of control.

2. The Press Complaints Commission does not have the power to hold journalists accountable for the harm they so often cause.

3. There's an urgent need to rethink what 'public interest' means and to redefine the press's relationship with police and politicians.

NO

1. The worst abuses exposed by the phone-hacking scandal were criminal offences: these will and should be punished in the courts.

2. Stricter regulations, as in France, tend to lead to cover-ups of the dubious activities of public figures.

3. A nation's tabloid press is part of its social and cultural fabric. You can't legislate away our fascination with sex and scandal.

Why is
Thomas Cromwell
controversial?

Because depending on *whom you ask, Henry VIII's powerful minister was either the great architect of modern, accountable government, or a brutal schemer with the blood of Catholic martyrs on his hands. Thomas Cromwell (not to be confused with his great-great-grandnephew, Oliver) is best known for writing the laws that framed the Reformation and created the Church of England. It was he who drafted the Act in Restraint of Appeals, passed by Parliament in 1533, to allow Henry's divorce to be granted without interference from the Pope; he who drafted the laws affirming the royal supremacy.*

And why has he been so detested?

As the King's ruthlessly loyal adviser, Cromwell carried out some of the most divisive and bloody acts of Henry's reign: organising the executions of Anne Boleyn and Saint Sir Thomas More; extricating England from papal authority; dissolving the monasteries, confiscating their property and helping himself to the spoils; initiating doctrinal changes in which many central features of Catholicism (the existence of purgatory, the value of monasticism) were rejected. He was also merciless in suppressing the Pilgrimage of Grace – the great northern Catholic uprising of 1536.

But it wasn't just his policies that made him such a hate figure – with Catholics in particular, nobles like the Duke of Norfolk seethed with resentment at the sight of a commoner raised above them.

So Cromwell was not high born?

Far from it. He was born in Putney in 1485, and his father was a blacksmith and alehouse keeper – in her Booker-winning novel *Wolf Hall*, Hilary Mantel portrays him as a petty tyrant (see box). Little is known of Thomas's early life, but he is thought to have left for Europe in his mid-teens, where he fought as a mercenary and represented an Italian banking family in the cloth trade, before returning to England in 1512 to study law. Within eight years he was legal secretary to Cardinal Wolsey, Henry VIII's first great adviser; and after Wolsey failed to secure Henry's divorce from Catherine of Aragon, Cromwell stepped over his master's dead body to become chief minister in 1532.

What brought him down?

His efforts to persuade Henry to marry the German princess Anne of Cleves in the hope of securing the support of the north German princes against the Holy Roman Emperor, Charles V. The marriage was a disaster, the alliance failed and Cromwell was doomed. Condemned for religious radicalism, he was beheaded on Tower Hill in 1540, and died repudiating all heresy and declaring himself a Catholic. His head was mounted on a stake, facing away from London in disgrace. Still, the picture that endures is of him in his pomp – cold, brooding, malevolent – best visualised in the famous portrait by Hans Holbein (above). That's why Hilary Mantel's depiction of him is so unusual.

In what way is it unusual?

Her novel, written in a highly coloured, impressionistic style, depicts him as a basically kind and decent man – a figure resembling neither Holbein's portrait nor his portrayal in Robert Bolt's 1960 play, *A Man for All Seasons*. In the subsequent film, Paul Scofield starred as the noble, upstanding Thomas More opposite Leo McKern's hideous, scheming Cromwell. Is Mantel alone in championing him? No. Shortly before Bolt began polishing More's reputation, the great Tudor historian Sir Geoffrey Elton was making a case for Cromwell as the man who put a brake on the personal, autocratic rule of England's kings by initiating the rule of law and developing the bureaucratic institutions that have governed it ever since. According to Elton, Cromwell introduced the first auditing procedures, making nobles answerable for how they spent the king's money, and formalised the work of the Privy Council, turning the king's circle of advisers into a collective decision-making body prefiguring the modern cabinet.

And was Elton's thesis widely accepted?

By no means. It was attacked by many other historians, not least Elton's own protégé, David Starkey. In his *Reign of Henry VIII: Politics and Personalities*, Starkey contends that most of Cromwell's so-called reforms had medieval precedents, and that many had actually been pioneered under Henry VIII's father, Henry VII. He also argues that, far from moving England to a more systematic, bureaucratic style of government, Cromwell's court was highly personalised and thick with cliques. Starkey's work led to a 'cosmic falling-out' with Elton, worthy of the Tudors themselves.

Do people agree about the scale of Cromwell's brutality?

By Elton's calculations, Cromwell's political revolution – the split from Rome, the transfer of the

---

It wasn't just his policies that made Cromwell such a hate figure – nobles like the Duke of Norfolk seethed with resentment at the sight of a commoner raised above them.

Catholic Church's vast wealth to the king – came at the cost of around 40 lives per year. 'A pretty cheap omelette', as the reviewer in the *New Yorker* put it. But there is no getting around Cromwell's role in the show trials of Anne Boleyn and Thomas More. And these were just the better-known ones. He also presided over the starving of 10 Carthusian monks in Newgate gaol, the chaining of a rebel to the walls of York Castle, where he died of thirst, and the burning of 14 Anabaptists. 'There is a reason,' wrote Melanie McDonagh, a Catholic writer, in her review of Mantel's book, 'why Cromwell has had a long-standing reputation as a complete bastard.'

What did Hilary Mantel make of that?

She doesn't hide his ruthlessness. 'Only you and me, master,' confides his servant, Christophe, 'we know stop some little fuckeur in his tracks, so that's the end of him and he doesn't even squeak.' But in Mantel's Tudor England no one is straightforward, and she takes particular issue with More, whose saintly reputation is also increasingly under attack from historians. More persecuted heretics just as Cromwell did, yet it is his outward displays of piety that have gone down in history. As Cromwell says to More in one of the book's climactic scenes: 'You will drag down with you God knows how many, who will only have the suffering, and not your martyr's gratification.'

CHILD ABUSE: AN EXTRACT FROM WOLF HALL

Mantel's novel is written in an unusual, immediate style, right from its opening lines. Throughout the book, Cromwell is often referred to as just 'him' or 'he'.

'So now get up!' Walter is roaring down at him, working out where to kick him next. He lifts his head an inch or two, and moves forward, on his belly, trying to do it without exposing his hands, on which Walter enjoys stamping. 'What are you, an eel?' his parent asks. He trots backward, gathers pace, and aims another kick.

It knocks the last breath out of him; he thinks it may be his last. His forehead returns to the ground; he lies waiting, for Walter to jump on him. The dog, Bella, is barking, shut away in an outhouse. I'll miss my dog, he thinks.

What **is** Huntington's **disease** ?

It was identified by George Huntington, a doctor from the seaside town of East Hampton, New York, whose 1872 account, based on a study of families in the town afflicted by the disease, is a classic of medical observation. His interest had been aroused as a young boy when, travelling with his father, he saw a mother and daughter beside the road, writhing and grimacing with jerky, uncontrollable movements. In line with nineteenth-century medical tradition, the disease became known as Huntington's chorea (chorea is Ancient Greek for 'dance'). Both neurological and psychiatric, it involves disturbances of movement, mind and mood.

What are the symptoms?

The first symptoms – jerky, uncontrolled movements, memory loss and lapses in concentration – typically occur when subjects are between 30 and 50. Sufferers develop a staggering gait that often gives the appearance of drunkenness, and eventually lose the ability to walk. Their speech grows incoherent, eating becomes a major challenge and swallowing is perilous. Often there are personality changes, sometimes involving serious depression: it's thought one in four sufferers try to take their own lives. It typically takes between 10 and 20 years for this gradual degeneration to end life. There is no cure. Sufferers need full-time nursing.

So is it common?

Genetic disorders are relatively rare, but Huntington's is one of the more common forms, reported in all racial and ethnic groups. Owing to its heritability – children of sufferers have a 50 per cent chance of developing the condition – it often occurs in clusters. In Britain, for example, it is more common in East Anglia. It was probably carried to America by two brothers from Suffolk called Knapp, who crossed the Atlantic with other Puritans in 1630 (followed three years later by another East Anglian Puritan, Simon Huntington, ancestor of George). The best-known victim is probably US folk singer Woody Guthrie, who died of the disease in 1967, and whose wife Marjorie, after his death, set up a committee to combat the disease and to fund research.

Do we know much about its genetic origins?

The gene involved was identified in 1983 by a team at Harvard Medical School, but it wasn't until 1993 that scientists managed to isolate and clone the gene itself. This discovery showed that the disease is caused by an extended 'genetic stutter': a stretch of DNA repeated over and over at one end of a gene on Chromosome 4. Most people have fewer than 36 copies of this stutter, but Huntington's sufferers have more than 36 – and the longer the stutter, the earlier the disease will strike. Despite predictions that the discovery would soon lead to effective treatments, there's still no cure in sight – though there is now a relatively cheap diagnostic test, and drugs have been developed that can alleviate some symptoms.

How many victims are there?

Far more than you might think. Statistics suggest the number affected in Britain may be double the official figure of 6,700, not least because the disease is stigmatised. Early studies in the twentieth century linked it with witchcraft, and it became a model for the sort of genetic disease that the eugenics movement wanted to target with programmes of compulsory sterilisation. It is thought that, even today, many people ask for it not to be put on death certificates. Yet there's another reason, aside from the stigma, that people may want to keep the condition secret.

What is that?

Fearing that newly developed tests for a range of genetic disorders might create an uninsurable 'underclass', the last government

---

The best-known victim is probably US folk singer Woody Guthrie, who died of the disease in 1967, and whose wife set up a committee to combat the disease and to fund research.

---

came to an agreement with the insurance industry that there would be a moratorium on the disclosure of test results until 2014. But there is one exception to this protocol: Huntington's disease. On life-insurance policies worth more than £500,000, and on critical-illness policies worth

more than £300,000, insurers can demand to see results from tests for Huntington's. It turns out that only 20 per cent of those at risk of Huntington's decide to take the gene test, and it's thought that some who might otherwise have taken the test refrain from doing so for fear of losing their insurance cover.

What does the insurance industry say?

That genetic testing is a refined version of gleaning information from family histories, something that insurers have been doing for years. Indeed, anyone failing to admit to a family history of Huntington's would lose their insurance if they then developed the disease. Besides, the Huntington's test, unlike tests for 'genetic predispositions' to certain cancers or Alzheimer's, has almost 100 per cent predictive accuracy – so those taking it are just as likely to be relieved (and better off) as they are to be distressed or to face higher insurance premiums. Of those who test positive, meanwhile, some will have a version of the gene linked to later onset of the disease, meaning they can obtain standard health insurance when they are younger. Hence, say the insurance companies, the overall level of premiums will go down if people have to disclose test results.

Are there dangers in following that principle?

Scientists predict that it will soon be possible to sequence entire genomes for as little as £500, and to offer such testing as standard.

And while that could open up an entire new field of medicine to help predict and prevent disease, the tests could create an uninsurable genetic underclass. That concern has led Belgium, Austria, France and Norway to ban the use of tests by insurers, and led the US Congress to pass the Genetic Information Nondiscrimination Act, which outlaws genetic discrimination for employment and health (but not life) insurance.

INSURERS SHOULD SEE GENETIC TEST RESULTS

AGREE	DISAGREE
1. Insurers already ask about family medical history when doing risk assessments; the principle is no different with genetic tests.	1. It would deter people from taking tests that could help save their lives or prevent them passing a disease to their children.
2. Why should the healthy majority be expected to subsidise people with genetic diseases or predispositions?	2. It would lead to the creation of a genetic underclass, denied access to insurance, mortgages and jobs.
3. People testing positive for serious genetic disorders would be motivated to insure themselves properly.	3. It would deter people from participating in genetic research that could lead to the development of new treatments and cures.

How many 'honour killings' are there?

No one knows *for sure. Ten years ago, the UN estimated that every year across the world 5,000 women and girls were killed for being seen to have 'shamed' their family in some way, usually to do with sex. But most human-rights groups think that this is a huge understatement, as many countries where honour killings occur fail to recognise them as murders, either recording them as suicides or ignoring them altogether. Egypt claims to have no honour killings, yet they are well documented by activists and journalists. In rural, highly patriarchal communities from Turkey to Afghanistan, women often disappear with no further information given. In a special report for The Independent, Robert Fisk put the annual total at more like 20,000.*

Are victims always female?

Not always. In Pakistan's province of Sindh, 137 men were thought to be victims of honour killings in 2002, compared to 245 women. And in Afghanistan, a man was stoned to death in 2010 after eloping with a woman who had been promised to her cousin. But the vast majority of victims are women. Human Rights Watch even defines honour killings as 'acts of violence, usually murder, committed by male family members against female family members, who are held to have brought dishonour upon the family'. In societies where they're treated as possessions of their fathers, brothers and husbands, women can bring dishonour for refusing an arranged marriage, seeking a divorce, even 'allowing' themselves to be raped. A 17-year-old Gazan girl was murdered by a brother in 2005 for becoming pregnant by her own father. In another case, a husband murdered his wife after a dream in which she had betrayed him – and got off. Honour killings can be strikingly brutal, and have a terrifying, ritualistic quality. Women are decapitated, electrocuted and buried alive.

Do honour killings mainly happen in Muslim countries?

Yes. Pakistan is thought to have the most (possibly as many as 10,000 a year), with large numbers also reported in Turkey and Kurdish Iraq, and among Palestinian refugees in Jordan. Yet in Jordan, the Christian minority is thought to be involved in more honour killings per capita than the country's Muslims; while

India was shocked by a series of 19 honour killings in 2010 in its mainly Hindu north. In short, honour killings have less to do with religion than with other features of tribal and feudal society: the role of dowries and inheritances, and the absence of effective recourse to a wider legal system.

Why is that significant?

Social anthropologists distinguish between cultures of law (whose members, confident that transgressors will be punished by the legal system, accept curbs on their freedom to defend themselves and retaliate for injuries); and cultures of honour, where in the absence of effective law enforcement, cultivating a reputation for swift, disproportionate revenge is seen as vital to ensure the safety of person and property (and to reinforce the control of the male patriarch over female dependents). Cultures of honour have occurred in groups as diverse as Bedouin, Scottish/English herdsmen of the Border country, cowboys and ranchers of the American West, aristocrats whose hereditary privileges put them beyond the reach of codes of law, and criminal gangs.

Are such killings tolerated by law?

They often are or have been. Article 340 of Jordan's criminal code stipulates that 'a husband or close blood relative who kills a woman caught in a situation highly suspicious of adultery will be totally exempt from sentence'. Attempts by King Abdullah II to reform the law have been rejected by Jordan's parliament. Pakistani law is notorious for allowing a victim's family to pardon the accused at any stage of a criminal trial and halt the prosecution. Since honour killings are usually committed within a family, cases almost never come to court. But again, Muslim countries aren't the only ones. In Brazil until 1991, wife killings were treated as non-criminal 'honour killings': in one year, nearly 800 husbands killed their wives. A 2002 report for the UN shows that the penal codes of such non-Muslim nations as Argentina, Ecuador, Venezuela and Peru all allow for the partial or complete use of the 'honour' defence.

Has 'honour killing' played a big role in Western cultures?

Not really, though in Italy the concept of 'honour' remained a legal defence right up until 1981: by appealing to it, men who had killed their wives, daughters or sisters could receive no more than a three- to seven-year jail sentence. Elsewhere, the 'crime of passion' did duty for the 'honour' defence. Under the Code Napoléon, crime passionnel

---

Treated as possessions, women can bring dishonour for refusing an arranged marriage, seeking a divorce, even 'allowing' themselves to be raped.

---

was a valid defence for murder in French law until the 1970s. In England, 'provocation' was allowed as a defence against murder – mostly to husbands accused of killing their wives – until 2009. Indeed, the civil laws in many ex-colonies that provide sanction for honour killings derive from precisely such defences in Western legal codes.

Can't these countries now reform their laws?

They can, and many have. But enforcement does not necessarily follow. Honour killing has been a capital offence in Pakistan since 2005, but that makes little difference when barely any cases are prosecuted. Seeking entry into the EU, Turkey has stiffened the penalty for such killings, but this seems to have led women to commit suicide instead: NGOs have found that 'dishonoured' women are being locked in rooms with a gun, poison or a noose, and left there until they kill themselves. In the town of Batman in south-eastern Turkey, more than 100 women are known to have attempted suicide between 2000 and 2006, twice the number of men. The grim truth, as Fisk notes, is that in many male-dominated societies across the developing world, honour killing is seen as part of the social order, and it will be as hard to get people to desist as it would have been to persuade 17th-century Englishmen to stop executing witches.

HONOUR KILLINGS IN THE UK

In 2004, the Metropolitan Police announced it was re-examining more than 100 murders in England and Wales that it believed could have been honour killings. Among them were the case of Surjit Athwal, a customs officer at Heathrow whose murder was ordered by her mother-in-law; and the disappearance of Tulay Goren, a 15-year-old Kurdish girl from north London, whose father was convicted of her killing (for falling in love with a Sunni Muslim) in 2009.

The cases, mostly among Pakistani, Bangladeshi and Kurdish families, went back a decade; police think there are now about 12 honour killings in the UK each year. Women's charities say there are far more, and point to the suicide rate of women aged 16–24 from South Asian backgrounds: a study has shown that they are three times more likely to kill themselves than their white counterparts. Hundreds of other women in abusive marriages in isolated communities are likely to suffer 'honour crimes' of a non-lethal sort. When in 2008 the Home Office set up a forced marriages unit, it received 5,000 calls and rescued 400 victims in the first six months.

Do coalitions produce the goods ?

In Britain, *in war and peacetime, they have helped leaders put aside party differences to act in the 'national interest' – although those leaders have often ended up being rejected by their own parties as a result (see box). And in Europe, coalitions have generally delivered stable, consensus-based governments: the countries above are regarded as some of the world's best-run. But coalitions have not always been popular or functional. Italy, for instance, has had 62 governments since 1945 because its alliances have collapsed so often. And they are often accused of being not nearly as democratic and representative as they appear.*

Why is that?

Coalitions mean that the real politics – the haggling and the arguing – takes place out of the public eye and behind closed doors. 'The people do not get a look-in,' says Lord Norton, one of Britain's leading constitutional experts. 'Compromises are reached which may bear no relationship to what electors want.' They can give a disproportionate amount of power to the smaller parties, such as the religious groups in Israel's right-wing coalitions. And they have also been criticised for sustaining consensus when disagreement and decisive action would be more fruitful.

Thomas Kielinge, *Die Welt*'s London correspondent, says that in Germany the political process often 'descends into an unholy *fudge majeur*. Reforms are stymied because the "coalitionistas" can't agree on more than the lowest common denominator for fear of making life impossible for the other guy. The public is increasingly cynical.'

So they're not 'The New Politics'?

No. They are a very old kind of politics – one that has broken out in Britain several times in the last 150 years, particularly at moments of national crisis. The country had several recognisable coalition governments in the nineteenth century – including one formed between the Tories and breakaway Liberals in 1886. Coalitions have helped steer Britain through dark and momentous times, such as the two world wars. They have also produced great leaders. But they have often been profoundly uncomfortable – a deviation from our normal, adversarial style of parliamentary politics. 'Coalitions, though successful, have always

found this,' said Disraeli in 1852, 'that their triumph has been brief.'

Do hung parliaments always produce coalitions?

Not necessarily. In 1974, and between 1976 and 1979, Jim Callaghan's Labour Party could not command a majority in the House of Commons, but it did not form a coalition. Instead, Labour ruled as a minority government but made a pact with the Liberals, who promised not to bring down the government. Roy Hattersley, who served as a minister under Callaghan, has described the constant tension of serving in such a fragile administration – the endless consultations and compromises that were made to stay in power. 'Inevitably,' he says, 'much time and energy was spent struggling to survive.' Coalitions are designed to have more stability.

How do they try to achieve that?

By sharing government posts among two or more parties, and compromising on key policies, coalitions can claim to reflect the opinion of the electorate far more accurately than a single party. Thus, in the past, they have made it possible to pass legislation at difficult moments, sometimes with enormous parliamentary majorities to help them. In 1918, David Lloyd George's 'National Liberal' coalition of Liberals and Conservatives promised to build a land 'fit for heroes to live in' after the First World War, and won 525 out of 707 seats. During the Second World War, Churchill ordered the Labour

---

In Germany the political process often 'descends into an unholy *fudge majeur*. Reforms are stymied because the "coalitionistas" can't agree on more than the lowest common denominator.'

---

and Tory whips to share an office in the House of Commons to make sure legislation passed without a hitch. But such cooperation has not only been associated with wartime.

When else has it occurred?

During moments of extreme political stress. There were a series of coalitions between 1846 and 1867, as Britain wrestled with the changes wrought by the Industrial Revolution. In the 1840s, the Conservative Prime Minister, Sir Robert Peel, formed a coalition with the opposition Whigs to repeal the Corn Laws, a set of agricultural tariffs that enhanced landowners' profits and were fiercely defended by his own party. Other landmark laws – introducing universal suffrage, and home rule for India and Ireland – have also been passed by coalitions. In a parallel closer to the current situation, a National Government was formed in 1931 to tackle the Great Depression. More recently, the assemblies of Scotland and Wales have been run by coalitions.

What about coalitions abroad?

In democracies around the world, particularly those with proportional representation, coalitions are very common. Much of northern Europe – including Germany, Sweden, Norway, Denmark and Belgium – has been ruled by coalitions for most of its recent history. The Netherlands and

Finland have been governed by coalitions since the end of the First World War. In Switzerland, a group of four or more parties has governed since 1959, dividing power via an arithmetical device known as the 'magic formula'.

So will coalitions catch on in Britain?

They may have to: the electoral share of the smaller parties has grown steadily (in 1951, only 3 per cent of votes did not go to the main two parties; in 2010, it was 35 per cent). But the adversarial two-party system, for all its faults and name-calling, is deeply embedded in Britain, and the country has reverted to it whenever possible. Even in 1941, when the House of Commons was bombed during the strongest coalition of the century, it was rebuilt along adversarial lines.

THE CURSE OF THE COALITION

Some of Britain's greatest prime ministers, from Sir Robert Peel to David Lloyd George to Winston Churchill, have led coalitions – and they have, almost without fail, suffered a degree of rejection by their parties as a result.

Peel's decision to repeal the Corn Laws led to such antipathy from his fellow Tories that some refused to mourn when he died after a riding accident in 1850.

Lloyd George may have been the dominant British politician of the early twentieth century, establishing national insurance and state pensions, and helping to win the First World War, but he destroyed the Liberal Party in the process: in 1922, Labour became the official opposition.

Ramsay MacDonald, who led Labour into the National Government of 1931, in which the majority of MPs were Conservatives, ended up expelled from his own party, which accused him of 'betrayal'.

Even Churchill, who was invited by King George VI to lead the wartime coalition on 10 May 1940, was initially cheered only by the Labour benches and had to wait six months before being elected to lead his own party.

Neither David Cameron, a moderniser suspected by traditional Tories, nor Nick Clegg, a Lib Dem with long-standing links to Conservative politicians, has history on his side.

What was the
world's worst
industrial accident?

Just after midnight *on 3 December 1984, water got into the machinery at Union Carbide's chemical plant at Bhopal, a lakeside town of 800,000 people that's home to one of India's largest mosques and capital of Madhya Pradesh state. The water reached a tank containing 40 tonnes of methyl isocyanate (MIC), a highly unstable and deadly chemical used to kill insects. The water reacted with the MIC, causing a sharp increase in temperature, and in the process creating a derivative of phosgene, a poison gas used in the First World War. It began to escape, and within hours had enveloped half the city.*

Was the gas lethal?

Five hundred times as poisonous as hydrogen cyanide, the escaping MIC killed hundreds of people in minutes. Some died in their beds, others as they shielded young children, or on roads as they fled. 'We woke with eyes crying, noses watering. The pain was unbearable. We were writhing, coughing and slobbering froth,' said Champi Devi Shukla, a leader of the survivors. 'Among the crowd of people, dogs and even cows were running and trying to save their lives.' Officially, 3,000 people were reported dead that night, but campaigners and journalists put the actual number nearer 8,500. The Indian Council for Medical Research says that around 25,000 people have died as a result of the leak. A further 100,000 remain chronically ill with symptoms of chemical poisoning. Bhopal's miscarriage rate is seven times India's national average; the proportion of babies born with deformities is similarly skewed.

Was the disaster totally unexpected?

'Wake up people of Bhopal, you are on the edge of a volcano!' So wrote Raj Keswani, a journalist in Bhopal, two years before the gas leak. Keswani was covering the deteriorating safety record at the Union Carbide plant, where the US-owned company had imposed $1.25m in cuts in the four years before the disaster. Built in the 1970s to provide fertilisers for India's agricultural revolution, the Bhopal plant was losing money in the early 1980s. So the workforce was halved, and the team looking after the toxic MIC cut from 12 to 6. Refrigeration, to stabilise the chemical, was stopped to save money, and the plant's warning siren was turned off because it kept being triggered by minor

leaks. According to the *Guardian*, an audit of the plant by engineers in 1982 identified 11 critical safety hazards in the MIC unit, and warned of a possible major release. On the night of the disaster, none of the four safety devices to control an MIC leak were in working order. Days after the disaster, police arrested Union Carbide's chairman, Warren Anderson (see box).

Did the company admit fault?

No, neither Union Carbide nor its parent company – Dow Chemical, the maker of napalm, which bought the company in 2001 – accepted legal responsibility for the Bhopal disaster. An internal company investigation concluded that adequate safety systems had been in place, and that the disaster could only have been the result of sabotage. This conclusion, they claimed, was endorsed by an expert committee working on behalf of the Indian government, and by Arthur D. Little, the engineering consulting firm that conducted its own investigation.

Did Union Carbide do nothing to help?

Union Carbide did accept 'moral responsibility' for the MIC leak, and set up a $100m charitable trust to build a hospital for victims. In 1989, it also reached a settlement with the Indian government, under which it paid $470m to compensate victims. In return, the government agreed to drop a suit which might have cost the company $3bn in compensation payments. India's Supreme Court called the settlement 'just, equitable and reasonable', and it was given similar praise in a report by the Reserve Bank of India. In a statement to mark the 25th anniversary of the disaster, Dow Chemical said that the 1989 deal 'resolved all existing and future claims. [The company] did all it could to help the victims and their families.'

How much money reached the victims?

The Indian government limited the number of claimants to 105,000, meaning thousands of survivors and families in Bhopal who believe they are entitled to compensation have received nothing. Some were given as much as £1,200, but the average was around £300, or 7p per day. There were considerable problems distributing the money. As recently as 2004, 15 years after Union Carbide offered its settlement, half of the funds remained in an Indian government bank account. But even that scandal pales next to the continuing health risks associated with the disused chemical plant.

'We woke with eyes crying, noses watering. We were writhing, coughing and slobbering froth. people, dogs and even cows were running and trying to save their lives.

Has it not been cleaned up?

No. The factory lies abandoned, and investigators say thousands of tonnes of toxic chemicals remain there, seeping into the ground every time it rains. Tests show that pesticides and heavy metals, such as mercury, which are still at the site, have contaminated the groundwater that the 30,000 local people have to drink. Water from a hand-pump near the plant was tested by Greenpeace in 2009 and found to contain levels of the industrial solvent carbon tetrachloride 4,800 times higher than limits permissible in the USA. The Centre for Science and the Environment, an Indian science and advocacy group, said that the disused site had brought 'chronic toxicity' to the surrounding area. But these findings were disputed by the state government of Madhya Pradesh, which has been in control of the plant since 1998. Babulal Gaur, the minister in charge of the clean-up, said the factory was safe, although he dropped plans to open it to the public. Dow Chemical insisted that it was the government's responsibility to clean up the factory.

WHERE'S WARREN?

After years of faltering court cases and inadequate compensation, the annual survivors' pilgrimage to the Union Carbide plant in Bhopal has become a symbolic exercise as much as anything else. 'For the past 25 years we've taken out rallies and burnt hundreds of effigies of Union Carbide and its former chairman Warren Anderson. We are doing the same today. We will burn yet another effigy and beat the scarecrows with sticks. This has been the only way of calming our frustration," said Abdul Jabbar Khan, an activist, last week.

Warren Anderson is still facing prosecution for the Bhopal disaster. The former chairman of Union Carbide was arrested in Bhopal, when he visited the city four days after the leak in 1984, on suspicion of negligence and corporate liability. He was later charged with manslaughter. But Anderson skipped bail and flew back to the USA in a private jet, where he has remained. In 2002, the *Daily Mirror* tracked him down to the Hamptons, the well-heeled tip of Long Island, near New York. Union Carbide and Dow Chemical insist that all legal issues surrounding Bhopal were resolved in 1989 and, although a judge in Delhi issued another warrant for Anderson's arrest, the USA refused to extradite him in 2010. The same year, seven ex-employees were convicted and sentenced, but bailed.

Who are the 'Palestinian refugees'?

There are around *4.7 million of them, including almost half of the 3.9 million population of Gaza and the West Bank. That compares to the 7.5 million people living in Israel (of whom 5.5 million are Jews). There are so many because, uniquely under international law, 'Palestinian refugees' are not just those who fled the Arab-Israeli wars of 1948 and 1967, but their descendants too. This is also the obstacle to their 'right to return', recognised by the UN. If they all went home, Israel would lose its identity as a Jewish state. But the longer the problem lasts, the larger it grows. According to UNRWA, the UN organisation which looks after them, the number of Palestinian refugees has doubled in the past 20 years.*

Is their future part of the peace talks?

No. It is too contentious. Although there is not much of a peace process to speak of at the moment, the leaders of Israel and the Palestinian territories are still supposedly following the 'road map' agreed with the Bush Administration in 2002. The plan set out a series of steps – curbing Palestinian violence, dismantling Jewish settlements – leading to a two-state solution, but the refugee problem was too fraught even to talk about. And yet it is impossible to imagine a lasting peace without it being resolved.

So where do all the refugees live?

The largest group of refugees, almost 2 million, is in Jordan, where they comprise around a third of the population. Syria and Lebanon both have around 400,000 refugees, while Saudi Arabia has 240,000 and Egypt 70,000. The remainder (1.8 million) live in the Palestinian Territories, where tented camps have evolved into permanent slums with some of the highest population densities on Earth. In the Beach refugee camp in Gaza, 82,000 people live in half a square kilometre. Although their circumstances vary from country to country, what is unusual about the Palestinian refugees is not only how long they have been in limbo, but also how they have failed to integrate with the populations that took them in.

And what accounts for that?

While most Arab countries cling to UN Resolution 194 of 1948, which says that 'refugees wishing to return to their homes and live at peace' should be allowed to do so or receive compensation from Israel, they have ignored their own obligations under international law to 'facilitate the assimilation and naturalisation of refugees'. With the notable exception of Jordan, all Arab states with sizeable Palestinian populations have for decades denied them jobs, citizenship rights and access to public services. In the past, keeping the refugees in camps was seen as a shrewd tactic to draw world attention to their plight and put pressure on Israel; but that tactic was eventually overtaken by the realities of poverty, ill health and segregation.

Just how dire is their situation?

'The systematic refusal of Arab governments to grant basic human rights to Palestinians who are born and die in their countries,' claimed *The Independent*, 'recalls the treatment of Jews in medieval Europe.' The worst offender is Lebanon, where factional fighting in the camps spilled over to become a key part of Lebanon's civil war from 1975 to 1990. Lebanese laws bar Palestinians from more than 20 professions, and from voting or owning property. A law of 2001 also prevents Palestinians from passing on any land they may have acquired to their children. Politicians across Lebanon's religiously and ethnically mixed population all oppose the naturalisation of the refugees.

Are conditions better elsewhere?

Yes. Palestinians have better lives in Syria and Jordan, but even there

---

1.8 million live in the Palestinian Territories, where tented camps have evolved into permanent slums. In the Beach refugee camp in Gaza, 82,000 people live in half a square kilometre.

---

they suffer constraints. In Syria, where 70 per cent of refugees no longer live in camps, Palestinians run their own businesses and have government jobs; but they cannot vote, buy more than one house or own agricultural land. Jordan, meanwhile, is the only country to have granted full citizenship

to Palestinian refugees, with the vast majority holding dual nationality and contributing to the political and economic life of the nation. Queen Rania of Jordan, for instance, is a Palestinian. But even in Amman, the refugees don't feel entirely secure. In 2009, the government was forced to deny that it was revoking the citizenship rights of thousands of Palestinians.

Why is the Palestinians' situation so precarious?

They have not been straightforward settlers. The awfulness of their plight and the complexity of their politics have made them volatile – and sometimes threatening – guests (see box); nowhere more so than in Jordan, where in the late 1960s, the Palestinian Liberation Organisation under Yasser Arafat fought the army of King Hussein. In the 'Black September' of 1970, 3,500 men died as the two sides clashed for control of the state. The following year, Palestinian gunmen killed the Jordanian Prime Minister, Wasfi al-Tal, in Cairo. On the other hand, receiving countries have also exploited their Palestinian refugees for their own ends. The leadership of Hamas, the Islamist faction which controls the Gaza Strip, for instance, is based in Damascus, and the group is often seen as a proxy for Syria in Gaza and the West Bank.

So what do the refugees want?

The official Palestinian line is that they want to 'return home': but this remains as politically improbable as the alternative – mass granting of citizenship and relinquishing the whole idea of going back to Palestine. However, the fact is that most Palestinian refugees have never lived in present-day Israel, and it is not at all clear that they would go back if they had the chance. In 2003, a leading Palestinian pollster, Khalil Shikaki, interviewed 4,500 refugees and found that 90 per cent would not act on their 'right to return' if they were given it. They would rather stay where they were, or live in a Palestinian state. Shikaki's findings were so optimistic – suggesting that the refugee problem could be solved after all – that they were considered incendiary. His office in Ramallah was attacked and smashed up by rioters.

AL-QAEDA IN THE CAMPS

The hopelessness of the refugee problem is considered a major source of radicalisation among young unemployed Palestinians in camps across the Middle East. Disillusioned by the peace process, they have adopted more religiously based, global ideologies, such as those of al-Qaeda, who see the wars in Iraq and Afghanistan, and the Arab-Israeli conflict, as all part of the same struggle.

Hundreds of Palestinians travelled to fight in Iraq, while in 2007, the Nahr al-Bared camp in Lebanon was all but destroyed after months of fighting between an al-Qaeda-inspired movement called Fatah al-Islam and the Lebanese army, which cost almost 500 lives. Increasingly violent and hardline groups have also sprung up in the Palestinian territories. In 2009, Hamas killed 22 members of a new faction called Jund Ansar Allah, which had accused Hamas of being too liberal and secular and declared the territory an 'Islamic emirate'.

Is deep-water **drilling** inherently **dangerous**?

From 20 April *until 15 July 2010, when BP finally managed to bring its leaking deep-water Macondo well under control, almost five million barrels of oil escaped into the Gulf of Mexico from the sea bed. The largest oil spill in history, it was a direct result of the hazardous, highly unpredictable conditions under which BP was trying to extract it (see box). And though 75 per cent of the slick had dispersed by August 2010, according to the US government, the effects on the deep undersea environment remain unknown. That's why environmental groups such as Greenpeace are calling for a moratorium on all deep-sea drilling projects around the world until the risks are better understood. And that includes off the coast of Britain, where the big oilfields of the North Sea are exhausted and the future of exploration lies deep under the sea to the east of the Shetland Isles.*

How did the White House respond to the disaster?

As the scale of the Gulf of Mexico spill became clear, President Obama declared a popular six-month moratorium on deep-water drilling off the USA – halting oil production on 33 rigs in the Gulf. And to pay for the clean-up, federal officials began considering a new tax on oil production – one of the most heavily subsidised businesses in the USA, with tax breaks available at every stage of the exploration and extraction process. Congressional Budget Office figures showed that oilfield leases, drilling gear and other capital investments were effectively taxed at 9 per cent, compared to an overall business average of 25 per cent.

What was the reaction to such proposals?

A rising backlash from the friends of Big Oil, who argued that such drilling and such subsidies were essential to America's economic and energy security. The six-month ban, they said, would put at least 20,000 jobs at risk. The Gulf – which according to the American Petroleum Institute accounts for 30 per cent of US oil production, 80 per cent of which comes from deep-water areas – was losing precious rigs as they move away to other seas, increasing US reliance on foreign oil. The US moratorium ended in October 2010, and the issuing of new drilling permits resumed. Meanwhile, Norway, New Zealand, Canada and the UK all continued deep-water

drilling after the disaster. Australia offered 31 new off-shore leases, some for drilling at depths twice as great as the Macondo well; Brazil committed to spending $200bn in five years to extract oil from newly discovered reserves four miles beneath the sea.

Why the focus on deep water?

Because in Western-friendly regions of the world, easily accessible oil and gas have largely been extracted, while in the main oil-producing regions – places such as Saudi Arabia (which claims to have 25 per cent of global reserves), Russia, Iran and Venezuela – Big Oil has, over the past 30 years, found itself frozen out by the state-controlled national oil companies. In 1978, the 'Seven Sisters' – the big seven Western multinationals – controlled 78 per cent of the world oil reserves. Now there are only five (ExxonMobil, Royal Dutch Shell, BP, Total and Chevron), controlling less than 10 per cent. 'The days of easy oil,' says Michael Klare of the Institute for Policy Studies, 'are over.'

So they have to drill in deep water?

Pretty much. There are still regions – West Africa, Angola, the Peruvian Amazon – where oil is more accessible, though as critics point out, Big Oil's pollution record in such areas is worse than in the Gulf of Mexico: it is thought that there are about 2,000 untreated spills in the Niger Delta alone. And though there are untapped reserves on land, such as Canada's tar sands, these are just as hard and costly to work. By contrast, deep-water drilling has presented Western governments with potentially vast new supplies of energy right on their doorsteps, and oil firms willing to undertake the risk of exploring them. Consider the Gulf of Mexico: in 1995, it was thought to be largely exhausted of oil. Then the USA gave deep-water exploration a boost by exempting companies from paying royalties on new oil finds – a policy that paid off last year with BP's discovery of the 'giant' Tiber oil-field, with its estimated four billion barrels of reserves. This was the field that the Deepwater Horizon rig was drilling when it exploded.

So is deep-water drilling inherently dangerous?

Oil companies say not, and point to their improving record in human and environmental safety. Spills in the USA have fallen by two-thirds since the 1970s, they say. But the BP disaster did much to challenge that impression. Meanwhile, the nature of deep-water exploration means companies reach ever-greater depths and use ever-more

---

Norway, New Zealand, Canada and the UK all continued deep-water drilling after the disaster. Brazil committed to spending $200bn in five years.

---

ambitious techniques to extract the oil. Big Oil is now moving into such environmentally sensitive areas as the Barents Sea off Norway, the deep seas off the Falklands and – if it can get its hands on the oil underneath it – the Arctic itself.

Why do they bother?

Because the sums still add up.

The early twenty-first century has been a rollercoaster for oil, with prices swooping from $10 a barrel to nearly $120 and then down again. In an ordinary market, this uncertainty might have prompted a switch to alternative fuels, but in such a carbon-dependent world that threat has been nullified, and Big Oil has managed to reap big profits while looking forward to years of rising demand. Deep-water drilling accounts for just two per cent of world oil consumption (in the end, BP's 'giant' find in the Gulf of Mexico may be enough to supply the world for a single weekend), but the rewards of pursuing it still outweigh the costs. World oil demand is expected to increase from today's 86 million barrels per day (mbd) to 115mbd in 2030. With old fields being depleted all the time, there are still great prizes to be found at the bottom of the sea.

PLUMBING THE DEPTHS

The average depth for off-shore oil wells off the US coast has tripled since 2000, to 644m (2,114ft), with some – such as BP's Tiber field – much, much deeper. When it exploded in 2010, Deepwater Horizon, a rig responsible for some of mankind's deepest oil finds, was drilling at around 1,524m (5,000ft). At such depths, there is no sunlight, the temperature is just above freezing, and water pressure is 2,300lbs per square inch (enough to crush an ordinary submarine), placing such wells far beyond the reach of divers and most submarines. Only specially built Remote Operated Vehicles (ROVs) were able to intervene and attempt to plug the Macondo well.

The huge pressure and temperature differences between the top and bottom of the well – the surface of the Gulf of Mexico is 30°C warmer than the floor – make deep-water exploration inherently prone to 'blowouts'. Water, oil, debris and methane shoot up in a slushy, liquid form, expanding and changing their state: from solids to liquids and explosive gases. Being so far from the surface also makes deep-water drilling a messy business. At extreme depths, companies can only extract around 10 per cent of reported finds, while a further 2–5 per cent is wasted at the sea floor. The risk of such wastage – or, in the case of the BP well, spillage – is little understood, owing to our scant knowledge of the deep undersea environment.

What
causes
a tsunami ?

Typically, an earthquake under the seafloor. The plates that form the Earth's crust grind against each other, sometimes moving the seabed up and down. If this happens, hundreds of cubic miles of water can be displaced in a moment, and a massive wave or series of waves is formed. In the open sea, these waves can be imperceptible, even though they can move at speeds of around 500mph. When they approach shallower waters, however, they slow down, the volume of water piles up, and they can rise to heights of 30ft or more. This tremendous build-up of energy creates the tsunamis' destructive force and drives the water much further inland than other freak waves. Tsunami means 'harbour wave' in Japanese.

How often do they happen?

Small ones occur frequently as a result of minor earthquakes. Major tsunamis are rare. An asteroid collision 3.5 billion years ago is thought to have caused the greatest wave of all time, which swept around the Earth several times. In the past century, there were around 25 tsunamis, one of which created the highest wave ever recorded (see box). Most occurred in the Pacific Ocean, triggered by the intense geological activity in the 'Ring of Fire', a jigsaw of tectonic plates reaching from Indonesia to the coast of Chile. The 2011 Tohoku tsunami, which killed more than 15,000 and caused a series of nuclear accidents, and the 2009 disaster in Samoa, American Samoa and Tonga both occurred in this region, as have around 60 per cent of all known tsunamis. A further 25 per cent of tsunamis have happened in the Mediterranean, 12 per cent in the Atlantic and 4 per cent in the Indian Ocean. However, the catastrophe of 26 December 2004 in the Indian Ocean killed 230,000 people and was the most devastating ever recorded.

Are tsunamis becoming more frequent?

Probably. There is a theory that the 2004 tsunami, which was caused by a magnitude 9 earthquake, was so powerful that it weakened geological faultlines around the world and caused intense and ongoing seismic activity. Scientists in the journal *Nature* reported that there had been an unusually high number of magnitude 8 earthquakes in 2005 and 2006, and that the 2004 quake had caused increased seismic energy in the San Andreas fault, 5,000 miles away.

Have tsunamis struck the UK?

Not recently. The most significant occurred in 6100 BC, when a huge landslide off the coast of Norway caused a 70ft-high tsunami that swept over the east coast of Scotland. Sediment from the event has been found up to 50 miles inland. In 1607, 'mighty hilles of water' were seen surging up the Bristol Channel. They killed an estimated 2,000 people and flooded an area of 200 sq miles. Some scientists think it was a tsunami caused by a landslide on the Irish coast. In November 1755, the great Lisbon earthquake, which killed between 60,000 and 100,000 people, caused a tsunami that reached as far as Finland and the West Indies. Cornwall was struck by waves 6ft high.

Is there any reason to expect more?

No immediately obvious ones, but geologists say we should not be complacent. If the Cumbre Vieja volcano in the Canary Islands erupted, for instance, a mass of rock could slip into the sea and cause a tsunami that would overwhelm Europe's Atlantic shore, threaten the eastern United States and hit the south coast of England with waves 32ft high. There is also a possibility of a repeat of the ancient Norwegian slide. In 2003, geologists noticed that frozen methane beneath the ocean floor was melting, weakening a

---

If the Cumbre Vieja volcano erupted, the tsunami could overwhelm Europe's Atlantic shore, threaten the eastern United States and hit the south coast of England with waves 32ft high.

---

section of the continental shelf. They concluded that it could fall away in the next 200 years.

Is that down to climate change?

Almost certainly. Scientists have warned that earthquakes, volcanic eruptions, landslides and tsunamis could become more common as climate change affects the Earth's crust. They say that when ice sheets and glaciers melt, a weight is lifted from the tectonic plates below, which rise up, causing seismic events. 'Climate change doesn't just affect the atmosphere and the oceans but the Earth's crust as well. The whole Earth is an interactive system,' says Professor Bill McGuire, director of the Aon Benfield Hazard Research Centre of University College London.

Can tsunamis be predicted?

Up to a point. When an earthquake happens under the sea, geologists can determine within minutes whether a tsunami is likely. The Pacific Tsunami Warning System (PTWS) works this way, and most countries that border the ocean practise evacuation procedures. The Indian Ocean now also has a similar system. However, as the 2009 disaster shows, warnings are only useful if the earthquake occurs hundreds of miles off the coast. On that occasion, the PTWS headquarters in Hawaii issued an alert just 18 minutes after the earthquake, but by that time waves had already started crashing into Samoa and American Samoa, which were only 120 miles away from the epicentre. The problem is that scientists are still not able to predict earthquakes. The best defence for communities in high-risk areas is to recognise the signs – an earthquake, an unusual receding of the sea – and then head for high ground as fast as possible.

What about sea defences?

Japan has built walls up to 15ft tall to protect its coast from tsunamis, but they haven't always helped – the tsunami in March 2011 was as much as 20ft high in places. And 100ft waves swamped the small island of Okushiri in the Sea of Japan on 12 July 1993. The harbour of Aonae was surrounded by a tsunami wall, but the waves washed over it, destroying all the wood structures in the town. More than 100 people died, and the tsunami caused $600m of damage to Japan's west coast. That said, natural barriers, including shoreline trees, have been known to slow tsunamis. In 2004, the village of Naluvedapathy in southern India suffered minimal damage because the wave broke against 80,244 trees that had been planted two years earlier in a bid to enter the *Guinness Book of Records*.

'ALL HELL HAS BROKEN LOOSE IN HERE'

The highest wave ever recorded tore through a narrow bay in Alaska on a summer's night in 1958. Three boats were in Lituya Bay when a magnitude 7.7 earthquake hit at 10.17pm. The bay, long associated with bad luck, lies on top of the Fairweather Fault, one of the most active in the world, and during the earthquake 90 million cubic feet of earth, rock and ice were torn from a glacier at its inland edge.

'Have you ever seen a 15,000ft mountain twist and shake and dance? I hadn't either,' said Howard Ulrich, who was with his seven-year-old son on their fishing boat, the *Edrie*. Ulrich saw the landslide fall into the bay and cause a wave which was 1,720ft (524m) high when it struck the opposite side – taller than the Empire State Building. By the time the wave hit the *Edrie*, it was 120ft tall. 'Mayday! Mayday! All hell broke loose – I think we've had it – goodbye!' he radioed. Amazingly, the *Edrie* and another boat survived. A third boat, carrying two people, was lost. No one else in the bay was killed.

Are public libraries finished?

Britain still had *just over 4,500 public lending libraries in 2010 – one for every 13,000 or so people. But there are unlikely to be so many a few years from now. Around 500 libraries, just over 10 per cent, have been identified as likely victims of the government's ongoing spending cuts, as local authorities across the country contend with reductions in their budgets – 20 per cent, in some cases. Oxfordshire County Council initially said that 20 out of its 43 libraries might close; Dorset could shut 20 out of 34; North Yorkshire 24 out of 42. The Isle of Wight may soon have only two left – nine of its 11 libraries are facing closure.*

Why are libraries so hard hit?

Because of the way local authorities were asked to cut back. The total budget for councils will be cut by 27 per cent by 2015, and more than half the cuts came in 2011–2012. This 'front-loading' made standalone services like libraries the most obvious targets to pick. Libraries were also targeted because, on most indices, they're in decline: anachronistic places with shrinking book collections, shabby exteriors and inconvenient opening hours. The idyll of the workingmen's reading room, or the quiet corner where children come and experience literature for the first time, no longer exists.

How long have we had libraries?

They first appeared in ancient Greece and Egypt: an inscription above the door of the library at Thebes called them 'the medicine chest of the soul'. Around 300 BC, under the guidance of Aristotle's disciple Demetrius, King Ptolemy I of Egypt began collecting scrolls for the library at Alexandria, eventually amassing half a million. In Britain, libraries for scholars, the clergy and other respectable citizens became common in the seventeenth century, before the novel and the growth of reading for pleasure gave rise to commercial circulating libraries run by W.H. Smith, Boots and the Times Book Club in the nineteenth century. But it was the Public Libraries Act of 1850 – part of the great wave of Victorian social reforms – that recognised the library as a key public service.

Was it a huge success?

Not at first. The Public Libraries Act was introduced in the teeth of resistance from the Conservative Party, one of whose MPs argued: 'The more education people get, the more difficult they are to manage.' At first councils were forbidden to raise more than a halfpenny in the pound in taxes for their libraries, or to spend the money on books – funding had to come from philanthropists such as Andrew Carnegie, who helped stock around 380 of the new public libraries. But the libraries were popular among temperance campaigners and working people – miners in South Wales contributed to the building of more than 100 – and by the 1920s they were fondly regarded across the UK. 'I ransack public libraries and find them full of sunk treasure,' Virginia Woolf wrote in her diary in 1921. Public libraries reached their zenith in the 1960s, under Harold Wilson's Labour government, when councils increased funding by 50 per cent and set about buying 250 new books per year for every 1,000 people they served.

When did the decline begin?

With the oil shocks and spending cuts of the 1970s, after which came a gradual, seemingly unstoppable, fall in the number of books, users and loans. In 1984, public libraries in England

239

made about 650 million loans; in 2007–2008, they made just 269 million. The eroding of funding meant that by 2000, only 25 libraries in the country stayed open for more than 60 hours a week, to provide a place for people to read in the evenings. Library campaigners describe a vicious circle in which a local library (often a dilapidated Victorian hall) begins to cut its new acquisitions and opening hours and slowly becomes inaccessible, unwelcoming and unwanted: the public starts to get its books elsewhere. Book sales in the UK have increased by 13 per cent since 2004, and bookshops increasingly offer places to sit, drink coffee and spend time.

So are libraries finished?

Not at all. The number of loans and books on the shelves may have declined, but libraries have actually maintained their visitor numbers in recent years, at around 300 million a year. People now come for more than the books. Since 2000, libraries have been the mainstay of the 'People's Network', a Labour government attempt to spread digital technology which helped thousands of people find new jobs. Libraries also host book groups and local literature festivals. And at a time when people's lives are dominated by commercial transactions – buying and selling – anthropologists argue that libraries represent one of the last places that we borrow, return and share. And many still do it: more than 13 million Britons borrow at least one book, DVD or video from their local

The Public Libraries Act was resisted by the Conservative Party, one of whose MPs argued: 'The more education people get, the more difficult they are to manage.'

library each year. Not bad for 1 per cent of local authority funding.

So what should libraries do now?

Fighting back is not such a bad idea. In February 2011, more than 100 'Save Our Libraries' events were held across Britain, with 'National Libraries Day' following a year later, and some councils appeared taken aback by the depth of feeling among their library users. Northamptonshire immediately agreed to reconsider the closure of four libraries; Gloucestershire and Surrey also announced changes to their plans. More generally, libraries appear to be a likely early test case for David Cameron's Big Society: several councils hope to turn over dozens of libraries to volunteer groups to run in whatever way they see fit, while keeping a smaller number of council-run reading rooms open in the evenings, with a better supply of books. In the longer run, though – especially as electronic reading devices become more popular and books ever cheaper – libraries are going to have to work out whether they still exist primarily for books and reading, or for a wider range of social goods.

DO LIBRARIES STILL HAVE A ROLE?

YES

1. The number of visits to libraries has stabilised – at 300 million a year. Libraries still provide a service that people need.

2. Rebuilding programmes, late opening hours and reading groups have all been shown to reinvigorate libraries.

3. Libraries are civic institutions arranged for sharing. They fulfil an important role in an increasingly atomised society.

NO

1. More than 60 per cent of British adults never go to a public library, and many of the 40 per cent who do never open a book.

2. The internet, cheap books and comprehensive schooling have robbed the public library of its autodidactic function.

3. Libraries are for reading. If people want to use the internet, find jobs and have meetings, then let's have social clubs instead.

Why did the Rwandan genocide happen?

There is no genuine ethnic difference *between the two peoples involved: the Tutsi ('rich in cattle'), historically the ruling caste controlling the monarchy and army, are said to be taller than the Hutu ('servants'), who make up at least 80 per cent of the people of Rwanda and neighbouring Burundi. But both groups share the same language and inhabit the same regions. Once Rwanda and Burundi became independent in 1962, the Hutu's numerical supremacy enabled them to wrest power from the Tutsi who kept trying to reverse the new status quo only to find themselves the victims of reprisals. In fact, during the three years before the 1994 genocide there were 16 massacres of Tutsis organised by government officials, in each of which hundreds of civilians were killed.*

What triggered the violence in 1994?

The failure to secure a power-sharing agreement between Rwanda's Hutu-led government and the Tutsi-led rebels of the Rwanda Patriotic Front (RPF). The pact was to be supervised by a UN mission headed by Canadian general Romeo Dallaire, but the day before he arrived, in October 1993, the Hutu president of neighbouring Burundi was assassinated by Tutsi officials and Burundi slipped into civil war. This convinced Hutu extremists in the Rwandan government that it was time to eliminate the *Inyenzi* – or Tutsi 'cockroaches' – once and for all.

Was the genocide carefully organised?

Yes. Lists were drawn up of those to be killed and vast quantities of machetes, axes, hammers, razors and guns were bought with aid money and stockpiled. From this time on 'genocide hung in the air', as one observer put it. Then, on 5 April 1994, the new Hutu presidents of both Burundi and Rwanda were killed when the plane they were travelling in was shot down. In the ensuing political vacuum, Hutu militants – *Interahamwe* ('those who fight together') – set in motion long-laid plans for the eradication of the Tutsis. The first massacres were carried out by militias, but soon it became a free-for-all, as hundreds of thousands of men, women and children, urged on by radio broadcasts, became *genocidaires*, slaughtering friends, neighbours and even family members. 'Cut down the tall trees,' was their cry (see box).

Didn't the world try to prevent it?

In the spring of 1992, the Belgian Ambassador to Rwanda warned Brussels that the extremist Hutu clan, the Akazu, was 'planning the extermination of the Tutsi', yet Belgium did nothing to alert the world. The behaviour of France, which for geopolitical reasons had replaced Belgium as the foremost protector of Hutu power, was even worse. Akazu death squads received military training from France; Hutu extremists were always assured of a warm welcome in Paris and the flow of French arms to the Hutus continued throughout the genocide. Bill Clinton's government did consider jamming the genocidal radio broadcasts, but decided that the cost ($8,000 an hour) was too high. When the Czech Ambassador to the UN Security Council described the killings as a 'Holocaust', he was taken aside by British and US diplomats and told such inflammatory language was 'not helpful'.

How was the genocide reported?

There were very few reliable press

reports since there were at most
15 reporters in Rwanda to witness
the atrocities, though no fewer than
2,500 were celebrating the birth
of South Africa's new democracy
further south. Both General Dallaire,
leader of the UN peacekeepers, and
Jacques-Roger Booh-Booh, the UN
secretary-general's representative
in Rwanda, sent reports back to
the UN Security Council, but the
Council secretariat preferred to
believe Booh-Booh's optimistic pro-

When the Czech Ambassador
described the killings as a
'Holocaust', he was taken
aside by British and US
diplomats and told such
inflammatory language was
'not helpful'.

Hutu reports rather than Dallaire's
desperate pleas for help. So,
two weeks into the genocide, the
Council actually agreed to withdraw
most of the peacekeepers, reducing
their numbers from 2,548 to just
270. By mid-May, when it was
at last decided to send in 5,500
peacekeepers, it was too late.

Why did the UN handle things so badly?

Partly because the then UN
secretary-general, Boutros
Boutros-Ghali, was the wrong
man to deal with the crisis. As
Egypt's foreign minister, he
had developed links with Hutu
extremists, had singlehandedly
reversed Egypt's traditional ban
on selling weapons to Rwanda and
so was responsible for providing
the Hutus with much of the
weaponry used in the genocide.
Moreover he chose for the key
post of special representative in
Rwanda Jacques-Roger Booh-
Booh, a francophone African who
was also openly pro-Hutu and
kept putting an optimistic gloss
on developments. So did a third
African involved – Kofi Annan –
then head of UN peacekeeping
operations, who forbade the
peacekeepers in Rwanda from
engaging in arms inspections
despite repeated warnings from
General Dallaire of impending
massacre; and who failed to
pass on such information to the
Security Council – for which he
was later censured in a UN report.

Could the massacres have been prevented?

When the killings began, Boutros Boutros-Ghali refused to interrupt a European tour to deal with the situation and didn't allow any change in the role of the Rwandan peacekeepers on the grounds that he wasn't sure what was going on. Had their mandate been broadened to allow offensive action, and had they received support from the elite French, Belgian, and Italian troops sent in to evacuate their own citizens, many experts believe that they could have saved many lives, not least by deterring many ordinary Rwandans from joining in the killing.

And has Rwanda now returned to calm?

The genocide finally ended in July 1994, when the Tutsi rebel movement (the RPF), led by current president Paul Kagame, took power, forcing two million people into refugee camps in neighbouring Tanzania and Zaire. Kagame's Tutsi-dominated government brought a measure of stability to Rwanda, pursuing a policy of what might be called de-ethnicisation. People are told to think of themselves not as Hutu or Tutsi, but simply as Rwandan. And in some ways at least, they now appear to do so. Kagame was re-elected president with the support of over 90 per cent of voters. Yet the genocide left a terrible legacy. Moral ambiguities fester in every village as survivors of the massacre still live side by side with the perpetrators, most of whom remain unpunished.

ANATOMY OF A MASSACRE

Between 800,000 and one million Rwandans were butchered in just 100 days – shot, killed with grenades or hacked to death with machetes. Neighbours killed neighbours: even nuns and priests are known to have taken part. Most of the victims were Tutsi, but moderate Hutus who refused to take part in the killings were also slaughtered. The barbarity was truly horrific: mothers ordered to bury their children alive, mass slaughter by machete, babies having their brains dashed out on stones, the lopping off of limbs and genitalia before the final death thrust, the killings in churches of crowds who had sought refuge. The genocide left the country nearly 70 per cent female and an estimated 10,000 babies were born as a result of rapes perpetrated on women and girls in those three months.

The Khmer Rouge: can justice be done?

The trial *of Kaing Guek Eav, aka 'Comrade Duch', began in July 2009 in Cambodia. Duch was the commandant of 'S-21', a prison in the capital, Phnom Penh, where thousands of Cambodians were interrogated, starved and tortured, before being sent to the 'killing fields' outside the city to be beaten to death with an iron bar. Around 14,000 people were sent to S-21: only seven are thought to have survived. Duch admitted that he was responsible for what happened at S-21, but said he would have been killed himself if he had not obeyed orders.*

Who was he taking orders from?

The Communist Party of Kampuchea (Cambodia) – better known by its French colloquial name, the Khmer Rouge. Founded by a group of former exchange students who had studied at the Sorbonne, the Khmer Rouge began as a conventional Marxist movement. But when a former technology student called Pol Pot became the party's leader in 1962, it moved towards an extreme Maoist ideology that glorified rural peasantry and insisted on the subjugation of the individual to the 'Angka', or 'Organisation': the ruling body of the party (and Pol Pot was to become known as 'Brother Number One').

How did the Khmer Rouge come to power?

During the Vietnam War – under pressure from its Chinese and North Vietnamese neighbours – Cambodia allowed the communist Viet Cong to set up bases on its territory. As punishment, America launched a massive, secret bombing campaign against Cambodia. During one three-month period in 1973, American B-52s dropped more bombs on Cambodia than were dropped on Japan in the whole of the Second World War – the equivalent of five Hiroshimas. Between 1969 and 1973, American bombs killed at least 150,000 Cambodians. The effect was to destabilise the country and provoke a five-year civil war, which only ended in 1975, when 68,000 black-clad Khmer Rouge guerrillas marched into Phnom Penh.

Did they have popular support?

Initially people greeted the Khmer Rouge with joy, hoping they might bring peace. But within days, the new regime set about constructing its peasant utopia – by force. 'Year Zero' was declared. Thousands of people were driven out of cities and forced to work on collective farms. Private property, currency and religion were abolished. The national library was turned into a pig pen, and ancient Buddhist parchments were used by Khmer Rouge soldiers to roll cigarettes. In an effort to destroy family ties, children were separated from their parents and raised in collective nurseries. Strangers were forced to marry each other in mass ceremonies.

How bloody was the regime?

In four years of Khmer Rouge rule, between 1.7 million and 2.2 million Cambodians died – out of a population of 8 million. Most were killed by exhaustion and starvation on collective farms. But at least 500,000 people were deliberately murdered by the paranoid regime. Having an education, speaking a foreign language, wearing glasses or using a toothbrush could mark you out as a capitalist traitor. Even picking wild fruit was deemed 'private enterprise', punishable by death. 'Angka has as many eyes as a pineapple,' warned posters. 'Angka sees everything you do.' Suspects were tortured, made to 'confess' and beaten to death because bullets were scarce. 'To keep you is no benefit. To destroy you is no loss,' was the regime's motto.

How was the regime toppled?

The Khmer Rouge turned against communist Vietnam and began cross-border raids in the late 1970s. In 1978, Vietnam invaded Cambodia, drove out the regime with the help of a Khmer Rouge defector, Hun Sen, and installed its own government. Pol Pot and his comrades fled into the jungle bordering Thailand; but they were not yet finished. Cold War America and the West refused to recognise communist Vietnam's government in Phnom Penh, and gave secret support to the Khmer Rouge's guerrilla campaign against the new regime. Refugee camps just inside the Thai border were used by the Khmer Rouge to regroup. Many former Khmer Rouge leaders got jobs with NGOs and UN agencies. Comrade Duch became a Christian and took a job with the American Refugee Committee. Pol Pot, meanwhile, directed guerrilla

operations from his comfortable headquarters in Thailand.

When did the Khmer Rouge admit defeat?

After 1993, when UN-backed elections established a new coalition government headed by Hun Sen, the Khmer Rouge lost its international backers. Its power base dwindled away, and in 1997 it agreed to lay down arms. That

---

In four years of Khmer Rouge rule, between 1.7 million and 2.2 million Cambodians died – out of a population of 8 million.

---

same year, the party – now eager to disassociate itself from past crimes – arrested Pol Pot and charged him with treason. The former leader died in their custody in 1998, still insisting: 'My conscience is clear.'

Why were no Khmer Rouge members tried before Duch?

Partly because suspects were hard

to find – Comrade Duch was tracked down by a journalist, Nic Dunlop, in 1999 – and partly because much of Cambodia's leadership was drawn from the Khmer Rouge. Hun Sen remains PM, and the head of his parliament and party are both former Khmer Rouge comrades. Although it was Hun Sen who first asked the UN for a tribunal, he soon showed a marked lack of enthusiasm for the court – suggesting that it would be better to 'dig a hole and bury the past'.

What did the trials achieve?

It is hard to say. Cambodia does not have the death penalty, so Duch was sentenced to 35 years in prison, which was extended to life imprisonment in 2012. His trial took so long that the other suspects awaiting trial were not even indicted until 2010 – three of their trials began in 2011; proceedings against a fourth were suspended pending a 'health evaluation' of her mental fitness. But the trials have a symbolic value: although most Cambodians are too young to remember the atrocities, polls show that 69 per cent want some kind of justice.

SURVIVING S-21

The trial of Duch allowed the handful of people who survived S-21 to come forward and describe their experiences. One, a 79-year-old man called Chum Mey, told the court how he was arrested in 1977 and accused of spying for the CIA. He was taken to the prison with his wife, whom he never saw again. 'I will never forget my suffering at S-21, as long as I live,' said Mey, who was electrocuted and had his toenails torn off. 'When I entered the room, I didn't expect to survive. I just laid on my back, waiting to be killed.' He was allowed to live because his guards discovered he was a mechanic who could fix cars, sewing machines and tractors.

Another survivor, Vann Nath, told the tribunal he escaped death by painting a portrait of Pol Pot for his jailers. He was ordered to keep painting portraits, and kept alive on six teaspoons of rice porridge a day. 'We were so hungry, we would eat insects. We would quickly grab and eat them so we could avoid being seen by the guards,' said Nath. 'When the guards saw it they hit me until I spat out the grasshopper or insect. I even thought eating human flesh would be a good meal.'

Homeopathy:
quackery
or cure
?

Homeopathy originated *in the late eighteenth century. A German physician, Samuel Hahnemann, developed a form of medicine based on the idea that like cures like. His 'Law of Similars' proposed that patients could be cured by taking a diluted dose of a substance that caused symptoms similar to those afflicting them. Coffee, for example, could be used to treat insomnia, stinging nettles skin complaints. Modern homeopathic remedies are prepared by repeatedly diluting substances in water and shaking the bottle. Homeopaths believe that dilution strengthens the remedy – so much so, that many remedies do not even contain the original substance, but rely on the water's 'memory' of it to induce the cure.*

And did homeopathy quickly gain a following?

It became extremely popular in the nineteenth century, when dozens of clinics opened in Europe and the USA to treat cholera, yellow fever and influenza. Anecdotal evidence suggests that their water-based remedies proved more effective than the unsanitary, uncertain, often downright dangerous rival medicines of the day, and homeopathy thus established a reputation that has not only endured – the Queen, Prince Charles and other members of the royal family are well-known advocates – but grown. The European homeopathy market grew 60 per cent in the last decade, while the British market is worth more than £40m, with 54,000 people receiving homeopathic treatment on the NHS in 2009.

When did the NHS start offering homeopathy?

Since its inception. Back in 1948, ministers declared that homeopathy would be publicly funded for as long as there were 'patients wishing to receive it and doctors willing to provide it'. Today there are four NHS homeopathic hospitals (a fifth closed in 2009) run at a total cost of around £4m per year. But the treatment is controversial because homeopathic remedies – unlike all other medication offered by the NHS – are not evaluated by the National Institute for Health and Clinical Excellence (Nice), for their efficacy and value for money. A recent survey found that 80 per cent of GPs want the NHS to stop offering homeopathy.

And is there any scientific basis for it?

The NHS's own website sounded

the doubts. 'The claim that water has a memory,' it said, 'is a controversial one to say the least.' (The website's homeopathy content was removed in late 2011, to be 'revised as part of our regular content review process'.) And the Commons Science and Technology Committee, in one of its regular 'evidence checks' of government policy, concluded that, on available evidence, there was nothing to suggest that homeopathic remedies had any benefit beyond a 'placebo effect', and recommended that homeopathy no longer be funded by the NHS. It also questioned the rigour of homeopathic doctors. The director of the Royal London Homeopathic Hospital, for example, was unable to say exactly how much shaking a typical remedy required. 'That has not been fully investigated,' admitted Dr Peter Fisher. 'You have to shake it vigorously ... if you stir it gently, it does not work.'

How do homeopaths counter that?

They argue that, on the contrary, there have been more than 140 medical trials on the subject and that 44 per cent of these reported positive results. Presenting evidence to the MPs, the British Homeopathic Association (BHA) put forward five reviews of the practice, four of which, it claimed, had 'reached the qualified conclusion that homeopathy differs from placebo'. But it appears that the BHA had seriously misrepresented the conclusions of three of the four reports. For example, the author of one of them, Jean-

---

Britain's first professor of complementary medicine said that, although initially sympathetic to homeopathy, he had changed his mind. 'You may as well take a glass of water.'

Pierre Boissel of the University Claude Bernard in France, had indeed argued that homeopathy 'differs' from the placebo effect – but only to say that, according to the best-designed studies, it appears to make things worse. Another expert cited by the BHA, the University of Exeter's Edzard

Ernst, Britain's first professor of complementary medicine, said that, although initially sympathetic to homeopathy, he had changed his mind after carrying out trials on the efficacy of homeopathic remedies in treating asthma and bruising. 'You may as well take a glass of water,' he concluded.

Doesn't that put an end to the argument?

No: homeopaths and supporters of complementary medicine insist that mainstream medicine, with its randomised trials and peer-review system, is prejudiced against them and has yet to uncover the sub-atomic physics that would validate homeopathy. For now the real test, they say, is how patients feel after treatment. 'It doesn't matter how it works,' says Dr Michael Dixon of the Foundation for Integrated Health, a body set up by Prince Charles. 'What matters is whether it helps them get better.'

And how do patients feel after treatment?

A six-year survey of Bristol's NHS homeopathic hospital found that 70 per cent of patients felt some improvement, supporting the BHA's claim that, for people with chronic or otherwise untreatable conditions, homeopathy offers a cheap, safe and comforting alternative. Indeed, a large part of its appeal, argues Professor Ernst, is that cared-for feeling. While a GP might only give a patient ten minutes, a homeopath might give them an hour. 'Homeopaths tend to be gentle, understanding people,' says Prof Professor. 'In my view, it is this care and attention that helps people feel better.'

So where lies the harm in that?

In the danger, say critics, that people come to see homeopathy as a credible alternative to life-saving, conventional medicine. There are many cases of patients shunning vaccines and drugs for heart problems, malaria and even cancer, in favour of homeopathic remedies. When David Colquhoun, professor of pharmacology at University College, London, asked several pharmacists which 'natural' pills they would prescribe for his grandchild's severe diarrhoea, he was horrified that only one advised him to choose a conventional rehydration treatment or go to the doctor. 'It really is very simple,' says Colquhoun. 'There is nothing in the pills.'

SHOULD THE NHS PROVIDE HOMEOPATHY?

YES	NO
1. 70 per cent of patients, many with chronic conditions, report good results with homeopathy. Why reject their experience?	1. NHS endorsement gives homeopathy a spurious legitimacy which can lead people to reject effective medicine.
2. Compared to conventional medicine, homeopathic remedies are incredibly cheap and in 200 trials they've been found effective.	2. It is immoral to waste money on homeopathy while denying people access to medicines that are proven to work.
3. The NHS funds lots of people/ practices that have no 'evidence base': hospital chaplains, for example. Why not homeopathy?	3. The 'science' behind homeopathy is eighteenth-century hokum as the evidence before the Commons' committee well attests.

What is
high-
speed **trading** ?

It's money-making by the millisecond. *By harnessing massive computer power to spot momentary, minuscule changes in value, and buy and sell stocks in the blink of an eye, high-speed traders can make huge profits. The technique was pioneered in the early years of this decade by a New York hedge fund, Renaissance, which hired astrophysicists, mathematicians and statisticians to devise electronic trading programs. Other firms, including Goldman Sachs and Credit Suisse, quickly followed suit. Few outside the securities industry knew much about the practice until computer glitches helped cause the Dow Jones Index to plummet 700 points in about 15 minutes in May 2010 – a 'flash crash' unprecedented in its depth and speed. High-speed trading (also called 'high-frequency trading' or HFT) now accounts for up to 70 per cent of all trading in shares listed on the New York Stock Exchange. In the London market, the figure is at least 40 per cent, and growing.*

What advantage does HFT provide?

Two-tenths of a second is enough to give traders an edge. Using a high-speed system, they can buy into a stock rally or sell into a decline slightly ahead of the pack, gaining a more favourable price than ordinary investors making the same trade a fraction of a second later. The advantage rarely amounts to more than a couple of pence, but over millions of transactions it can add up to tens of millions of pounds. High-speed trading 'is where all the money is getting made', said William Donaldson, former head of the New York Stock Exchange. 'If an individual investor doesn't have the means to keep up, they're at a huge disadvantage.'

How does it work?

HFT trading firms, from Wall Street powerhouses like Goldman Sachs to little-known shops with a handful of employees, electronically scan markets to exploit tiny price differences in the same stock as it trades on different exchanges. This was impossible when big stock exchanges had monopolies over trade in their stocks, but deregulation of exchanges in the USA has resulted in a complex matrix of nine exchanges and dozens more trading platforms. In 2007, Europe also deregulated, ushering in a welter of new exchanges, each with slightly different trading systems, speeds and fee schedules (the London Stock Exchange's share of trading

in British stocks fell from 96 per cent to 51 per cent in just two years). The resulting variation in what traders call 'latency' – the time it takes for data to travel through a given system – is what has created the opportunities for high-speed trading.

Do exchanges encourage HFT?

Yes, because they live or die by their ability to offer clients faster and faster transactions. Seeking to offer ever-lower latency, many stock exchanges now allow some traders – for a fee – a few milliseconds' preview of bulk orders for the buying or selling of a given share. 'It's a rigged game,' said Sal Arnuk of brokerage firm Themis Trading. Some HFT traders go further, paying a stock exchange for the right to install computer servers right next to the exchange's own servers, a practice known as 'co-location'. The physical proximity to the exchange server can shave crucial milliseconds off the time it takes for a firm's buy or sell orders to be executed. Academic studies have found that shaving one millisecond off every trade can be worth $100m a year to a large high-speed trading firm.

Does HFT distort markets?

Its fans claim it makes markets more efficient by constantly adding liquidity, meaning they generate so much activity that normal market participants can quickly find buyers and sellers for their trades. Critics counter that high-speed traders are simply exploiting an expensive technological advantage – high-speed computer systems can cost $250m – to gain unearned profits. 'They're like locusts,' said professional trader Joe Saluzzi. 'They come in, swarm the market, squeeze as much as they can, and when they're done they'll just move on to the next market.' There is growing concern that the practice is at odds with the traditional function of stock markets: to raise capital for companies by means of orderly and fair price discovery. And the perception that HFT traders are gaming the markets for their own ends (a large part of the business is in proprietary trades) could deter companies from floating shares in the first place.

Do small investors get hurt?

Yes, but without knowing it. High-speed traders take some of the profits that would have gone to slower investors. Institutional investors, such as pension funds and insurance companies, also suffer. Such large institutions conduct massive, multimillion-dollar stock trades: high-speed traders can sniff these out using pattern-recognition algorithms and

---

Many stock exchanges now allow some traders – for a fee – a few milliseconds' preview of bulk orders for the buying or selling of a given share. 'It's a rigged game.'

---

then use their speed advantage to buy before an institution buys (which sends the price up), or sell before it sells (sending the price down). This 'front-running' reduces the returns to the big funds, and ultimately, to pensioners.

What's being done about it?

The major stock exchanges

installed 'circuit breakers' to temporarily halt trading in a stock if its price moves more than ten per cent up or down within five minutes. But even if breakers reduce the risk of a huge collapse, they can't level the HFT playing field, which is still largely unregulated. All it takes to set up an HFT firm in the UK is company registration and the necessary technology. But regulators may be about to take firmer action. In 2010, the Bank of England's director of financial stability, Andy Haldane, attacked HFT on the grounds that the rest of society gains nothing from such trading, yet must bear its potentially disastrous risks. It is no coincidence, Haldane argues, that the rise of high-speed trading coincides with the lowest equity returns for ordinary investors for almost a century – but extraordinary profits for City and Wall Street financiers.

THE SERVERS THAT RUN THE WORLD

'Guys, this is probably the craziest I've seen it down here ever!' shouted a trader at the Chicago Futures Exchange on 6 May 2010 as, in full panic mode, he and his fellow traders frenziedly sold off stocks. Meanwhile, in a quiet, air-conditioned room in Jersey City, the only sound was the hum emitted by hundreds of Dell and Hewlett-Packard computer servers, all serenely spitting out sell orders by the hundreds of thousands.

Like the plot of a sci-fi movie, the 'flash crash' appears to have been a triumph of machines over humans. Securities regulators suspect it started when a clerk entered an erroneous price for a transaction. High-speed trading algorithms spotted the anomaly and reacted with a cascade of orders to sell, sending markets plunging before humans could intervene. Three other cases of algorithms running amok have been reported in the past six months – the latest at the Osaka Stock Exchange. 'Why pretend that people are in control?' asked *Wall Street Journal* blogger Evan Newmark. Our wealth is at the mercy 'of a bunch of computers making ugly, messy love with each other'.

What's the point of
a £30bn
train set
?

The plan is *to build a new high-speed rail (HSR) route between London and Birmingham on which trains will travel at 250mph. Eighteen trains an hour, carrying 1,100 passengers, will cut the current journey time from 84 to 49 minutes. Costing £17bn, the line will be the first phase of a £30bn, Y-shaped network that extends to Manchester in the North West and Leeds in the centre of the country, eventually cutting around one hour off journey times between the capital and Britain's largest cities. It will take a while to happen though: construction will not begin until 2017, and the London to Birmingham line will not be running before 2026.*

And what's it for?

The idea is to unify the 'economic geography' of the UK, improving the movement of goods and people between the country's largest conurbations. According to the Department for Transport, Britain's main railway lines will be suffering serious overcrowding – of both passengers and freight – by the 2020s, and no amount of tweaking and expanding our original nineteenth-century network will change that. Motorways and air travel are unattractive alternatives, given Britain's pledge to cut its carbon emissions by 80 per cent by 2050, which leaves HSR, in the government's view, as the cleanest, fastest option. A study by accounting group KPMG predicts huge economic benefits in better connecting the UK's major cities, with up to 42,000 extra jobs being created – and increased tax receipts of £10bn per year by 2040.

Didn't the rest of Europe go high-speed ages ago?

Yes. France has more than 1,200 miles (1,950km) of fast track on which TGV trains reach speeds of 200mph, more than double the 335 miles that the UK is planning. Spain, which didn't start building HSR until the 1990s, now has 1,000 miles (1,600km) in operation and a further 1,300 miles (2,100km) under construction. And HSR is not just a European phenomenon. There are 1,400 miles (2,250km) of high-speed track in Japan – where the first HSR line opened in 1964 – and China will have 6,000 miles of high-speed track open by 2012. In the USA, where there are plans for a nationwide HSR network by 2030, President Obama has dedicated $8bn of stimulus funds to the project.

And have these schemes been judged a success?

France delights in its TGV (Train à Grande Vitesse) service, which celebrated its 25th anniversary in 2006 and has now been exported to South Korea, Italy and Taiwan. The TGV's 250,000 daily passengers make journeys that, in terms of distance travelled, would take twice as long in the UK, and which are the major source of revenue for the SNCF, France's national rail operator. In Spain, high-speed trains began running between Madrid and Barcelona in 2008, cutting a four-hour journey to 2hr 38min. Before the line opened, 90 per cent of travellers flew between the cities, but rail passengers now outnumber those who travel by plane, despite higher ticket prices. Proponents of HSR claim that it will soon replace air travel as Europe's preferred method of transport for journeys of up to 750 miles – the distance between London and Florence.

Won't it carve up the countryside?

Yes it will. The UK's proposed route will require the demolition of

440 homes (mostly around Euston station in London and the site of a new station, on Curzon Street, in Birmingham). And the building of a swathe of track, tunnels and viaducts through the Chiltern hills will do irreparable damage to an area of outstanding natural beauty. The Campaign to Protect Rural England has voiced 'major concerns' about the route, but there is no conceivable alternative that would not also face fierce

---

The environmental case for HSR is most clear-cut when it reduces the need for domestic air travel. But there is no air travel between Birmingham and London.

---

local opposition. But even if that is seen as a necessary cost, there are still doubts about the overall cost and environmental benefits.

Surely there is no doubt it will help cut carbon emissions?

The environmental case for HSR is at its most clear-cut when it reduces the need for domestic air travel – as in Spain and Japan – or diverts passengers from roads. But currently there is no air travel between Birmingham and London (and only 21 flights a day from Manchester, out of a total of more than 2,000 flights to the capital). What's more, the government envisages that 20 per cent of passengers on the new line will be 'induced' or extra travellers, in other words, people who would not otherwise be making the journey and who thus can't be said to be diverted from the roads. The railways themselves are only as green as the power stations supplying electricity. And with the UK behind schedule to meet its target of 40 per cent of energy from 'low-carbon' sources in 2020, the environmental impact of the new HSR network would be, at best, neutral.

And is this really a time to be spending an extra £30bn?

Britain's motorway network was planned in 1943, at the height of the Second World War, so there is no necessary reason why a government should be deterred from handling major capital projects – such as London's Crossrail and Olympics – during a recession. But with most areas of public spending being severely cut, there are plenty who argue that the money could be better spent. For that sum, says the consultancy group ANS, it would be possible to equip every business in the UK with a high-definition video-conferencing unit, reducing the need for business travel in the first place. Critics of HSR in Europe say the schemes have redirected investment from regional and suburban routes – where commuters still choose cars over trains – in favour of intercity lines that were pretty good already. 'The last thing people want is service cuts, higher fares and more potholes,' says Stephen Joseph, of the Campaign for Better Transport, 'while the executive classes are treated to gleaming new high-speed trains.'

DOES BRITAIN NEED A HIGH-SPEED RAIL LINK?

YES

1. It is a disgrace that the world's first railway nation is lagging behind its international competitors, by decades in some cases.

2. In the long term, HSR will help control carbon emissions by attracting traffic away from cars and planes.

3. The trains will bring Britain's cities closer together, creating thousands of jobs and billions in tax receipts.

NO

1. HSR benefits countries where cities are far apart – like the USA or Spain. Speed is not the UK's main rail problem.

2. The carbon impact is likely to be neutral, and the new line will ruin one of Britain's most precious 'green lungs'.

3. £30bn of transport investment could be better spent on improving commuter rail networks.

Why did the Catholic **Church cover** up **child abuse** ?

The received wisdom *was that bishops and archbishops in the Irish Catholic Church were as surprised as anybody by the avalanche of allegations of sexual abuse that followed the first high-profile prosecution for child abuse of an Irish priest (Father Brendan Smyth) in 1994. But a three-year commission led by Judge Yvonne Murphy, investigating the way the Dublin Archdiocese had handled the issue, concluded in 2009 that the last four archbishops of Dublin had known about the crimes of their priests, but had concealed them for over 20 years.*

What sort of crimes?

The full extent of the scandal was spelled out in the five volumes of the Ryan Report, a horrifying catalogue of sexual, physical and emotional abuse meted out to thousands of children who passed through Catholic-run institutions between 1914 and 2000, notably those run by the Christian Brothers (see box). The Murphy Report also contained confessions by abusers (one priest estimated that he had abused a child every fortnight for 25 years; another that he'd attacked more than 100 children). But the inquiry's focus was on the cover-up, not the abuse itself.

What did Murphy find?

That bishops and the Garda

(Irish police) colluded to head off investigations of child abuse, and shuffled sex-offending priests from parish to parish, without letting their new congregations know why. Some offenders were promoted. 'The Dublin Archdiocese's preoccupations in dealing with cases of child sexual abuse, at least until the mid-1990s, were the maintenance of secrecy, avoidance of scandal, protection of the reputation of the Church and the preservation of its assets,' said the report. Rather than being on 'a learning curve' about child abuse, as church authorities claimed in the 1990s, successive archbishops had kept the details of allegations against 28 priests in a safe to which only they had the key. As early as 1986, the Archdiocese sought special insurance to protect it from lawsuits arising from child abuse.

How did it get round the law?

Because the archbishops were treated as if it didn't apply to them. For years, senior Garda officers deemed the church to be outside their remit: right up until November 1995, when Archbishop (now Cardinal) Desmond Connell handed over the names of 17 suspected child abusers, the state allowed 'Church institutions to be beyond the reach of the normal law-enforcement processes'.

In some cases, the Garda even handed over allegations to bishops rather than investigate themselves. In the 1980s, during a criminal investigation of Father Bill Carney – a notorious abuser who preyed on boys and girls at swimming pools – the report found that one of the archdiocese bishops used to visit the officer handling the case, 'maybe once or twice a month'. And as the Ryan Report noted, the education authorities were no better than the police.

How did they collude in the abuse?

The Ryan Report showed how Ireland's Education Department had aided the abusive culture through infrequent, toothless inspections that deferred to church authority. Inspectors were meant to restrict the use of corporal punishment and ensure children were adequately clothed and fed, but the inspectorate was grossly understaffed, schools were warned of visits in advance, and inspectors rarely talked to the children. And if they did raise concerns, they were ignored. As far back as the 1940s, school inspectors reported broken bones and malnourished children but no action was ever taken, so dominant was the church's influence.

How did it become so dominant?

Partly because of the links between Irish nationalism and Irish Catholicism which rigidified at independence. The bitterness caused by '800 years of oppression', and the sense of unfinished business with Protestant England left by the partition in 1921 between Ulster and the rest of Ireland, gave Irish Catholic politics a siege mentality. That mentality was given institutional support by Éamon de Valera, the leading figure in Irish politics for almost five decades, whose 'grand vision' was that Ireland should be a rustic, devoutly Catholic state, where rigidly enforced traditional morality would prevail over materialism or modernism. To that end, De Valera forged a close partnership with John McQuaid, the ultraconservative Archbishop of Dublin from 1940 to 1972, and one of the figures investigated by the Murphy commission.

Where is McQuaid's influence most conspicuous?

In the 1937 Constitution, which enshrined the 'special position' of the Church in Ireland, banned divorce and contraception

---

The archbishops were treated as if the law didn't apply to them. In some cases, the Garda even handed over allegations to bishops rather than investigate themselves.

---

and defined women solely as homemakers and mothers. McQuaid ensured that the Church continued to run the vast majority of hospitals and schools. The committee for banning unacceptable books, set up in 1929, was also retained. (As late as 1976 it banned a family-planning leaflet.) The depth of McQuaid's effect on public life was evident at the funeral in 1949 of Douglas Hyde, Republican Ireland's first president, and a Protestant. Members of the government had to sit outside the church in their state cars during the service, because the Church hierarchy would not then allow a Catholic even to enter a Protestant church.

What happened after the Murphy report?

Not a great deal. 'I am aware that no words of apology will ever be sufficient,' said Diarmuid Martin, Dublin's current Archbishop. The Garda commissioner also apologised for the police failure to investigate the clergy, and Justice Minister Dermot Ahern promised to open investigations into some of the crimes. (Only 11 of the 46 priests mentioned in the report were ever convicted.) 'The bottom line is this: a collar will protect no criminal,' he said. Priests expressed their regret during Masses across Dublin. They were greeted with applause. Four bishops offered their resignations in December 2009; Pope Benedict accepted two of them, but later refused the others. He also released a 'pastoral letter to the Catholics of Ireland', conceding that the Irish clergy had made 'serious mistakes', and said he was 'truly sorry'.

THE CHRISTIAN BROTHERS

The order was founded in 1802 by a Waterford merchant called Edmund Rice, to educate the children of the poor ('to keep themselves unspotted in the world') and to resist the onslaught of proselytising radical Protestant groups in Ireland. The Christian Brothers were arguably the most important force in shaping the identity of an independent Ireland: seven of the fourteen leaders of the 1916 Easter Rising executed by the British, and five of the seven men who formed the first Irish cabinet, were old Christian Brothers boys. Many products of their schools, including Cambridge English don John Casey, have expressed gratitude for the education they received. Other alumni include actors Liam Neeson and Gabriel Byrne, and bowler Dominic Cork.

But they always had a darker side. Critics accuse them of fostering a narrow, exclusively Catholic view of what it meant to be Irish. Conor Cruise O'Brien described their teaching of history as 'concentrated Anglophobia'. 'Dreadful human beings,' Pierce Brosnan called them. But it's the revelation of systematic abuse meted out in their institutions that has done most harm. Not long ago there were 1,300 of them in Ireland: now there are 250. There have been no new vocations in 20 years.

Why is
Haiti
so disaster-**prone**?

Sitting between two *fault lines, and in the path of hurricanes that make their way through the Caribbean, it has suffered earthquakes and storms throughout its 206-year history. Since 2001, there have been 15 natural disasters – hurricanes and storms accompanied by floods and mud slides that have necessitated international relief efforts. Three hurricanes hit Haiti in 2008 alone, killing 800 people and leaving a million homeless.*

Is it just a question of geography?

No. The impact of any natural disaster is magnified by Haiti's chronic inability to cope with it – as comparison with its neighbour, the Dominican Republic (with which it shares the island of Hispaniola), makes plain. Both have a population of around 10 million, yet life expectancy in the Dominican Republic is 13 years longer than in Haiti, and its economy is 7 times

larger. While tourists fear to travel to Haiti, the Dominican Republic is the Caribbean's most popular tourist destination. Hunger, disease, infant mortality, literacy: on every indicator Haiti is worse off.

Has Haiti always been so chronically poor?

On the contrary. From 1697, when (as Saint-Domingue) it came under French rule, it was one of the richest colonies in the New World. Its sugar, coffee and cotton accounted for a third of France's trade. But its riches were built on slavery. In 1789, the population consisted of around 30,000 Europeans, a further 25,000 mixed-race *affranchis* and half a million African slaves. In the 1790s, inspired by the French and American revolutions, the slaves rose. Their leader, an educated slave called Toussaint L'Ouverture, was heralded by Wordsworth as the 'morning star' of the Americas. But L'Ouverture presented himself for peace talks with the French in 1802 and was shipped in chains to Paris, where he died. Two young generals, Jean-Jacques Dessalines and Henri Christophe, fought on – and in 1804 Haiti became the world's first independent black state.

And did it prosper?

Destitute and divided by race, language and religion (Haitian culture is permeated by voodoo, a fusion of West African beliefs and Catholicism), the state soon fell into civil war. In 1810, Henri Christophe (later crowned King

Henri I), restored some order, but only by sending some slaves back to their plantations. King Henri, who built the huge 'Sans Souci' palace killed himself in 1820. There followed a motley succession of emperors, kings and presidents-for-life. Since 1804, there have been 33 coups, and the country remains in thrall to the idea of the *gwo neg* ('big man'). A tiny French-speaking elite, centred on a handful of Lebanese and mulatto billionaires, and making up less than 1 per cent of the population, still controls 50 per cent of Haiti's meagre wealth.

Did European nations help Haiti?

Far from it. The prospect of slaves achieving independence terrified Europe. France persuaded Spain and the USA to join an embargo of Haiti, and by 1825 the country was so isolated that it had to agree to pay 150 million francs to France in compensation for its uprising. The settlement crippled Haiti. In 1900, it was still spending 80 per cent of its national budget on the debt, which it finally paid off in 1947. In 2004, it was estimated that Haiti paid France a total of $21,685,135,571 for its freedom.

Is France to blame, then?

Not solely. In the twentieth century, the USA became the shadow hanging over Haiti. In 1914, wary of the country's instability and Germany's influence there, President Woodrow Wilson sent in the marines to remove deposits from the Haitian National Bank and bring them to New York for safekeeping.

Since 1804, there have been 33 coups, and Haiti remains in thrall to the idea of the 'big man'. A tiny French-speaking elite still controls 50 per cent of Haiti's meagre wealth

---

A full-scale US invasion followed in 1915, and the invaders stayed for 19 years. During the occupation, the USA overturned Haiti's ban on the foreign ownership of land – one of its founding principles – and installed deeply unpopular, race-based policies including the *corvée*, or forced labour. Washington retained control of Haiti's finances until after the Second World War, and has intervened in Haiti's affairs ever since.

Has that intervention been to good effect?

Haiti seemed to make a fresh start when a doctor, François 'Papa Doc' Duvalier, won the presidency in 1957. The USA backed him as a buffer against Fidel Castro, and Port-au-Prince briefly flourished as a destination for tourists and US-owned factories. But Duvalier's rule soon turned Haiti into 'the nightmare republic' familiar to readers of Graham Greene's *The Comedians* – 'an evil slum floating only a few miles from Florida', as Greene described it in the novel. Securing his rule with the thuggish militia known as the Tontons Macoutes or 'Bogeymen', Papa Doc created a cult with himself at the centre as Haiti's President for Life, Professor of Energy and Napoleonic Electrifier of Souls. He modelled his image on Baron Samedi, a voodoo god of death, and would only leave his palace on the 22nd of the month. As many as 30,000 people are thought to have died under his rule. After his death in 1971, his 19-year-old son, Jean-Claude ('Baby Doc'), came to power and ruled until 1985, when riots drove him from power. With American help, he fled to the south of France.

What happened after Baby Doc?

With the Cold War thawing, the USA lost interest in Haiti. But in the late 1980s, a Catholic priest called Jean- Bertrand Aristide began to attract a following in Port-au-Prince. In 1990, Aristide was swept to power by the Lavalas movement, named after Haiti's flash floods, and was hailed as the Caribbean Mandela. But, seen as dangerously left-wing, he was toppled eight months later by a CIA-backed coup (see box). In 1994, Bill Clinton atoned for this by sending 20,000 troops to reinstate him, but since then corruption and flip-flops in US policy have undermined Haiti's stability. Aristide was driven into exile in 2004. He was succeeded, after the two-year acting presidency of Boniface Alexandre, by his protégé, René Préval – seen by many in Haiti as Aristide's *marassa*, or voodoo twin. Préval was replaced by Michael Martelly in the wake of the 2010 earthquake.

HAITI'S CHARISMATIC PRIEST

'We are ready to leave today, tomorrow, at any time to join the people of Haiti, to share in their suffering, help rebuild the country, moving from misery to poverty with dignity,' said Jean-Bertrand Aristide, while still living in exile in South Africa, after the earthquake. The former Catholic priest, forced from power by the Bush administration after it questioned his 90 per cent majority in the 2000 elections, finally returned to Haiti in 2011. But he remains a divisive figure. In the ten years in which Aristide and the Lavalas held power, Haiti was dogged by its old curses of corruption, endemic infighting and powerful gangs, known as chimeres.

Despite the genuine appeal of his 'liberation theology', Aristide's government, and that of his successor, Préval, were and are dominated by cronies and family members seeking to get rich – politics being one of the few routes to wealth in Haiti. Aristide, though, has remained very quiet since his return to Haiti. But to his supporters, Aristide is a leftist leader never given a chance by the USA, and he remains the only politician with a mandate to guide Haiti's recovery.

What is the
Great Pacific
Garbage Patch **?**

Plastic refuse. *Fifty years ago, most flotsam was biodegradable. Now it is 90 per cent plastic, and practically indestructible. In 2006, the United Nations Environment Programme (UNEP) estimated that there are now 46,000 pieces of floating plastic in every square mile of ocean. Around 20 per cent of it is rubbish from ships and harbours – buoys, fishing nets, that sort of thing – but the rest is carrier bags, bottles, flip-flops, children's toys, tyres, yoghurt pots: in short, the detritus of modern consumer societies. Last year, rescuers searching for the wreckage of Air France flight 447, which disappeared over the South Atlantic, were astonished to find that instead of pieces of wreckage, their instruments were detecting vast amounts of rubbish.*

How does so much plastic get into the sea?

If it's not dumped there directly, plastic rubbish is blown out of littered streets and landfills and conveyed by rivers and drains to the sea. It's also washed off beaches. Once in the water, around 70 per cent sinks to the ocean floor, while the remainder floats, usually within 20 metres of the surface. Out to sea, the rubbish is drawn into huge circular currents known as 'gyres', and accumulates in their centres. Huge pools of plastic are building up in each of the world's five major gyres (two in the Atlantic, two in the Pacific, one in the Indian Ocean), but the greatest known concentration is in the North Pacific, where around six million tonnes have come together to form what campaigners call the Great Pacific Garbage Patch – a pool of rubbish twice the size of Texas.

How long has this been a problem?

Scientists have worried about plastic rubbish in the oceans since the 1980s, but it wasn't until 1997 that the scale of the problem was discovered by a Californian sailor called Charles Moore, who was on his way home from a race in Hawaii. He and his crew were motoring a catamaran across the top of the North Pacific Gyre, a route that boats normally avoid because of the lack of wind. As he made his way, Moore watched an unending procession of bottle caps, toothbrushes, Styrofoam cups, detergent bottles and plastic bags pass by. 'It took us a week to get across, and there was always some plastic thing bobbing by,' he says.

Why on earth hadn't it been noticed before?

The idea of a raft or island of trash is misleading. The plastic is impossible to photograph from aircraft or satellites, and hard to see unless you're in the middle of it. Even then, the larger pieces of plastic are only the beginning of the problem. They swim in a soup of tiny particles that are either plastic fragments worn down by friction and exposure to sunlight, or resin pellets – no more than 2mm across – known as 'nurdles', the micro-ingredients from which disposable plastics are made. Billions of tonnes of nurdles are shipped around the world every year, and a lot are spilled, lost and flushed down drains. Beachcombers call the nurdles 'mermaids' tears'.

What damage do they do?

Biologists are only just beginning to work out the threat posed by nurdles and other flecks of plastic. Fish, birds and whales mistake them for tiny fish and zooplankton, and then find them impossible to digest. More worrying still is the fact that they attract heavy metals and toxins in the ocean – industrial chemicals such as DDT and polychlorinated biphenyls (PCBs) that would otherwise have stayed out of the food chain. Once consumed by smaller animals, the pollutants become more concentrated as those animals are eaten in turn – eventually by humans. 'You can buy certified organic farm produce, but no fishmonger on earth can sell you a certified organic wild-caught fish,' says Charles Moore, who has now spent more than fifteen years studying the problem. 'This is our legacy.'

Are the nurdles worse than the larger pieces of rubbish?

None of it is good. According to UNEP, general plastic rubbish kills a million seabirds a year worldwide, and 100,000 marine mammals and turtles. The animals die strangled by discarded fishing nets and choked on rubbish they have eaten. Albatross populations in the northwest Hawaiian islands, a marine sanctuary, have been devastated by plastic. The giant birds have been found dead, their stomachs full of toothbrushes

and syringes. The plastic in the stomach of a typical Pacific albatross, says Moore, 'could stock the checkout counter at a convenience store'. A similar fate awaits fulmar petrels (sea birds related to the albatross). The bodies of fulmars washed up on North Sea coastlines have been found to contain an average of 45 pieces of plastic per bird.

Albatross populations in the Hawaiian islands have been devastated by plastic. The birds have been found dead, their stomachs full of toothbrushes and syringes.

Can't we clean it all up?

Moore is convinced it's too late. It would take an enormous amount of resources to remove six million tonnes of plastic from the North Pacific Gyre – and a total of around 100 million tonnes worldwide. What's more, the mesh required to gather up the tiny plastic particles would be so fine that it would also entrap millions of fish, devastating the ocean's ecology. 'Trying to clean up the Pacific Gyre would bankrupt any country and kill wildlife in the nets as it went,' he says. The challenge is to rethink the way plastics are used and to stop them reaching the oceans in the first place. Many of plastic's best qualities (see box) make it difficult and uneconomical to recycle. Whatever happens, much of the plastic in the ocean will be there for centuries to come. Some predict that it will eventually form a layer in the geological record.

THE TWO FACES OF PLASTIC

In 1909, when Leo Baekeland, a Belgian chemist, developed the first synthetic polymer, Bakelite, he could not have foreseen the problems it would create for the environment. After Baekeland's breakthrough, scientists and companies competed to investigate hydrocarbon chains and the wonderful materials they could create. The First World War saw the first synthetic leathers (PVC) and rubbers; nylon was invented in 1935; and after the Second World War came acrylics, carbon fibres and polyurethane, to name but a few. Since then, plastic bags, films and containers have revolutionised packaging and food-supply chains, extending shelf lives and reducing the amount of food that's wasted before it comes to market.

The qualities that make plastics such ideal materials in the industrial process – their lightness, cheapness and efficiency (plastic manufacturing accounts for just four per cent of annual oil production) – are the same qualities that make them so hard to recycle. Even if collecting plastic rubbish was economical or environmentally sound (which it rarely is), the fact that manufacturers combine several polymers into the same product makes reprocessing impossible. The other option, incineration, produces carbon dioxide.

Were the Vikings really so **fearsome**?

Apparently not. *Historians claim there was a lot more to the Vikings than pillage. Most of the seafaring peoples who came from Norway, Sweden and Denmark between the eighth and twelfth centuries – the 'Viking Age' – were farmers and merchants, rather than violent raiders, and wherever they settled they brought advanced skills in leather and woodwork and soon integrated into local communities. You might even call them 'progressive'. Women, who were free to trade and participate in political and religious life, were afforded considerable respect, as witnessed by the riches found in their graves. Vikings were also in touch with their softer side, fussy about appearance and hygiene and very fashion-conscious. Archaeologists find more Viking combs than either swords or axes.*

So how did they acquire their evil reputation in Britain?

The first recorded Viking landing was in 787, when three ships from Norway landed in Dorset. According to the Anglo-Saxon Chronicle, compiled more than a century later, the man sent to meet them was chopped up into little pieces on the beach, after which Viking raids became a byword for mayhem. 'Behold, the Church of St Cuthbert, splattered with the blood of its priests,' wrote Alcuin of York, a religious scholar, of the sacking of the monastery at Lindisfarne, Northumberland, in 793; and over 1,200 years later, Denmark still felt the need to issue apologies for Viking raids. 'We are not proud of the damages to the people of Ireland that followed in the footsteps of the Vikings,' said Brian Mikkelsen, the Danish culture minister, in 2007. Some scholars maintain that the raiders made themselves crazily violent by taking magic mushrooms and that from this arose the myth of the 'berserkers', warriors who in the heat of battle were impervious to pain.

And are these stories wrong?

They're almost certainly exaggerated. While raiding was a Viking tradition – fragments of bibles from British and Irish monasteries have been found in Denmark – there's scant evidence of extreme violence. There's not one case of rape reported in contemporary sources, and when Alcuin wrote his account of the destruction of Lindisfarne, he was at the court of King Charlemagne in Aachen, more than 500 miles away. Extensive archaeological surveys at Lindisfarne, meanwhile, have failed to come up with any evidence of a massacre: no signs of burning or mass graves of monks. There are even doubts about how much the Vikings looted from the monastery. In broader terms, excavations of Viking sites do still find the odd skull split in two, but most of the surviving evidence suggests that they were peaceful settlers.

What sort of evidence?

Many Viking archaeological sites contain no weapons at all, merely brooches, needles, coins and other examples of an everyday existence. 'Most people's image of the Vikings centres on their arrival and the disruption it brought, but that only continued for a very short time,' says Dr Máire Ní Mhaonaigh, a professor of Celtic studies. 'Afterwards, they started building settlements and interacting with the locals.' Raiders adopted the host language and, over one or two generations, took local wives, adopted local names, adapted to local social structures, often converted to

Christianity and became part of mainstream society. Modern Britons, says Dr Mhaonaigh, can take a lesson from such a positive example of immigration.

If they were so nice, why invade?

The Vikings' big problem was their native Scandinavia: arable land was scarce, the seasons hostile, so they were always looking for greener pastures.

Some scholars maintain that the raiders made themselves crazily violent by taking magic mushrooms and that from this arose the myth of the 'berserkers', warriors who were impervious to pain.

And they had the technology to do so. Their longships were fast and seaworthy, their crews astoundingly adept at navigating them. By salting and storing cod, they could make extraordinary journeys. These included the five recorded Viking expeditions to North America between 985 and 1011 and settling as far afield as Constantinople, Greenland and Newfoundland. This global diaspora is the truly remarkable thing about the Vikings: they travelled as far as the Volga River in Russia and fought as mercenaries for the Byzantine Empire, reaching North Africa, Jerusalem and Baghdad.

What about their influence in Britain?

Danish raids during the reign of King Alfred the Great (871–899), split England in two: Wessex and English Mercia on the one side, and the Danelaw (the East of England) on the other. Alfred and his descendants eventually reclaimed the Danelaw, but it kept its own identity. Things got even more complicated in the early 11th century, when the Danish King Sweyn Forkbeard and his son Canute invaded, defeating the English king, Ethelred the Unready, himself backed by Danish forces. Once Canute became King, even more Danes settled, so by 1066 almost all English leaders, including King Harold, were at least half Danish. Even the Normans, when they arrived, were partly Viking (Danish Vikings conquered Normandy as early as the 8th century): so at the Battle of Hastings there was Viking blood on every side. In a sense, Vikings have ruled England ever since.

So have we now changed our minds about the Vikings?

Not entirely. The authoritative *Cultural Atlas of the Viking World* still maintains that the Vikings attacked Britain with 'startling and unparalleled ferocity'. Alfred Smyth, emeritus professor of medieval history at Kent University, insists there must have been something uniquely terrifying about them. 'When they got psyched up,' he says, 'they could butcher an entire population – something new to warfare in the early Middle Ages.' Historian David Hipshon insists that attempts to reinvent the Vikings smack of trendy moral relativism. 'The Nazis may have to wait a few years,' he wrote to the *Daily Telegraph*, but sooner or later 'someone will organise a conference to highlight their technological prowess and cleanliness.'

WHAT DID THE VIKINGS EVER DO FOR US?

They gave us words for a start. The Vikings enriched the English language with essentials like 'law', 'egg', 'happy', 'anger', 'box', 'clumsy', 'cunning', 'fast', 'rotten' and 'ruthless'. Viking place names also litter the East of England including anywhere ending in 'by' (farmstead), 'thwaite' (meadow) and 'beck' (stream).

But more importantly, in many cases, the Vikings are the British. The chances are, if you are from Scotland or the East of England, you have Scandinavian blood.

DNA research for the BBC series *Blood of the Vikings* found the highest percentage of Viking DNA in the North and East of England, with the highest concentration in York, a well-known Viking settlement site. On the West coast, in Cumbria, traces of Norwegian Viking DNA turned up in Penrith, while studies of Orkney and Shetland have shown that the invading Norsemen were probably accompanied by equal numbers of Norsewomen.

Is the US President
the world's
most powerful **man** ?

On the face of it, yes. *As chief executive of the world's only superpower, he is boss of 2.7 million employees (two per cent of the US labour force) and Commander-in-Chief of the mightiest army on Earth. At all times he is accompanied by the so-called 'football', a briefcase containing America's nuclear launch codes. He can negotiate treaties, pardon criminals and appoint around 4,000 senior officials (though many require the Senate's consent), including ambassadors, judges, generals and cabinet ministers.*

Whence does he derive his powers?

In contrast to the ill-defined powers of the British Prime Minister, his are defined in a document: Article II of the US Constitution (signed in 1787). Yet the powers thus assigned don't sound that impressive. Scarred by memories of war with King George III, most of the 56 Founding Fathers wanted to create a weak central leader (a 'foetus of monarchy'), to let Congress make the laws, and to keep most power in the hands of state and local legislatures. But they were also in thrall to the trustworthy figure of George Washington, the revolutionary general widely expected to be the first man to hold the new office. That helps explain the ambiguous nature of some of his defined powers (e.g. the duty 'to take care that laws be faithfully executed'), an ambiguity that over time the President has systematically exploited.

And how did the presidency develop in the early years?

Washington, elected in 1789, was conscious of his role in shaping the office ('If I may use the expression, I walk on untrodden ground'). Sensitive to public fears of an over-mighty executive, he enshrined many self-limiting customs – an egalitarian term of address ('Mr President'), cabinet meetings and term limits that only later became law. His minimal activism, and that of the next five presidents, reassured the public. Only when the seventh – Andrew Jackson, a firm believer in a strong presidency – took on both Congress and the Supreme Court in the 1830s, were the constraints on presidential power put to serious test.

What are those constraints?

The structure of American government, it's often said, is 'an invitation to struggle': power is divided between executive and legislature, while authority to interpret the Constitution rests with the Supreme Court. The President's cabinet, unlike the British PM's, cannot contain sitting members of the legislature; and 'Potus' can never be sure of a legislative majority. The Founding Fathers wanted Congress to initiate policy and, for a century after Andrew Jackson, it largely did so; the President playing a mainly oppositional role. Only after the New Deal of Franklin Roosevelt (1933–1945) did the kind of presidential programme now being prepared by Barack Obama and Mitt Romney become institutionalised.

Is he now America's lawmaker?

He has certainly become the largest source of new legislation. And though he may not vote in Congress, if he doesn't like a bill he can veto it. His veto can only be overridden by a two-thirds majority in the Senate, which has only happened 107 times (4 per cent of attempts) in the history of the USA. But then again, he too finds it hard to get his own way.

Between 1953 and 1996, only 46 per cent of proposals submitted by presidents were passed into law.

How else does Congress limit him?

Although the Constitution grants him some leeway to begin a sudden, defensive war, he still in theory depends on Congress to do so (see box). Congress's real power over the White House, however, lies in its control of the purse strings – 'the most complete and effectual weapon with which any constitution can arm the immediate representatives of the people', as 'father' of the Constitution James Madison put it. And so it has often proved. In the mid 1990s, the federal government shut down for 28 days when the Republican-controlled Congress refused to approve Bill Clinton's budget.

And what about impeachment?

The House of Representatives, by a simple majority, can vote to impeach a president (i.e. subject him to trial by the Senate) for 'Treason, Bribery, or other high Crimes and Misdemeanours'.

But though three have faced impeachment proceedings – Clinton, Nixon and Andrew Johnson – none has been sacked. Nixon resigned before the House could vote; Clinton survived his trial. Johnson, who succeeded Abraham Lincoln after his assassination, was dubbed 'King Andy' for his resistance to Congress. In 1866, for instance, he vetoed the Civil Rights Bill giving freedom

---

Congress's real power over the White House lies in its control of the purse strings – 'the most complete and effectual weapon for the immediate representatives of the people'

---

to the slaves. Desperately unpopular (Congress overrode his vetoes 15 times), he survived impeachment by a single vote.

Is the Supreme Court easier for presidents to control?

The President's power to nominate judges gives him scope to shape the politics of the court. But it doesn't always work out that way. The Senate can reject appointments; and in any case, once installed, judges are hard to control. George Bush Snr's appointment, David Souter, ended up being one of four justices to side against his son in the Florida recount of 2000.

How do they get anything done?

By ignoring the rules: most great presidents have become so while acting outside their authority. Jefferson carried out the Louisiana Purchase (buying the land of 15 states from Napoleon) despite having no constitutional right to spend $23m. Lincoln suspended the right of habeas corpus during the American civil war. In the 20th century, President Theodore Roosevelt pioneered the use of Executive Orders, presidential decrees that have the force of law. They have since been used to desegregate the US army (Truman), ban the use of federal funds for abortion (Reagan) and start an air war in Kosovo (Clinton). As Paul Begala, one of Clinton's advisers, said: 'Stroke of the pen. Law of the land. Kinda cool.'

VIETNAM, IRAQ AND THE WHITE HOUSE

'Congress shall have power to... declare War,' reads Article I, section 8 of the Constitution. And so it has done five times in US history. That just leaves about 120 other occasions when the President has sent US troops into battle. Like the UK, America has largely stopped declaring its wars. The President instead asks for an 'authorisation of force' from Congress, as in the case of the Vietnam war – in which 58,000 Americans and up to four million Vietnamese died; or in the case of the Korean war, no authorisation at all.

After the Vietnam war, Congress tried to reassert its authority with the War Powers Resolution of 1973, which would force the President to consult Congress and regularly seek reauthorisation for an ongoing conflict. But every President since Richard Nixon (who tried to veto it) has ignored it. The White House continued to fight the war in Iraq under an authorisation to remove (the long dead) Saddam Hussein. And in 2011, Barack Obama was criticised for exceeding his constitutional authority by ordering attacks on Libya without Congressional permission.

Index